Heretics to Heroes

A Memoir on Modern Leadership

Cort Dial

Printed in the United States of America

First Printing, 2016

ISBN 978-0-9973817-3-3

Library of Congress Control Number: 2016904813

www.CortDial.com

*To my high school sweetheart,
wife, mother to our children,
and best friend, Julie.*

Welcome to *Heretics to Heroes: A Memoir on Modern Leadership.*

You may not consider yourself a heretic, but I have news for you: your decision to pick up this book was an act of heresy.

Congratulations. That means you're well on your way to becoming a hero.

Heretics to Heroes is unlike any other business book you've ever read. In fact, it undermines many traditional tomes that have shaped industry for far too long.

You've begun an important journey that can change not just your life, but the lives of countless others, and I want to support you along the way. To learn more about how to develop the All-In Leadership™ described in these pages, access special offers available exclusively to you as a reader of *Heretics to Heroes*, connect with me, and more, go to:

http://www.cortdial.com/heretics-to-heroes-readers-page.

What follows is my story, but I believe you'll find your own in it as well. Together, let's go All-In.

— Cort Dial

Table of Contents

Acknowledgments
Foreword

PART 1: MY INTRODUCTION TO LEADERSHIP 1

Chapter 1: The Hero Journey 3
Chapter 2: My First Leader 7
Chapter 3: The Fire 15
Chapter 4: Growing Up 25
Chapter 5: How'd We Kill This Man? 33
Chapter 6: Taking My Stand 47
Chapter 7: A Quality Opportunity 59
Chapter 8: He's a Witch! 73
Chapter 9: You're an Executive Coach 81

PART 2: MY JOURNEY TO ALL-IN LEADERSHIP 103

Chapter 10: Paying Penance.. 105
Chapter 11: Falling in Love 117
Chapter 12: The Grand Tour 135
Chapter 13: I'm So Ashamed 147
Chapter 14: Inshallah 157
Chapter 15: Juliana's Declaration 167
Chapter 16: I Am a Father 179
Chapter 17: Baton Rouge—Part 1 195
Chapter 18: No Shit 203

PART 3: ALL-IN LEADERS IN ACTION 209

Chapter 19: The Chicken-Shit Principle 211
Chapter 20: Navel-Gazing 233
Chapter 21: Slaying Dragons 239
Chapter 22: A Coonass in the Rough 259
Chapter 23: The Drift 271
Chapter 24: Baton Rouge—Part 2 279
Chapter 25: The Pinnacle of Leadership 299
Chapter 26: The Vision 315
Chapter 27: The Corporate Audit 333
Chapter 28: The Summit 341
Chapter 29: Mr. Drift 351
Chapter 30: A Day in My Life of Bliss 361
Chapter 31: The 5 Conditions of Performance 371
Chapter 32: The Big Leadership Lesson 381

EPILOGUE: THE TURNAROUND 389

Acknowledgments

I wrote this book for those of you who spend your days toiling in organizations, waiting for someone in leadership to understand you and your heretical ideas. My request to you is simply this: get off your butts and start leading!

Thanks to my clients for their courage in risking a partnership with a rascal such as me (and of course, for paying their invoices on time). I am honored that you allow me to accompany you on your hero journeys.

Thanks to all the coaches who have partnered with me over the years. I have learned much from all of you and am grateful for your work in service of our clients. Special thanks to Laura Pankonien, Stephanie Qualls, Will Hewett, and Roy Flores, the very best with whom I've worked.

And last but not least, thanks to my branding team at Root + River: Justin Foster, Emily Soccorsy, Alyssa Patmos, and Jennifer Lawhead; my editors: Stacy Ennis, Elizabeth Carroll, and Kim Foster; and my graphics wizard at Ellis Graphics, Jeffrey Breckenridge.

Foreword

I will never forget the BP Deepwater Horizon disaster in the Gulf of Mexico. The oil and natural gas industry that I've been a part of for more than forty years will always remember the men who lost their lives that day and their loved ones.

As my colleagues and I left the memorial service for the Macondo victims, my deep sadness was matched only by a sense of urgency. I promised myself I would do everything I could to ensure something similar never happened again. At the same time, I was not sure how I would keep that promise.

My uncertainty definitely wasn't caused by a lack of experience tackling complex problems. As General Manager of Drilling and Completions at Chevron, I've faced plenty of challenges. One of the biggest hurdles I've cleared was getting to where I am in the first place. My path to senior-level executive was not traditional. In 1975, I began pulling slips, driving trucks, and doing roustabout work. It took me seventeen years to earn my degree while holding down a full-time position and raising a family.

It's in the DNA of people in my industry to work hard and enjoy taking on what seems to others as insurmountable challenges. I guess it was that tenacity, coupled with my moral compass and passion to do more both for my people and my industry, that made me seek out Cort's coaching.

I first met Cort when Chevron hired him as a performance coach. As I observed him coach, what immediately struck me was his approach, which is different than any of any of the other consultants I've ever encountered. While other performance coaches are often what we call "red"—in your face and excitable in ways that definitely work wonders for a lot of folks—Cort is pensive and calm. He listens more than he speaks, and when he does speak, he chooses his words carefully.

The early months of our coaching relationship consisted almost entirely of Cort asking me pointed questions about my past, beliefs, and goals. I answered honestly, not knowing exactly what he had up his sleeve.

When Cort revealed what he had been working on, I realized the role I had defined for myself in my industry was about to change forever.

Cort had taken all of my answers and turned them into a narrative that described the future I see—not just for me or for my team, but for my industry.

I see a future where it is unthinkable that anyone could be seriously hurt, let alone killed, doing our work. It's a future where the public recognizes that our industry provides security, powers achievement, and enables freedom with a devotion and dependability on par with heroes such as first responders and our military. Twenty years from now, I believe the world will value our people as stewards of the earth and architects of great societies.

Cort helped me articulate that vision. Then he helped me share it.

Together, we organized and executed the most important event of my career, the Clear Leading from the Future Summit. Staged in Galveston, Texas, in 2013, the Summit was where I first publicly declared my vision. I got up in front of my staff and peers and shared something people are not accustomed to hearing in a corporate gathering: I shared my heart.

After I told my team about the future I envisioned, it was time for more honesty. I admitted that I didn't know how to realize the future I'd just painted for them. But I told them what I did know, which was this: We have the people, commitment, and passion to achieve it.

At my Summit, Cort also helped me earn buy-in from the participants by allowing them to work through the four-stage process all human beings rely on when we grapple with a new future: denial, resistance, exploration, and finally, making the decision of whether or not we're willing to commit. My understanding of these steps has helped quell my own frustrations that inevitably pop up when individuals don't immediately join my cause. An emotional response from me can threaten the entire initiative, but my patience and support of followers as they work through all four stages ensure the strongest possible commitment.

The Summit created such commitment and empowerment that still fuel us as we work toward what is now a shared vision. Did everyone opt in? No, some people excused themselves from our mission. And at the end of the day, that is okay. You don't need all people to join you—just the right people.

Our Clear Leading from the Future Summit was a watershed event for me and my people, but it is not the only way Cort has helped us. Two years ago, while struggling with a stretch of poor performance, Cort helped me challenge my leadership team to craft a mission and instill priorities, goals, and accountability to motivate our people to higher performance and standards.

My team developed the mission and with Cort's and my help, enrolled their teams. The clarity of purpose, intent, and accountability generated by this initiative led to exceptional results. We brought millions of dollars and credibility back to my unit, and we could not have done it without Cort. My executive leadership now sees us not as a problem, but as an example of drilling and completion done better than others dreamed possible.

Today, our industry is facing perhaps our most daunting challenge yet. There is a human face to the drop in oil prices that does not get much attention in the media. More than 300,000 jobs are being lost. Watching families and skilled workers with decades of experience face extreme uncertainty is painful. As an industry, we must unite to create a solution that is sustainable for generations to come, and as one of this industry's leaders, I know this is something I want to do with Cort. Cort has become an inspiring guide and indispensable partner.

Cort's concept of All-In Leadership isn't for everyone. It demands the greatest commitment from a leader, and sometimes it goes against convention. But you cannot lead an organization to new highs with just one foot in. Today, there are numerous All-In Leaders in my unit whom I love and admire greatly, and we all employ our own unique approaches. Cort's All-In Leadership may look different on different people, but the core tenets of valuing and understanding people remain constant no matter who is practicing them.

If I had met Cort fifteen years ago, I'd be on a whole other level—not in terms of my specific job, which I love, but in the way I lead, motivate, and influence others. Take this book and explore Cort's ideas and the journey he traveled as he established and lived out his principles. I cannot tell you if you are ready to go "All-In," but I can tell you this: If you do, you will never regret it.

—Marcel Robichaux, 2016

Part 1:

My Introduction to Leadership

Chapter 1:
The Hero Journey

"For those who have not refused the call, the first encounter of the hero-journey is with a protective figure (often a little old crone or old man) who provides the adventurer with amulets against the dragon forces he is about to pass. . . . What such a figure represents is the benign, protecting power of destiny."

—Joseph Campbell

Author and educator Joseph Campbell wrote often of the "hero journey." For Campbell, the hero journey provided a template for a common adventure found in mythology, film, and literature. Essentially, every hero journey follows the same archetype. Regardless of the adventure, the hero eventually ends up at the place he started—though he's not the same.

This hero journey is one I believe all who are to become true leaders must undertake. The adventure often begins when leaders find themselves in a predicament or crisis that calls for their transformation. Those who successfully answer the call, confront an adversary (often within themselves), overcome the challenges, and return home transformed are what I call All-In Leaders™—the rarest but most powerful form of leaders.

This is the journey I took, one I will share with you in this book. I will also describe how, after my transformation into an All-In Leader™, I have guided other leaders through their personal adventures.

There are three ways a person can begin the hero journey. Some fall unintentionally into the quest. A common tale is of a hunter lost in the forest. This hero comes upon a village threatened by a dragon and chooses to lead the villagers to defeat the beast. She doesn't choose this journey but instead happens upon it.

A leader often finds himself in an unintentional quest, a situation that calls for a major change in himself, his organization, or even his industry. He does not ask for or intentionally create these conditions; he stumbles into them. He may not even be fully aware he is in a new reality. But regardless of whether he is conscious of it or even wants to go on a quest, he's going. The adventure has begun.

A person can also begin the hero journey by eagerly seeking the adventure. Just as Luke Skywalker in *Star Wars* yearns to leave his home and join the rebels in their fight for freedom from the Galactic Empire, this person wants to lead and is actively in search of the opportunity—he seeks to go to war, to climb a mountain, to champion a risky cause.

Finally, a person can begin the hero journey by being tempted, persuaded, or recruited into undertaking the adventure, just as Alice in *Alice's Adventures in Wonderland* is lured to the tree by the White Rabbit. In other cases, a person is invited into the journey by a friend, associate, or manager who sees potential in her, but which she has yet to recognize. Ultimately, she must choose to take on the challenge before her.

Regardless of how the journey begins, a guide or protector figure exists in virtually every hero journey. In the case of the hunter, it may be an old warrior who trains her in the art of dragon slaying. For Luke Skywalker, it was the Jedi Master Obi-Wan

Kenobi. Alice was mentored and protected by the Mad Hatter. There is always a character who assists, guides, and when required, protects the hero as he undertakes the quest and grows into the person he must become in order to triumph.

It is this role of guide that others have played for me and I play for my clients. I spot individuals who are consciously or unconsciously ready for the adventure. They may be seeking improvement but lack the capacity to achieve it. They may have stumbled into a perilous circumstance to which they are oblivious or have consciously chosen to champion a new, outlandish idea. Or they may be overwhelmed by their predicament and actively seeking help. In some cases, I see the opportunity they cannot and provoke them to take on the adventure. Like the White Rabbit, I often find myself standing at the threshold of the forest, looking back at an emergent leader and saying, "Follow me, and I will guide you on a journey that will help you get results that seem impossible, and in the process you will develop yourself into a more effective leader than you can possibly imagine."

Once such a leader crosses the threshold, there is no going back. The journey has begun and there is no way to halt it. She must complete the journey and become an All-In Leader or be defeated by the dragon forces. Completing the quest, whether through triumph or failure, is a key part of forming the "all-in" aspect of the All-In Leader.

In my experience, five things must be already present within emergent leaders if they are to successfully complete the hero journey and become an All-In Leader. First and foremost, they must be coachable. They must be willing to be guided and mentored, if they expect to grow and develop into the leader they strive to be.

Second, emergent leaders must have some idea of who they are and what they stand for in the world. This includes an interest in serving their people and the greater good, rather than themselves.

Third, these leaders must be predisposed to lead. Emergent leaders are people who have acquired at least some of the realizations All-In Leaders possess. While they do not have to be completely aware they possess these realizations, they are unlikely to succeed in their journey without them. The most critical realization I look for is simply, "The most effective tool I have to create performance is me; therefore, I am the only one who needs to change."

Fourth, emergent leaders must be up to the big adventure, the one lesser leaders shy away from—the adventure of confronting oneself, one's paradigms, one's limitations, and one's fears. This requires a leader who is willing to have intimate conversations with a coach or guide. I help my clients explore personal aspects of themselves. These leaders allow me to speak in a manner in which very few people in their lives will interact with them. I will likely be the only person who tells them the truth.

Fifth and finally, emergent leaders must be willing to have their guide step in and protect them, when necessary, from things they cannot yet see or take on. This will most likely occur early in the journey when they have not yet acquired the faculties, realizations, and skills necessary to do battle on their own. During critical moments, I sometimes intervene and instruct leaders as to exactly who they need to be and what they need to say and do. It is difficult for many leaders to accept direction from an advisor. When they resist, I remind them they are new to this forest, but I've made this journey myself and have successfully guided dozens of others.

No matter what the situation, it is my role to help the emergent leaders see and embrace the situation that calls for their transformation. If they choose to answer the call and engage me as their coach, I will guide and protect them as they face trials and tribulations on the way to their victorious transformation into All-In Leaders.

Chapter 2:
My First Leader

"And so, my fellow Americans: ask not what your country can do for you—ask what you can do for your country. My fellow citizens of the world: ask not what America will do for you, but what together we can do for the freedom of man."

—John F. Kennedy

It's funny how time tends to sculpt a person. It's as if we are born concealed within a pillar of stone, and day after day, year after year, time chips away, revealing the person we are intended to be. For some of us, this is completed early in life; for others, much later, if at all. The process began for me as a young boy living in Dallas, Texas, with my mom, dad, and three brothers.

We were your typical Catholic family. All three of us older boys attended Catholic school. Mom was an excellent homemaker and a wonderful mother. Dad was a savvy businessman and a generous father. We all enjoyed each other and life.

But one day, and much younger than most, I was awakened to the dark reality of life.

The year was 1963. I was sitting in my kindergarten class at St. Pius X, watching my teacher call roll. My mind shifted to my two older brothers across the building in their classrooms, and I wondered if they were feeling the same excitement. Today was a special day: our president, John F. Kennedy, was visiting Dallas.

Every Catholic citizen in Dallas was proud that one of us had risen to the highest position in society. To us, it meant we were OK, we fit in, and we were not weird "rosary bead lovers," as some saw us in the sixties.

My teacher, Sister Rosa, was playing radio reports of the president's visit. A tweed-covered speaker with a brown, wooden frame hung high on the wall at the front of the classroom, its sound filling the room. I could hear radios all over school playing the same broadcast.

Later that morning, after we had returned from recess, Sister Rosa had the speaker volume turned up.

"President Kennedy has arrived in Dallas and is traveling to a hotel, where he will give a speech," she told us, her voice just over the drone of the radio reporter. "This is an important day for us and all of Dallas." And it was. In fact, it was so important she had arranged for us to bring our lunches from home so we could eat in the classroom during the broadcast.

We sat there listening, enjoying our sandwiches and chocolate milk. We were too young to understand the true meaning of what was going on, but we got the main idea. The president, who was one of us, was in our town today. I don't recall a day of school when everyone was as happy.

Then, all of a sudden, the tone in the reporter's voice began to change. As young children, we had no idea what that meant, but we all understood something was different when Sister Rosa leaped from her desk, ran to the speaker control, and turned it off. When we asked why, she simply replied, "That's enough radio for now. Please put your heads on your desks and remain silent. I will be back in a moment." Then she dashed out of the room.

Being obedient Catholic children, we did as we were told. I did not think much of Sister Rosa's odd behavior as I placed my head on my desk and soon fell asleep. I was awakened some time later, not by Sister Rosa but by my two older brothers, Greg and Gary, who were in fifth and third grades. I looked up at Greg, the oldest, as he whispered, "Cort, wake up. We're going home."

I raised my head, still groggy from sleep. "Why?" I asked.

Just come with us," he replied. "We're going home."

As I rose from my desk and began gathering my satchel, I became aware that people in the room were crying. I looked to the front of the room to find Father Robert hugging Sister Rosa as tears slid down their cheeks.

"What's wrong with Sister Rosa, Greg?"

"Get your books. We're going."

Greg took my hand, and we walked through the school. The radios were now off; the halls quiet. There was no noise except for the sound of people crying. As we left the elementary hall, we passed older boys and girls, administrators, nuns, and priests, all weeping and embracing each other. I knew something very sad must have happened for so many people to be crying, but I also knew it would not be proper for me to ask about it, so I just walked along with my brothers and observed the horrible spectacle.

Our home was not far, and I was used to walking to and from school with my brothers, but this walk was different. There was no talking, no laughing, no arguing, no whining, and no fighting. We were totally silent. Greg, the heftier and more steadfast of my two older brothers, wearing awkward glasses way too grownup for his age, kept his eyes facing forward as he dragged me along. Gary, the shorter, sleeker, and ornerier brother, hung a step or two behind us, uncharacteristically placid, staring at the ground.

"Why are we going home?" I finally asked. "What's wrong at school?"

Greg spun around. "Cort, I told you to hush. Mom will tell you when we get home."

That response did not satisfy me. I asked again what was going on.

Finally, Gary stepped in front of me with tears in his eyes. "They shot Kennedy!" he said.

"Gary!" Greg yelled. "Mom will tell him!"

"Who shot Kennedy? You mean our Kennedy?"

"Yes," Gary said, his voice quieter.

"Is he OK?"

"We don't know," Greg replied, nudging Gary aside. "We don't know for sure that he was even hit, but someone shot at him. Now, come on. Mom is probably worried about us."

Nothing else was said the rest of the walk home. We entered the house at the mudroom entrance, took off our shoes, and put away our things.

Greg yelled out, "Mom, we're home." There was no response.

We walked through the house, peeking into rooms, each of us calling out for Mom. Silence. Finally, the three of us made it to the rear of the house and stood looking at our parents' bedroom door. We could hear mom crying.

Greg knocked. "Mom, we're home. I got Gary and Cort with me. Do you have Corbin? Are you OK?"

"Corbin's with me," Mom replied. "Greg, you come in, but leave your brothers in the hall."

Greg went inside. Through the narrow door opening, I could see a dark room, lit only by the glow from mom and dad's black and white TV. I caught a glimpse of Mom cradling Corbin in her arms. Mom's hair and fashion very much mimicked that of the president's wife, Jackie, as did many of the women of that time. Today she was wearing her Sunday dress, its white fabric stained across the front with black smears from her running mascara. We'd all dressed our best that day.

Greg closed the door behind him. Gary and I sat outside in the dark hall, waiting, leaning our backs against the wall. We could hear the mumbling of Mom whispering to Greg, but it was impossible to understand what she was saying. All I heard over and over was Greg saying, "Yes, ma'am . . . yes, ma'am."

Finally, Greg returned, shutting the door quietly as he exited. "Mom's fine," he said. "She wants to be left alone."

We slowly walked to the family room, Gary running his right hand along the wall, Greg holding his head up and shoulders back. Greg sat us on our long, red couch and looked at each of us in turn.

"Kennedy was hit," he began. "I heard it from the TV, but Mom wouldn't tell me whether he was hurt bad. She's really upset, so I'm worried he might be in bad shape."

"Why would anyone want to shoot President Kennedy?" I asked.

"Best not to think about it, Cort. Mom will tell us when she thinks we're ready." He paused and looked toward our parents' bedroom, then turned back to us. "Stay in here and keep quiet. We don't want to disturb Mom. I'll go get you something to eat."

"Can we watch TV?" I asked.

"No!" Greg and Gary both yelled.

"No TV until Mom says we can," added Gary.

"Mom said Dad's on his way home," Greg offered. "She told me to make sure we don't watch TV until he says it's OK."

We sat on that red couch, watching the door for Dad. Several minutes later, we heard his car pull up, a door slam, and fast footsteps making their way to the house. Dad was a blur, dashing down the long hallway to the bedroom and flying through the door. As he closed it, I heard him say, "Dode, I am so sorry. Is he alive?"

It was several days before we were able to be with our parents. Dad moved the family TV into a small den with folding vented doors. They remained in there for three days with the doors closed, sitting on a small loveseat and watching news reports.

During that entire time, there was not a single moment in which my parents interacted with me in any significant way. There was only the quiet lull of the TV from behind the folding doors and the occasional glimpse of Mom and Dad when the doors opened, the TV beams reflecting off their faces and bodies as they sat staring. We boys didn't play. Whenever we spoke, we whispered.

Greg took care of us. He woke us, fed us, and put us to bed. Any time we spoke louder than a whisper, he would shush us and remind us to not disturb Mom and Dad.

Over those days, Greg did his best to answer my questions about the president's welfare, but he was intentionally vague. When I pushed him for answers, he would always say, "Mom or Dad will answer when they think it's time."

One afternoon a few days after the shooting, I put on my coat and went outside into the alley behind our house to bounce the basketball. It was a bright, crisp winter day, and I needed to get outdoors and do something physical, away from the dark sadness of my house. I looked around at the empty alley before I began playing. But after no more than a few bounces, I heard the neighbor from across the alley screaming. She came rushing out of her back door, sprinted over to me, and kicked the ball down the alley.

"Damn Dial boys!" she screamed. "Don't you know the president's dead?"

I ran down the alley, chasing after my ball, my eyes wet with tears. From behind me, I heard Greg yell, "Hey, get your hands off my brother, you old witch!"

I turned just in time to see Greg run up to the lady and push her back a few feet. "If you ever hurt one of my brothers," he said, "I'll whoop your ass." I had never heard Greg curse before.

Greg ran to me and grabbed the ball. "Let's go before she gets her jerk husband to come after us."

We ran back into the house, put the ball away, and sat silently on the red couch, waiting for the woman's husband to knock on our door. He never did.

After a while, I whispered, "That old bag said Kennedy is dead."

Greg scooted a little closer to me. "He died a few hours after we left school, but Mom and Dad don't want us to know. They blew his head off. Never had a chance. They got Connally, too, but thank goodness the governor's OK."

"But if he's been dead for days, why are Mom and Dad staying in the den?" I asked.

"Because there's a lot more stuff going on. They caught the guy who killed Kennedy, but this morning some guy shot him—right in the hands of the Dallas police! And today's Kennedy's funeral. It's all on TV, and Mom and Dad are watching it."

"Why would anyone want to watch junk like that?" I asked.

"For some reason, grownups think it's important to watch that stuff. Do me a favor, Cort. Just stay inside and stay quiet for a few more days until this is all over."

As I looked at Greg, I realized what it meant to have a big brother. He modeled the best for us younger siblings, standing up for us when we were unfairly attacked and stepping in for Mom and Dad in their absence. He was my protector. He has since played that role for me many times in my life, both good and tragic.

Many of Greg's qualities, I learned as I grew into adulthood, were attributes leaders possess. In that context, Greg was the first leader in my life. He would be one of many family members who helped me develop my image of a great leader.

Chapter 3:
The Fire

"A hero is someone who has given his or her life to something bigger than oneself."

—Joseph Campbell

Seven years passed. The shock of Kennedy's death had faded, and in its place was the anxiety of my first day of junior high in Houston, Texas. Years earlier Mom and Dad had moved us from Catholic to public school. At the time, they would not share with me why, but I heard from my brothers and their friends that my feisty brother Gary had decked a priest who was beating him for misbehaving in class. Apparently, Gary broke free of the priest's grasp and punched him right in the face. Dad had regularly schooled us in boxing, and at that moment, Gary's training paid off. Gary was expelled from school but quickly became folk legend among the kids within our neighborhood.

I entered Spring Woods Junior High and took out my schedule to double check first period: Mr. Henderson's history class. I found my place in the first seat in the far right row, nearest the classroom door. Mr. Henderson, a handsome, young, and enthusiastic black man and the first person of color I came to know well, began taking attendance. My body tensed. I dreaded the moment when he would call out my name, "Cortney."

My name was given to me by my father. As my parents told it, Mom had wanted to call me Dennis. If they ever had another boy, she reasoned, she would call him David. "That way, we would have Greg and Gary and Dennis and David," she'd explained.

But Dad had thought otherwise. While Mom was recovering from giving birth, Dad took advantage of her absence and completed my birth certificate with the name Cortney Mark Dial.

Dad was an American Indian and Irish mix. My grandmother was Sioux Indian and my grandfather was Osage. As Dad told the story, "When you came out of your mom, you were completely calm and at peace. Your grandmother said there is an Indian word that means calm and peaceful, which she pronounced as cort-ney, so I decided to give you that name. It took your mom a while to come around, but she came to like it. Of course, when your little brother came along, David would no longer do, so Mom named him Corbin."

Although I was never sure whether my dad's story was true, the story did cause me to feel that my name was special. The name Cortney and the story behind it influenced how I felt about myself. Consequently, I grew up a serene person, always the calm in the storm, the consensus builder, the negotiator, and when necessary, the peacemaker. This made me effective in influencing my friends and family and also appreciated and trusted by adults. As a teenager, when someone persuasive and trustworthy was needed, I was often the one called upon. This gave me opportunities my peers did not receive, and it's one reason I developed into a responsible adult well before most young men did.

But as I entered junior high, I became uncomfortable with my name. Some of the other kids would tease me, saying it was a girl's name. It did not help that the most popular girl in my grade was named Courtney.

As I anticipated, when Mr. Henderson called out "Cortney Dial," the classroom filled with restrained laughter.

Mr. Henderson looked up. "What are you snickering about?" he asked.

The class became quiet. Mr. Henderson walked toward me, gesturing at me as he said, "You wouldn't be laughing at Cortney's name, would you?"

The room remained silent.

"Why, he's got a great name," he said with a rascally smile. He turned to me. "You've got a cool name, Cortney."

Mr. Henderson turned back to the room. He changed his accent to urban black as he said, "Coatney Doll! That's a cool name. That's as cool as batman or supaman. Who would laugh at a name as cool as that?"

From a couple of rows to my left, Calvin Bale, a boisterous redneck youth if there ever was one, replied, "You gotta admit, it's a purty funny name." Cal grinned at his friendly joke.

Mr. Henderson turned to look at him. "People who live in glass houses shouldn't throw stones, Cal."

"What do you mean?"

"Well"—Mr. Henderson changed his accent to a Texas drawl similar to Calvin's—"if I had a name like Cow Bell, I'm not sure I would be making light of anyone else's."

This comment brought laughter from the entire room and even Cal himself. Cal then said, "You think that's bad? I got a brother named Door." The room erupted.

From that day on, two things changed. First, Cal and I became friends, and second, no one ever again made fun of my name, or if they did, I never noticed—maybe because I no longer cared. I had a cool name. I liked my name.

Mr. Henderson had made me feel comfortable with myself and proud of who I was. To him, I was not just another name on the attendance roll call. I was significant. I mattered. Mr. Henderson's ability to make students feel worthwhile was a capacity, I would later learn, that leaders possess.

Later that year, while sitting in class, a hall monitor entered the room and handed Mr. Henderson a note. My teacher's eyes moved over the paper and his expression deepened.

"Cortney," he said, "please pack up and go to the vice principal's office. Calvin, please escort Cort." I wondered if I was in some kind of trouble, but the tone in Mr. Henderson's voice told me that it was something else.

Minutes later, I pushed open the vice principal's office door to see her standing with the school nurse. Mom was on her way to pick me up, the vice principal explained, and I was to go to my locker, put away my books, and collect my belongings. When I asked why, they avoided answering. I was to hurry to my locker before Mom arrived. I did as I was told.

Mom finally came with my little brother, Corbin. Mom did not summon Greg and Gary, who were in a separate high school. I think she needed someone to be with her, and for some reason, she chose me. Without a word, she put her arm around my shoulders and led me out of the office, through the hallways, and eventually into the car.

Finally, I asked, "Why am I leaving school?"

Mom looked at me for a moment. "Your dad was in an accident today. He's been burned on his neck. He's at the hospital being treated. He's going to be OK, but some other men got hurt really bad."

It was not that unusual for Dad to be burned; he was a firefighter. His company sold firefighting equipment, and Dad often taught at different fire schools around the country. On that day, he was teaching at Texas A&M University, a few hours from

Houston. Mom told me they had transported him to a burn center in Houston.

The drive to the hospital seemed to last weeks. As I leaned my head against the window, I thought about my dad. Dad was an extremely handsome and athletic man. He had dark tanned skin, a huge white smile, opal blue eyes, and dark curly hair, which earned him his nickname, "Corkey." Once, we were in the grocery store when a thrilled woman approached us and began shaking Dad's hand. She thought he was John Kennedy, who at that time was only a senator but running for president. Dad smiled widely and with a puffed chest said, "I appreciate the compliment ma'am, but I'm just an everyday citizen like you."

Always the life of the party and never sitting still, Dad was the guy who had hundreds of friends and was liked by all. He traveled a lot, and so we did not see him for long periods. Mom ran the house and managed us boys. But when Dad was home, he always spent his time with us, playing ball, giving us the best equipment money could buy, hopeful that at least one of us would become a big leaguer.

Dad had taught at A&M, as it is known in Texas, many times prior. In fact, one very hot summer, he took me with him. We stayed together at the Aggieland Inn. I was not allowed to go to the fire school itself, so I spent my days at the swimming pool while Dad fought fires.

One evening, I said to Dad, "It's so hot out here, even the pool water's warm."

The next day, Dad had large blocks of ice delivered to the inn and placed in the pool. It was quite an experience to lie on a large block of ice and float in a swimming pool, but it did wonders to help me forget about the scorching Texas heat.

My attention was drawn to the hospital parking lot, where Mom was putting the car in park. Mom led us across the scorching pavement, through the front doors, and upstairs to the burn unit, where she located Dad's doctor. We got the good news that Dad would be released in a week or so. It didn't surprise me that he would recover quickly. Dad was tough.

But as we entered Dad's room, my happiness at the news quickly dissolved. He was lying in a hospital bed with a large bandage on the back of his neck, his gown loosely covering him, blankets pulled to his waist. The scene shook me up.

I had never seen my dad in that way. To me, he'd always been like a Texas Ranger: invincible. I was glad to see him and know he was going to be OK, but somehow the realization that he was not indestructible unsettled me.

As I stood at the edge of the room, I noticed Dad was not himself. His face was pale and tight and his eyes were sad. His customary smile and "howdy boys" were not forthcoming. He and Mom whispered to each other as Dad glanced in Corbin's and my direction. Mom patted him on the hand as she whispered, "It's not your fault. You did what you had to do."

Not long after, Mom, Corbin, and I said our good-byes to Dad; we'd be back that evening to visit. As we were walking to our car, I asked Mom, "Why is Dad so sad?"

"Shush. Not in front of Corbin," Mom whispered.

After we arrived home, Mom told Corbin, "Go play in your room, sweetheart, while I make lunch."

As Mom pulled out bread and peanut butter, I sat on a barstool at the kitchen counter next to her. I had sat at that counter many afternoons, eating one of Mom's snacks and telling her about my day. But this conversation was different. This was to be the first adult conversation I'd ever had with her.

As Mom spread jelly on pieces of bread, she told me Dad had been training some customers from a company in Mexico. They had planned and briefed the exercise with the trainees, as they always did. But as the exercise was underway, the wind shifted and unexpectedly blew the fire over Dad and two of the men.

Mom said Dad did exactly what a firefighter was supposed to do in that situation—he opened the fire nozzle to create an umbrella of water over their heads, shielding them from the heat. But the two trainees were so frightened that they tried to run away. Dad held the men's protective bunker coats to keep them from running while holding the fire hose under his right armpit, pressed between his chest and one of the men's backs. The nozzle was just above Dad's helmet, spraying water upwards and protecting the three of them. Dad clutched both men's coats with his hands and tried to pull them toward him to keep the three of them under the water umbrella. But as they continued to try to run away, they freed the hose and caused the nozzle to move, disturbing the umbrella and allowing the flames to enter and burn Dad and the men.

"Is that how Dad got burnt?" I asked.

"Yes," Mom replied. "In fact, Dad said he knew that the next time one of them tried to run, the nozzle would fall and all three of them could die. Dad said he decided he had to let go of the man on the left so he could hold onto the other man and the nozzle."

Mom placed my lunch in front of me on the countertop, sat down next to me, and said sorrowfully, "The reason Dad is so sad is that he had to let go of one of the men to save the other, . . . and when he let go, the man ran and died."

"Oh, my goodness!" I gasped. "What happened to the other man?"

"He got some burns, more serious than your dad's, but he's going to be OK," Mom answered. "But as I say, the other man did not survive. Do you understand what I am telling you, Cortney?"

"Yes, ma'am."

After a few moments of silence, I asked, "Why would he run? Didn't he know Dad would protect him?"

"We'll never know why, Cort. People sometimes do things when they're afraid that later on don't make a lot of sense."

"I bet Dad feels terrible."

"He does. But I want you to know your dad is a hero. He saved a man's life today. He held onto both those men with everything he had, but they were so frightened they couldn't stay put, and that's why your dad got burned."

"I wish those men had done what Dad told them," I responded. "Then everyone would be OK."

"Me too, but Dad said it was too loud for them to hear anything he was yelling," Mom explained. "Dad told me that if they had all remained together, he could have saved them. That's why Dad is so sad. He had to make a terrible decision.

"I know this is difficult for you to hear, but I want you to know what happened and to understand why your dad might not be himself for a while. I also want you to know that your dad would have given his life if there had been a way to save those two men. But there wasn't. The only way to save one of them was to save himself, since he was the only one of them capable of maintaining the water umbrella. Do you understand that?"

"Yes."

"Good boy." Mom patted me on the knee and turned to take Corbin his lunch.

Dad's wounds healed and he recovered quickly. Within a few weeks, he was himself again. I never spoke with him about that incident. I figured if he ever wanted to talk about it, he'd raise the subject.

I had told Mom that I understood, and I guess I did understand that Dad was a firefighter and that meant giving your life to save others. But that event had a profound effect on me that I never shared with any of my family. For the remainder of my junior high years, I was chronically worried that someone in my family would be hurt.

I know now I was suffering from some form of neurosis and should have told Mom, but in those days, you didn't share stuff like that. You kept it to yourself and dealt with it.

In addition to constantly worrying, my worst symptom was the need to constantly pray. During every waking moment when my mind was not occupied by other things, I would pray for the safety and well-being of my family. Over time, I developed a standard prayer that contained every family member's name. I would say it silently to myself, over and over, like a chant in my head.

Of course, I was worse when I knew Dad was involved with some sort of firefighting, but even when that was not the case, I still worried constantly. I prayed in class, when walking in the hallways, when playing sports, during meals, while in bed waiting to fall asleep, and upon waking up. I prayed continuously for two years. The entire time, I kept my condition from my family, friends, and schoolmates.

I often wondered, as I prayed for my family, what it was like for the family of the man Dad had to let go of . . . the man who died.

I don't know how or why, but for some reason, in my ninth year of school, I gradually stopped praying all the time. I guess I grew emotionally. Fortunately, time cured my wounds, as it had Dad's.

This event cemented in my mind that Dad was a hero and, although I would not have used the word at that time, a leader. I learned that leaders cannot always help everyone; sometimes they have to choose to let some of their people go in order to help the others. I also learned that leaders feel as bad as their people do when someone is harmed.

Dad's accident also transformed my relationship with my mom. From that day forward, when I would arrive home, Mom still waited for me at the kitchen counter with a snack. But instead of just talking about my day, we would discuss philosophy, history, religion, news, and even politics. I could ask Mom anything, and she would tell me what she thought and felt about the subject, and then listen to my point of view.

In those conversations, Mom never tried to get me to think or feel like she did. Whenever we'd discuss something controversial, she'd say something like, "Well, Cort, I've always seen it this way, but there are all kinds of ways to see anything. Which way of seeing it is best for you?"

I learned from Mom that leaders are always there for their people, ready to listen to what they have to say. Leaders don't sell or convince their followers of their ideas. Instead, leaders create a space where individuals can choose to embrace what's best for them and the greatest good of the enterprise. They step in and substitute for their counterparts when they are out of action, like Mom did for Dad.

Chapter 4:
Growing Up

"I feel sorry for the man who has never known the bracing thrill of taking a stand and sticking to it fearlessly. Moral courage has rewards that timidity can never imagine. Like a shot of adrenaline, it floods the spirit with vitality."

—Billy Graham

My ninth year of school was one of my happiest. I was starting on the basketball team, doing well in school, and our family's best friends moved from Dallas to Houston. My dad had helped their father get a job in his company.

The Fars had lived next door to us while growing up. They too were Catholic. Their four children went to our school: three boys, the same ages as Greg, Gary, and me, and a daughter Corbin's age, four years younger than me.

We six older boys were inseparable, going everywhere and doing everything together. When my parents sat us down and told us we were moving away, the first thing I thought of was how I'd miss the Fars. Yet our families remained close, and we vacationed together every summer. They were now joining us in Houston, and I assumed we'd all be lifelong friends.

For about a year and a half, it was like old times. I spent as much time at the Fars' house as I did my own. Although we attended separate schools, several of us played on the same ball teams, and on weekends we swam, hunted, and made trips to the Gulf to fish and surf together. We were growing into young adults, but that did nothing to change our friendship. In fact, we were closer than ever.

Then, the summer following my tenth grade, I was sitting with my mom in the grandstands, watching one of Greg and Gary's baseball games. Mom was especially quiet and distracted. When Gary ran across home plate, she didn't even seem to notice. I didn't think much of it but was a little concerned Mom was disturbed by something.

We had planned to go to the Fars' home for dinner after the game. But when I mentioned it to Mom, she uncharacteristically snapped back at me, "We're not going to the Fars' tonight."

"Why?" I asked.

"Because I said we're not. We may never go to that house again. Now stop pestering me and watch the game." The woman barking back at me was not my mom. Something had clearly happened between my parents and the Fars, but I was not about to ask why.

A few minutes went by, and Mom turned to me. "I'm sorry for biting your head off," she said. "I'm just angry about something, and it's not fair to take it out on you."

"What's happened, Mom?"

After a few moments of silence, Mom said, "Your dad quit his job yesterday."

"Why?"

"Because he decided he didn't belong there anymore."

"Why not?"

Mom took a deep breath, sighed, and then said, "Cort, all I can tell you at this point is that sometimes people you think you know and can trust, that you think are good people, turn out to be not so good. And when you find that out, it's best to get away from them."

"So Dad found out that the people at his work are people he wants to get away from?"

Mom looked down at me with a smile as if to say smart kid. "Yes, Cort. That's what Dad found out."

"But why can't we go to dinner at the Fars'?" I asked. I watched Mom's face, hoping she wouldn't snap at me again.

"Because, Cortney"—Mom used my full first name when she wanted to grab my attention—"your dad found out that one of those people he can't trust is Mr. Far."

Mom must have seen the change in my expression, because she reached out and patted my arm, then clasped my forearm for a moment before letting go. My eyes dropped to my lap as I thought about the Fars.

I would miss Mrs. Far and her kids, but I was not at all sad about not seeing Mr. Far again. I'd never liked Mr. Far, but I loved his wife. She always welcomed me into her home with a sincere smile and sometimes even prepared after-school snacks for her boys and me when she knew Mom wasn't home. She was a second mom to my brothers and me.

On the other hand, my only recollection of Mr. Far was of him griping at Mrs. Far or yelling at us kids. I often wondered why my parents were friends with the Fars, given that Mr. Far was so unfriendly. I guess, like me, they loved Mrs. Far and her kids so much they were willing to put up with him. After that conversation with my mom, I never again heard either of my parents speak of the Fars.

My aunt told me years later that Dad had quit because he'd discovered that Mr. Far and the founder's son were doing unethical things. When Dad reported his discovery to the founder, whom Dad had loyally served for nearly twenty years, the man threatened to fire Dad if he said anything to anyone. As my aunt told it, "You know your dad. He stood up, tossed the keys to his company car on the bum's desk, and took a cab home."

My Dad's stand cost him and Mom dearly financially, at least for a while. We sold things: our pool table, piano, and much furniture. Never one to sit and mope, when Dad was not job hunting, he was golfing, and it was during this time he introduced me to the game. I was sad and worried about Mom and Dad and their money challenges, but I was grateful for the time with Dad. He received several job offers, but Mom encouraged him to decline them, saying, "You can do much better, Corkey. Maybe it's time to start your own business."

Although we suffered the stress of significant financial hardship while Dad and Mom rebuilt their lives, I learned from my dad that there are times in life when a person must take a stand, regardless of the risk and consequences. Material things can be lost and regained, but a person's integrity, once gone, is very difficult to recover. I also learned when a parent loses a job, the children suffer as well. Lost jobs mean families must leave and find new homes and that children are ripped from their friends and have to assimilate into new environments while their parents are distracted by financial concerns.

My aunt told me that Mr. and Mrs. Far divorced sometime after Dad quit. Sadly, after his divorce, Mr. Far became an alcoholic and died at an early age from alcohol-related complications. As I mentioned earlier, time reveals a person. When it came to Dad and Mr. Far, it revealed two entirely different men.

Ultimately, my dad started his own company in Oklahoma. We didn't know it at the time, but Dad would eventually become extremely successful and acquire significant wealth. But not being able to see into the future, all I knew was that moving in the middle of high school was hard.

I found it difficult to assimilate into a new state. For a dyed-in-the-wool Texan, even stepping north of the Red River was abhorrent enough, let alone living there. I had nothing in common with the students or teachers at school. I might as well have been from a different country, and being from Texas, I pretty much was, or so I thought.

However, over time, I learned that Okies were pretty much like Texans, and slowly but surely, I made friends. As my parents' wealth grew, we moved to a wonderful home in a golfing and tennis community outside of Tulsa, where I discovered that I not only was very good at golf but I loved the game. My dad had always been an excellent and avid golfer. He even had an eighteen-hole putt-putt green installed in our backyard.

As my golf skills grew, my older brothers began to consider that I might be able to defeat Dad in a round of golf, something they had never been able to do. Each year, my brothers and their wives would come home for Thanksgiving, and every time, they would set up a round of golf with Dad, them, and me, in the hopes that I might defeat the old man. I came close a few times, but Dad always seemed to pull out the victory, and I could tell it meant a lot to him to have at least that over his sons.

One Thanksgiving season, when I was a senior in high school and at the peak of my golf game, my brothers called me several times as the holiday approached.

"Have you been practicing?" Gary asked during one call.

"This is the year that you're going to bring the old man down," Greg said during another discussion.

I couldn't understand why it meant so much to them that one of us beats Dad. I could care less if I beat him.

As was the family custom, over the Thanksgiving holiday, my brothers set up a round with Dad. By the time we reached the eighteenth and last hole, Dad and I were tied. We both reached the green in two shots. I was about ninety feet from the hole with an impossible side-hill putt, and Dad was just off the green. Dad went first and chipped within a few inches of the hole, then walked across the green and tapped the ball into the cup for a score of four. That meant if I somehow made my impossible putt, I would beat Dad.

I sized up my putt. As I began to address the ball, I heard my dad whispering to himself, "Miss it, miss it."

I backed away and turned to Dad, resting the putter on my shoulder while pointing at the ball. "If it means that much to you, Dad," I said, "I'll just pick up and we can call it a tie."

Upon hearing this, my brothers dashed over to me, yelling, "No, Cort, no! This is our big chance. You can make that putt!"

I turned to them. "If it means so much to you guys, then why don't you make the putt?" I said, holding the putter out to Gary.

"A tie? A tie is like kissin' your sister!" Dad said, quoting Texas football head coach Darrell Royal. "We ain't gonna tie, boy. You're gonna three-putt, and I'm gonna win again."

At that instant, like my brothers, I wanted to beat Dad. He had always told me I was not competitive enough, and I had always told Dad he wanted to win too much.

I reexamined my putt. At that moment, I got the feeling every golfer gets when they know, "I'm going to make this putt."

As I addressed the ball, I could hear my brothers chanting, "Make it, make it."

Dad chanted just as loudly, "Miss it, miss it."

I stroked the putt, and it glided along the side of the large mound in the green. The ball seemed to roll in slow motion as Dad and my brothers trotted alongside, continuing their chants.

When the ball was about forty-five feet from the hole, gravity started to take over. The ball began to fall left, toward the hole.

When it was about thirty feet from the hole, I knew I had hit a great putt and the ball had a good chance of going in.

As I stood there, marveling at the beauty of a graceful, long, curving putt and the spectacle of my dad and brothers, the ball glided the last fifteen feet to the cup's edge, paused for a microsecond, and fell into the hole.

My brothers began running all over the green, jumping up and down and high-fiving each other, as if they had won the match. Then I noticed Dad. He was slumped over and looking down at the green, shaking his head and tapping his putter on the ground. It was obvious how much it hurt him to lose the one last thing he had over his boys. I walked over to him as my brothers continued to celebrate.

"I'm sorry, Dad," I said. "It was a lucky putt."

Dad kept looking down and tapping his putter on the green. "Nah, Cort. It was bound to happen. I'm just glad it was you and not one of them." He pointed his putter at my brothers.

"Why's that?"

"Because you'll never mention beating me again," he answered. "They'd never let me forget it."

Then, still looking at the ground, Dad stuck his hand out to shake mine and added, "Hell of a putt, boy."

"Thanks, Dad," I replied. I shook his hand for the first time in my life.

It has always bothered me that I defeated my dad that Thanksgiving, especially since it meant so much to him and so little to me. But I learned a lot from Dad and my brothers that day. First, I learned to never let someone talk me into doing something I did not want to do. If they wanted it done, they should do it themselves.

Second, I learned how to win with grace and class. I had a choice in that moment to be like my brothers, running all over the green, pumping my fists and screaming. Dad helped me realize there was a more benevolent way to celebrate victory . . . the way I have taught my children and how I hope they celebrate wins in their lives.

Even more importantly, I learned something about myself. I do not play the game, either in business or life, to defeat my opponent or win, as so many do, and as is so often preached by coaches. I play the game for the joy of playing and developing myself. I find, at least for me and those I coach, that this approach leads to more wins and successes than the way Dad and my brothers approached winning.

I've passed this philosophy onto my daughter Katy and son-in-law Trent, who own a youth baseball player development business. I was proud and pleased when they shared with me their core business philosophy, which they instill in their employees and clients: baseball is for a season; character is for a lifetime.

Chapter 5:
How'd We Kill This Man?

"Evil . . . is the absence of the imaginative sympathy for other human beings. . . . [T]he inability to see your victims as human beings. To think of them as instruments or cogs or elements or statistics but not as human beings."

—Andrew Delbanco

"We are healed of a suffering only by experiencing it to the full."

—Marcel Proust

"[A]t the bottom of the abyss comes the voice of salvation. The black moment is the moment when the real message of transformation is going to come. At the darkest moment comes the light."

—Joseph Campbell

It was the early eighties: the Cold War was coming to a close, the Internet was beginning to revolutionize communication, and then there was me, a newly graduated engineer starting my career at a major chemical company. My first supervisory position was at a small chemical plant on the East Coast. I would go on to serve in various supervisory and managerial positions at five different manufacturing plants across the U.S. before moving into corporate, but that future was yet to be written.

I had been at the plant for a year, when one early spring morning, I decided to stroll out to the plant dock and watch the ships cruise upriver into the city. I often spent my mornings at the dock. As I watched the movement of the boats and felt the cool river breeze, my shoulders dropped and my face relaxed in a sort of peaceful meditation.

Sitting there, I had an overwhelming feeling of satisfaction. My career was progressing well. I was working in one of the most respected facilities in the company, which was considered the best performer in the corporation, especially when it came to safety. I thought to myself, I've made it, and I was feeling pretty good about my future.

Then, without warning, the wind shifted and a deep blanket of fog rolled off the river and covered the entire coastline about a mile inland. I snapped out of my trance and decided I should consider making my way back to the plant, despite being able to see only a few yards in front of me.

I remained for another ten minutes, hoping the fog might clear, but it did not. Then, as I stood and turned toward the shore, I heard a crackle on my radio. It was the plant medic, Tim.

"Cort Dial, come in, please. Cort Dial, come in, please."

I pushed the button on my radio. "This is Cort. Go ahead, Tim, over."

"Come to the contractor fabrication area," Tim replied. "Immediately, over."

"What's going on, over?"

"Cort, just get here as soon as you can."

My shoulders retightened. Tim was a real professional and one of the most respected leaders in the plant. If he wanted me there, he had a darn good reason. I immediately began walking to that section of the plant.

The dock was west of the plant, nearly a mile from the facility's center. The contractor staging area was approximately a quarter mile farther. I walked as fast as I safely could, but my pace was hampered by the limited visibility. I took each step quickly and carefully, continually surveying the patch of visible ground in front of me, until I finally passed through the tank farm and entered the main plant, which housed a number of chemical units.

As I passed each unit, I noticed the operators stepping out of their second-level control rooms. I could see their silhouettes turn to watch me as I walked by, but the fog hid their faces. Even through the haze, their body language told me I was walking toward something serious. I felt like a one-man parade. Whatever Tim was summoning me to, I hoped it wasn't too bad.

Finally, I reached the plant's main road that bisected the plant north and south. As I turned south and looked down Main Street toward the contractor area, the fog prevented me from seeing more than a block ahead.

I picked up my pace. Spectators continued to watch me as I passed building after building, which only exacerbated my apprehension. I began to notice my labored breathing, and I could feel the pulse of my heart against my chest. It was like I was inside a space suit, the outside world almost totally silent but my breath and heartbeats amplified. I wanted to run, but that was strictly against plant policy, and I was afraid of colliding with something in the fog.

As I walked, I narrowed my eyes, trying to get a glimpse of what might be happening, but the fog made it impossible. All of a sudden, I noticed a peculiar sound, one I'd never heard before. I thought, What the hell is that?

I knew it was not associated with the plant. It sounded like a record of a men's choir but as if someone had turned the speed of a recording up and down, causing the pitch to fluctuate. The eerie noise only heightened my apprehension, and I began to breathe even deeper. My heart was now beating through my chest.

When I was a few hundred yards from the contractor area, I began to make out a large, dark object on the horizon, just barely visible through the fog. It was a huge, shadowy mound, and to the right of the mound was a smaller, square, gray object with something long and thin sticking out its top. And that sound. It kept getting louder, but for the life of me I could not make it out. By now, I was near panic, and despite the plant rule, I began to jog toward the contractor area.

When I was about a hundred yards away, the objects began to take shape through the fog. I realized the smaller of the two was a crane, but I still couldn't make out the larger mound. At that instant, I realized that in the background of the entire scene was another object . . . an electrical tower. I said to myself, Oh, my God! Someone was operating a crane under the main electrical lines that power the plant!

I started to sprint. With each step, the objects became clearer and clearer, but I still could not make out that sound. It was creepy, and as much as the crane and power lines scared me, the sound was terrifying.

Then, as I reached about fifty yards from the scene, everything became clear. The crane had made contact with the plant's main power lines. The larger mound was made up of about fifty men, all huddled together, some standing and some on their knees. The eerie sound was men praying, crying, and wailing.

I stopped short from my sprint as I approached the group. The men stood and parted so I could walk into the center. As I walked past them, they all looked up at me, each with tears in his eyes, and continued to mumble prayers. Then I saw Tim.

Tim was at the center of the group, kneeling down next to an older man lying flat on his back. The man's arms and legs were sticking up in the air, and he was staring at the sky. It was as if he were reaching for the sky with his entire body.

Tim noticed me and motioned for me to come over, which I proceeded to do. It was at that moment I noticed that the man was missing most of his hands and feet. They had been blown off by the electricity that had rushed through his body. He had a massive open wound in his stomach, his organs visible. I later learned that when the crane struck the power line, he had been holding the load with both hands. The shock threw him several yards in the air, and he flew into a protruding piece of metal that sliced open his abdomen.

I looked at his hands. There was very little blood. What fingers he still had looked like peeled bananas, oozing and dripping clear liquid. The electricity had cauterized the wounds in his hands and feet. As I walked carefully around the man, I noticed that his deep blue eyes were still staring straight up at the sky. His handsome face was tight with fear as Tim stroked the man's silver hair.

"But I don't feel any pain," the man gasped. "I don't feel any pain."

As I approached, Tim grabbed my forearm and yanked me down next to him and the man.

"Cort, this is Harry," Tim whispered in my ear. "He's going into shock, and he's probably not going to make it. Stay with him, hold his hand, and comfort him. I'm going to meet the ambulance. I'll be back as soon as I can."

With that, Tim handed me Harry's arm. I placed my hand in what remained of his. Harry continued to look into the sky as I cried and prayed with all the other men.

"I can't feel any pain," Harry repeated, his gaze straight up. Then he lost consciousness.

I don't recall anything else. I can't remember if Tim and the ambulance ever returned, or how Harry was removed from the plant. I was a total blank until about forty-five minutes later, when I became aware that I was sitting in the men's locker room and Tim was undressing me.

As I came to, the sudden change startled me. Tim was removing my shirt. Reflexively, I reached for it and grabbed a sleeve to take it from Tim. I immediately recoiled when I touched the sleeve because it was soaked with a cold, slimy liquid.

"What the hell are you doing?" I asked Tim. "And what's that on my shirt?"

"Cort, Harry is gone now. I walked you down to the locker room because you need to take a shower and freshen up. There is an important meeting that you need to attend in about twenty minutes. You've got to get yourself together before that meeting."

"What are you talking about? What meeting? Where is Harry? Is he going to be OK?"

"Harry is on his way to the hospital. He had no vital signs when he left. He will probably be pronounced dead on arrival."

"Dead! Harry's dead!" I yelled. "You mean we killed a man?"

"Yes, we killed a man," Tim answered. He explained that the plant manager had called an emergency meeting of the staff to discuss the accident.

"But what's that on my shirt, Tim?" As I pointed at my shirt lying in the hamper, I began to panic. "What is that?"

Tim responded, "That's your shirt, and it's soaked with fluids from Harry's hand that you were holding. You did a hell of a job; I'm proud of you. Many guys couldn't have done what you did. You took Harry's hand and comforted him as best you could. Now, take your clothes off and get into the shower. You got a meeting to get to."

Tim's voice was steady, and though his body slumped slightly with the weight of the ordeal, he remained poised. I silently thanked God he was there for me in that moment. And then, I drifted away again, and the rest was a blur.

Suddenly, I was sitting in the main conference room of the document control building. I sat up, shifted in the soft leather seat, and rested my arms on the wooden conference table in front of me. I couldn't recall taking a shower, but apparently I had. I looked around for Tim, assuming he had helped me shower and dress. He hadn't arrived yet.

In those days, computers were just entering the workplace, so all plant drawings and documents had to be stored, cataloged, and archived in a special building. There were so many documents that this building was one of the biggest on-site. The conference room walls were lined with shelves packed with binders and documents. I had sat through many meetings in that conference room but nothing like the one that was about to happen.

As I sat in stunned silence, Tim took a seat in the chair to my right, two seats down from the head of the table; I was three seats down. The plant manager had not yet appeared, but some of the staff began arriving. I was astonished to see some of the staff members blaming each other, some screaming in anger. A fistfight broke out, men pummeling one another and continuing to curse and yell. The plant manager walked in, rushed to the men, and broke up the fight.

Once the commotion of the fighting died down, Bud walked to the front of the room.

"Shut up and get your ass in a chair," Bud ordered. "I have a question to ask, and no one is leaving this room until I get a satis-factory answer."

Bud was one of the best plant managers I've had the honor to serve. He was a Southern gentleman who treated everyone with respect and, until that day, I had never heard Bud curse. More than anything, he took pride in the fact that our plant had never experienced a fatal or disabling accident. I felt terrible for him at that moment.

Bud turned to the blackboard and wrote a question: How did we kill this man?

He then explained the process he would be using. One by one, starting on Bud's right and moving counterclockwise around the table, each of us was to give an answer to his question. This process would continue until someone gave him the answer he could live with.

The process went on for a couple of hours, with several rounds around the table. Bud refused to let anyone get a drink or use the restroom, and he declined any requests to bring food into the room. Still, the answers remained the same:

"I don't know how we killed him. That's not my department."

"Bud, he got himself killed. He's an electrician and should've known not to get anywhere near a crane under power lines."

Each time it became my turn to answer, I requested to pass, which Bud allowed, at least for a while.

After about three hours, Bud permitted the group to take a short break. Before he excused us, he said, "If we have to stay in here for weeks, we will. This meeting will not end until I understand how we killed this man."

Upon our return, Bud once again had each of us answer the question on the chalkboard. But this round, when he got to me, he said, "Cort, I want you to try and give me an answer this time. If you can, tell me what you are thinking and feeling."

"I don't know how we killed Harry. I feel as bad as anyone that this happened," I responded, my volume rising as I spoke. "For Christ's sake, I held what was left of his hand while he died. What more do you want from me?"

There was a long pause. Then Bud said in a quiet and calm voice, "Cort, all I want is to know how we did this. Don't you think Harry's family deserves an explanation? At least I can give them that much."

Bud sat back in his chair and let out a big, long sigh. Several moments of silence passed.

Finally, Bud leaned forward in his chair, turned to Tim on my right and said, "Tim, how did we kill this man?"

Tim gave the same answer that he had given each time prior. "Bud," Tim said, "if Harry had only followed our crane procedures—"

This time, Bud interrupted Tim by leaping out of his chair, grabbing the nearest three-inch binder—which happened to be the bright orange safety manual—and heaved it at Tim while screaming, "I don't give a f--k about the goddamn procedure, Tim!"

Unfortunately for me, I was sitting sideways to Bud, directly behind Tim. Tim ducked, and the binder struck me point-blank in the side of the head, knocking me out cold.

The next thing I remember was waking up flat on my back with a crowd looking down at me, while Tim revived me with smelling salts from his medic bag. Tim helped me stand, and Bud instructed him to put me back in my chair.

"Cort needs to go to the infirmary," Tim argued. "He's experienced a lot of trauma today and needs to rest."

Bud was resolute. "Cort can rest when I have my answer. Put him back in the damn chair."

Tim got me water and aspirin, and we all returned to our seats. To my surprise, Bud soon turned to me and said, "Cort, I know you have an answer. How did we kill this man?"

Looking back, I have to conclude that the safety binder knocked some sense into me, because when Bud asked me this time, I did have an answer. But I was too ashamed to say it out loud. Bud must have sensed this, because he started to gently interrogate me.

"Cort, do you know whether a hazard risk analysis was conducted before we decided to stage the contractors directly under the main plant power lines?"

"Yes, sir."

"Yes, you know, or yes, we did?"

"Yes, sir, I know we did."

"Did you participate in that exercise?"

Again, I answered, "Yes, sir, I did."

Bud continued. "And what was discussed during that exercise?"

"I don't exactly recall," I replied. Actually, I did, but I was too ashamed to say.

"Did you discuss the power lines?"

"No, sir."

"Did you discuss the cranes?"

"No, sir."

"If you didn't discuss the power lines or cranes, what the hell did you discuss?"

Never in my life have I felt more shame than at that moment. It took a while for me to muster up the nerve to answer. After several seconds, Tim leaned over and whispered, "Give the man your answer. He deserves to hear your answer."

I looked up at Bud through tearful eyes and said, "We talked about how contractors are dirty and that we didn't want them using our bathrooms or locker rooms." I started crying.

"What else did you talk about, Cort?" Bud asked.

"We talked about how we didn't want contractors parking in our parking lot . . . That's why we stuck them at the far end of the plant and put in that gravel lot," I said.

"And did you talk about anything else?" Bud asked.

I breathed in sharply and regained some composure. "Yes, sir, we did. We talked about how contractors steal things, and so we needed to put a temporary guard shack at their gate and inspect them any time they exited."

Bud paused for what seemed an eternity. He stared at me with a blank expression on his face. I wasn't sure if what I had said stunned him or if he was just utterly disappointed in me. I kept my gaze on the table in front of Bud, too embarrassed to meet his eyes or look in the faces of the other men in the room.

Then Bud broke his silence and rose out of his chair. He leaned over the table, looked down at me, and said in a voice so soft it was almost a whisper, "Cort, how did we kill this man? How did we kill Harry?"

I responded, "We killed him, Bud, because he was a contractor." Then I collapsed to the floor sobbing.

Tim knelt down next to me and patted me on my back. "It's not your fault," he said. "You didn't kill Harry. Don't put this all on yourself. We all played a role in this."

I appreciated that Tim was attempting to make me feel better, but deep down I knew that if I had done my job, Harry would probably be alive. I had to face that we'd killed him because he, being a contractor, didn't matter to us. Harry had not been worthy of our concern simply because of the station he held in life. I knelt on the floor, weeping and thinking to myself, How did I come to be such a person? Is that really who I am? Am I that heartless?

As I collected myself, Tim helped me back to my chair. I sat there, continuing to cry. Bud waited until I was completely composed.

"My friends, I have my answer," Bud said. "This meeting is adjourned. We will reconvene tomorrow morning at 6:00 a.m. in this room. Please say a prayer for Harry and his loved ones tonight."

Tim helped me up to leave, and as we neared the door, Bud said, "Cort, please stay behind. I want to discuss something with you."

I returned to my seat, and the room emptied except for Bud and me.

"I want to thank you for having the courage to fess up to what we caused here today," Bud said. "We killed a man, and you were the only member of my staff willing to say why. I knew you'd be the one."

"You're welcome, sir. But I don't deserve to be praised for what I did. I should be in jail for not doing whatever is necessary to protect anyone who sets foot on this site. That's our primary responsibility, and I failed at it miserably. And what disappoints me the most is that I failed not because I made an honest mistake; I failed because I'm an ignorant bigot."

"We all failed. This is not yours to shoulder alone," Bud replied. "We all will have to come to terms with what happened today."

Then Bud said something that surprised me. "I want you to go home tonight and not come back until Friday. Spend a few days contemplating the meaning you will give this event, what you will learn from it, and how it will make you a better person going forward. On Friday, I want to meet with you at 6:00 a.m. in my office, and you can share with me what you come up with. Will you do that for me?"

"Yes, sir, I will."

I followed Bud out of the conference room and headed to my office. A couple of my colleagues had arranged to drive me home, and someone followed with my car. They thought it best that I not drive myself.

When I arrived home, I acted as if nothing was out of the ordinary. I didn't share with my wife what had occurred. I could say I did this to spare her any pain, but that would be a lie. The truth is I didn't tell her because I was afraid of what she might think of me. Afraid of her reaction to what I'd done to Harry.

The next morning, I left the house at my normal time and spent the day driving around the area, contemplating what Bud had asked me to think about. I arrived home that night as if it was any other workday. I didn't want to explain to my wife why I was not going to work.

Friday morning, I met with Bud. I shared with him that I'd done a lot of introspective thinking and had made a personal commitment I wanted to share with him.

"I can't bring Harry back," I told him, "but I can commit to do everything in my power to ensure what happened Wednesday is never repeated."

Bud and I worked much of that morning to craft a joint commitment that we would vow to one another. We finally came to one we both agreed on: I am committed to the health, safety, and well-being of the men and women who design, build, operate, and maintain our world.

Since that day, my life's purpose has been to embody that commitment.

About six months passed. One day, Bud informed me he had nominated me for a position in another plant. The job, Bud said, would be an opportunity for me to start over. "Some fresh scenery will do you good," he added. I agreed and ultimately accepted the new position, and Julie and I once again relocated.

A few years later, I was sitting in my office when I got a phone call. It was Bud. He had recently moved into a corporate staff position.

Bud immediately said, "Cort! I've just been named project manager of a global project intended to totally revamp how our company relates to and partners with contractors. I'm starting the process of putting together the project team, and you are the first person I thought of. Can I count on you?"

"You know you can," I answered. "I can't think of a better pair to take this on than you and me. I say we start by basing our work on our commitment to working men and women."

"Agreed. I'll call you in a few weeks to let you know when we'll be launching the team."

I hung up feeling as though the universe had finally forgiven me for my past. In the few short minutes of that call, I felt as though I was allowed to flush my system of much of the guilt and shame I had carried for those three years. I was being given a chance to make amends.

Months later, as Bud and I traveled around the company introducing the new contractor approach, he and I would relate the story about Harry. It was difficult for me since I've never been able to tell that story without tearing up. That is true to this day. Regardless of how difficult it is for me to remember, I am sure it is much more difficult for Harry's friends and loved ones.

I am proudest of one aspect of the contractor approach that Bud, the project team, and I developed. It is its guiding principle: the only difference between a contractor and one of us is our paychecks have different company names.

Chapter 6:
Taking My Stand

"The world is a dangerous place, not because of those who do evil, but because of those who look on and do nothing."

—Albert Einstein

About a year and a half after my work with Bud and the contractor project team ended, I was promoted to a new position in the Midwest. As I drove onto the plant grounds the first day, I marveled at the expansive buildings—the facility was much larger than any I had ever worked in. The site contained three distinct manufacturing plants and employed seven hundred union workers. I was assigned to the senior staff of the largest, where we manufactured laundry detergent. The other facilities were a plastics plant and a plant that produced a sheet of glue used to laminate windshields for automobiles and aircraft.

My first day on-site, my new manager, Jake, arranged for us to have lunch in his office. Jake was the youngest site manager in the company and part of a new breed of leaders coming up through the ranks. Unlike his more traditional and formal peers, he was casual in his dress and manner. He may have been short in stature, but he was large in personality with a broad, white smile and a glint in his eye.

Always ready to pat someone else on the back while making fun of his own stocky frame or balding head, Jake oozed positive energy and humor.

I walked into Jake's office that afternoon, taking in the massive space, which was ornately decorated with mementos from his brief but impressive career. The furniture was crafted of the finest woods, leathers, and fabrics. He even had his own private restroom, with a shower and walk-in closet full of business casual attire, a few suits, and plant uniforms.

Jake sat behind a maple desk so large that five leather high-back chairs were lined up facing it. Behind and to the left of his desk were walls of ten-foot-high windows, giving him an excellent view of the entire site. It was as if Jake sat at the top of his castle looking over his entire domain. When I commented on how impressive his office was, Jake chuckled and said, "Nah, this was all built years ago with 'phosphate mafia' money."

Jake served me lunch in a sitting area as large as the average living room. It too was decorated with luxurious furnishings. The lunch was catered in from a local restaurant and served on china with silverware. I thought to myself, Does this guy eat like this every day, or does he think that I'm someone special? Over the next year, I learned that Jake thought everyone was special.

Jake was also fairly new to the site but was well experienced with leading union employees. As I was taking my last bite of food, Jake looked at me earnestly.

"Down the hall from your office is a large wood and frosted glass door with a big, round union seal painted on it," Jake said, leaning forward. "That door and that seal are over fifty years old. That's the office of the union president and his officers. If you are as sharp as Bud tells me you are, you will walk through that door and get to know, understand, and respect those people. They're the ones who really run this plant. It's their people, not ours, who do the work around here. Behind that door, you'll find some of the most committed and intelligent people you'll ever meet. It may be hard for you to see it at first. It'll be masked behind their bib overalls and profanity, but if you can look past all that, you'll see they have the same concerns and potential as anyone."

Jake paused for a moment, studying me as a father does a son.

"There will be those in this plant, possibly some of your counterparts on my staff, who will try to convince you otherwise," he continued. "They will try to get you to see the union as our enemy, not our partner. They'll tell you the union can't be trusted and that our job is to defeat the union with whatever means required. I suggest you let those comments go in one ear and out the other. Instead of listening to that crap, get to know our people, and make up your own mind about them."

Jake was right about one thing. Ever since I had announced I was moving to a union plant, all I'd been told by my associates was how bad unions can be.

"I will," I said. "I'll drop in on them after lunch."

Half an hour later, I found myself standing in front of the door with the big union seal. I suppressed a tremble. I wondered, Why are you so scared? They're just people.

Then I recalled something my dad had once said when I'd shared how afraid I was of making an important presentation: "Fear is just the feeling you get when your body is preparing to do something really important. Instead of trying to resist that feeling, welcome it. See it as a curtain that, as you walk through, showers you with energy. Just step through the fear, move on, and you will do great."

I looked right at that big union seal, inhaled and exhaled deeply, and stepped through the door.

Inside the room were about a dozen union officers, all clad in worn, khaki-colored company uniforms; as Jake had predicted, several were wearing bib overalls. Most were reading newspapers.

Each was smoking a cigar or cigarette, and the room was filled with a dense cloud of nicotine vapor. The officers were arranged haphazardly around the large room, each with his own table and chair signifying his space. The room décor was just the opposite of Jake's office: tattered and cheap. I got the feeling most of the furniture were "hand-me-downs" from the plant. I learned later it was worse than that—some of their furniture were from the plant dumpsters.

As I entered the room, all of the officers stopped and looked at me. I realized what they saw: a young, naïve man decked out in his spanking new, navy-blue management uniform. One of the men, a graying, unshaven gentleman whose 350 pounds was bulging out of his overalls, spun around in his chair. He had the air of a union president.

He bellowed, "Who the f--k are you?"

The rest of the group laughed for a moment and then turned back to their newspapers.

I approached the gentleman. "I was just having lunch with Jake, the new plant manager," I said. "He suggested I come visit your offices. He said I would meet some of the most intelligent and committed people he's ever known. My name is Cort, I'm a new member of Jake's staff, and this is my first day."

"Cort? What kind of name is Cort?"

"Actually, my full name is Cortney. Cort is my nickname."

"Cortney? That's even worse. Who would name a boy Cortney?" He snickered, meeting the eyes of the other men in the room as their faces widened with smug smiles.

"My dad did," I responded. "He's American Indian, and he named me Cortney because it's an Indian word that means calm and peaceful. Apparently, I was calm and peaceful when I was born."

"Indian?" he replied. "You don't look like no Indian to me. You're the palest damn Indian I ever saw." He laughed out loud. By now, most of the other men were laughing as well.

"That I am. I look like my mom, who is mostly Irish. My dad is Indian. His dad was Osage and his mom was Sioux."

"Well, Cort the Indian," he said, "I give you credit for having the balls to walk through that door. I've been union president for over ten years, and there is only one other member of management who's ever walked into this office, and that was Jake a few months ago."

He turned to his fellow officers. "Boys, it looks like we may have another Jake here. Maybe things are looking up. Let's welcome Cort, the pale-faced Cherokee, to the plant."

With that, they each stood up and welcomed me by telling me their names and positions and shaking my hand. And they did this in a manner as professional as any well-groomed executive might. In an instant, the room transformed from a room of "lazy union workers" to one full of professional businessmen. I started to understand what Jake was hoping I would see and learn and why he encouraged me to walk through the door with the big union seal.

I so enjoyed serving on Jake's staff, learning from him, and partnering with the union. We did a lot of good work, but it all ended way too suddenly.

One morning, I was headed over to Jake's office when his executive administrator met me at his door. She was crying.

I asked her what was wrong, but she just shook her head and continued to cry.

Finally, she raised her eyes to mine. "Cort, Jake died last night," she said. "He had a heart attack and died before he reached the hospital."

I tried to stammer a reply, but nothing came out. I made my way to my office and sat in silence.

Everyone on-site was devastated. A great man who was doing great things for a lot of good people was dead. He died so early, barely into his forties, and left a young wife and family, and his life's work undone. Each individual in the plant shared a profound feeling of sadness and incompleteness, but I may have felt it most of all. My mentor, my hero, was gone. I could only hope his successor would be as fine a leader as Jake was.

Soon, however, I realized my new manager was nothing like Jake or Bud. To say that Paul was a "dinosaur" would be to insult dinosaurs. Paul hated workers, and he especially hated the union. That's not just my opinion. He expressed those sentiments often, saying things like, "Goddamn, f--king union!" and "I hate those lazy bastards."

When in public, he showed a different side. His favorite lies were "The union has every right to exist" and "Union workers are the best workers." Suffice it to say, I did not care for Paul. I neither liked nor respected him. However, he was my boss, and my role was to serve him as best I could.

With Paul as our leader, we were unable to produce the same level of performance as we did with Jake. By every measure, our facility was becoming the poorest performer within the company. Safety performance was especially poor, and it seemed like every week we were transporting another person to the emergency room. But Paul had some close friends in high places. He was a couple of years from retiring, and the scuttlebutt was the company had put him "out to pasture" until he retired. His good fortune was our misfortune.

It seemed like Paul and I were constantly at odds. One source of regular friction was his tendency to blame the workers whenever anything went wrong.

Finally, one day as I was in the sitting area of Paul's office, a supervisor briefed the staff about an injury that had occurred in her department. One of her men had been riding on the tailgate of a truck. The truck hit a bump, and he was thrown away from the truck and severely fractured his skull.

Only a few minutes into the briefing, Paul interrupted the supervisor. "I've heard enough. I want this man fired. And young lady, if you have another injury in your group, you will soon join him."

The supervisor, whose name was Susan, looked to her manager for support, but none was forthcoming. Her head dropped and she turned to leave.

"Susan?" I said. She turned toward me.

"Can you answer a few questions for me before we conclude this briefing?"

Susan opened her mouth to respond, but her manager immediately interrupted.

"Susan works for me," he said. "Why do you want to ask her any questions?"

"Look, one of our people has been hurt bad, really bad," I replied. "I want to understand why and how that happened, and I think Susan can help add some insight."

I then turned to Susan, who had been standing during the entire briefing. "Susan," I said, "pull up a chair, and let's discuss this event."

Susan sat her helmet and radio on the coffee table, retrieved a chair, and sat down. At that moment, Paul rose and returned to his desk. The implication was obvious: he wanted nothing to do with the conversation I was planning.

I asked Susan, "Why was Jim sitting on the tailgate? Why was he not seated with his bottom on the truck bed, as is our policy?"

"He was the last man to be picked up, so the truck was full of men," she replied. "The guys lowered the gate so there would be room for Jim. He either sat on the tailgate, or he walked all the way back to the shop. It was the end of the day, and he needed to catch his bus. If he'd walked, he might have missed it."

"That makes sense. No one wants to be the one person left behind. We're all little boys and girls deep inside. And we'll all take a risk to avoid missing our ride."

From Paul's desk, way across the room, there came a loud, distinct scoffing sound. I ignored him.

"Do people ride on tailgates often?" I continued. "I mean, if I went out at shift change today and watched us picking people up, would I see anyone on the tailgate?"

"Yes. It happens all the time."

"Has it always been this way?"

At this point, Paul yelled from his desk, "What does it matter? All that matters is that it is this way today."

"It matters because something we've done might have caused this behavior, and I want to know what that might be. If we can figure that out, we might be able to make changes so people don't feel like they have to ride on tailgates."

Again, Paul let out a disapproving scoff. I continued questioning Susan.

"When Jim sat on the tailgate, did anyone who was in or near the truck say something like, 'Hey, Jim, wait a moment. That's not safe'?"

"No, no one said anything like that."

"Who was in the cab of the truck? Did they see this going on?"

Susan hesitated but finally said, "It's a little embarrassing. There were three supervisors in the cab."

At this point, Paul rose from his desk and started walking back to the sitting area.

"Did the supervisors see Jim on the tailgate?" I asked. "And if they did, did they say anything to try and stop him?"

"No, no one said anything. They saw it, but it happens every day, so no one thought twice about it."

I then asked Susan a question I knew would be very difficult for her to hear. I thought of the questions Bud had asked me a few years prior, and I knew it was in Susan's best interest to go through this process. I said as gently and softly as I could, "Were you one of the supervisors in the cabin who saw this going on and said nothing?"

Susan sat there, spinning her hard hat between her knees and looking down at her well-worn safety boots.

Finally, she looked up at me and said, "Yes, sir. I was driving. I saw what was happening. I knew it was risky, but I wanted to make sure my guys made their rides. Since you guys eliminated most of our trucks last year, we've had to make some compromises. I took the risk and now Jim's in the hospital. If you need someone to blame, blame me, not Jim."

I warmed with pride that she had told the truth and stood up for Jim. Susan looked ashamed.

"No one is to blame," I said. "These types of events can't be pinned on any one person. They are the symptoms of things that are wrong in our organization. We all hurt Jim. Jim hurt himself by taking such a risk, and his coworkers and supervisors hurt him by letting him do it. And this staff put good supervisors like you in the position to make bad compromises by eliminating most of your trucks, just to save a few bucks. As a result of all of that, one of our people is suffering and we are facing medical and liability costs that would pay for dozens of trucks."

To my dismay, Paul finally chimed in. "What's the point of all this? Why are you giving Susan the third degree?" he demanded, as if he actually cared about Susan.

That was the last straw for me. I stood and faced Paul.

"The point is, sir, this is exactly the type of inquiry that we need to make when we have an accident. Instead of firing the person who screwed up, we need to explore how we, all of us—including you, me, and this staff—contributed to his actions."

"I contributed? You're saying that I caused this accident? How the hell did I contribute to Jim getting hurt?"

"We all contributed. But since you asked, I'll tell you exactly how you did."

"Please do."

"You contributed, sir, by arriving on-site and making unilateral decisions like eliminating 80 percent of the plant vehicles, merely to make your costs look good to corporate and without considering the consequences to your people. You now have your consequences. One of your men is in the hospital with a seven-inch crack in his skull. But instead of owning up to your role in this matter, and instead of rushing to the hospital to console him and his family, you sit here in your plush office declaring you're going to fire his ass. That, sir, is how I say you contributed."

There was a long pause. Paul's face became violently red. He stared at me with wide eyes, clenching and unclenching his jaw.

He finally composed himself and said to the group, "Would you all please excuse me? I have something that I want to say to Mr. Dial." Everyone immediately left without saying a word.

Paul informed me that he was going to approach human resources and charge me with insubordination.

"If I can find a way to fire your ass, I will. But in case I can't, know this: You will never step in this office again. You will never attend another meeting I am in. And you will never speak to me or approach me in any way. Do you understand that?"

"I understand you loud and clear," I responded. "But you need to know this. I will not tolerate anyone in this plant doing anything that puts our people's health, safety, or well-being at risk, regardless of his rank. That commitment is something I will not relinquish. Do you understand that about me?"

"I will never understand you. It's time for you to leave my office."

"That seems to be the only thing we agree on. Good day, sir."

I turned and left Paul's office and proceeded immediately across the hall to the head of human resources, who was named Stanley.

As I entered Stanley's office, he said, "Good day, Cort. Sounds like you and Paul are having a stimulating meeting. Have a seat and tell me what's on your mind."

Without hesitation, I said, "Stanley, I will not work another day with that Neanderthal. Either we find me something else, or I'll have no choice but to start exploring other options."

Stanley nodded in understanding. "All I can say at the moment is I have been working on other options for a few weeks," he said in a low voice. "Come back tomorrow morning when you're not so upset, and we can chat." I accepted Stanley's offer and headed down the hall to exit the building.

A few doors down, someone whispered, "Cort, Cort." I turned around, and Susan was standing there.

"So, did the bastard fire you?" she asked.

"No, at least not yet," I replied. She exhaled in relief.

"Thanks for standing up to Paul and taking the heat off me."

"No worries. How 'bout you and I grab a couple of burgers," I offered. "We can visit Jim afterwards."

"That's a great idea," Susan replied. "Let's get the hell out of this asylum and go see what we can do for Jim."

Chapter 7:
A Quality Opportunity

"The race for quality has no finish line—so technically, it's more like a death march."

—Despair, Inc. Demotivational Poster

"Measurement is our drug in the business world, because we believe that by measuring everything and sending the good news upstairs to the C-suite we can ward off the bogeyman of business, namely Getting On the Boss's Bad Side."

—Liz Ryan

I entered the meeting with Stanley the following morning expecting him to give me the same old human resources sermon about having to support my manager. Or, at best, he'd say he's working on getting me reassigned. However, I quickly realized neither was going to be the case.

"I've got an interesting opportunity for you," he began, "that I think will achieve your objectives, while at the same time be a good move for the company."

Stanley was new to the facility, so I didn't know him well. I'd heard he was a former professional basketball player, which was evident by his six-foot-seven-inch frame. He was twenty years my senior and wore a pleasant expression, and it was clear he was doing his best to fill his predecessor's shoes. This was a challenge since his predecessor, Joe, was beloved by most employees. I especially thought highly of Joe since he'd gone out of his way to help me adjust to my new position and environment when I first started at the plant. For me, this was the first test of Stanley's capabilities. Little did I know that Stanley would not only pass the test, he would offer me an opportunity that would change the direction and trajectory of my life.

"You'll never guess who was in my office yesterday afternoon inquiring about you," Stanley said.

"Who?" I replied.

"Mick. He's been talking with me the last few weeks about whether you might be available for a position he is creating in his staff." My mind shifted to Mick, the manager of the plant that produced sheets of glue used to laminate automobile and aircraft windshields.

"Mick? What position is he creating?"

Outwardly, I remained calm, hiding my surprise from Stanley. Inwardly, I was shocked Mick would be inquiring about me since I had been a thorn in Mick's side since I arrived. In my eyes, Mick was an overly confident, aggressive manager who frequently took unwarranted risks.

"He's calling the position 'Manager of Customer Quality.' He says he needs someone like you to come into his organization and lead a major effort that is critical to the plant's future. Why don't you drop in on Mick today and talk with him about it?"

"I will. Thanks, Stanley," I said. "One thing, though. Do you have any advice for me when I speak with Mick?"

"I appreciate you asking. Yes, I do. Don't walk into the meeting being a guy who wants to get away from Paul. Walk into that meeting being the guy who is going to help Mick lead his plant into the future. Be that and you will do fine."

"I will. That's great advice."

I left Stanley's office and proceeded immediately to Mick's plant. On the way, I kept wondering, What the hell does Mick mean by "quality manager"? Why does Mick want me? How can I play a leadership role in a plant where I don't know the people, don't know the operation, and don't know a thing about quality?

I arrived at the plant's main lobby and was greeted by Mick's executive administrator, Janet. Immediately, I felt an entirely different vibe than in my current plant under Paul's leadership.

Janet rose from her desk and said, smiling, "Welcome, Mr. Dial. Stanley called and told Mick to expect your visit. I'm excited about the possibility of you joining our team. Mick speaks very highly of you. Let me inform him that you're here."

Again, I was shocked to hear that a guy who, I believed, thought I was a burr under his saddle was speaking highly of me and eager for me to join his team. At the same time, it felt good to be welcomed and thought of so positively.

Janet poked her head into Mick's office. "Mr. Dial is here," she said. "Do you have time to see him?"

"Of course," I heard Mick say in an excited tone. "Send him in."

Janet turned to me and said with a gentle, motherly whisper, "Go on in and good luck."

I entered Mick's office, expecting him to be seated behind his desk, just as Paul sat on his throne. But to my surprise, Mick greeted me a few feet within the door. He shook my hand briskly.

"Welcome, Cort," he said. "I was so pleased to hear from Stanley that you're open to discussing the role I have in mind for you. Can I get you some water or a soda?"

Mick was tall like Stanley and oozed confidence and business professionalism. His graying hair and slightly wrinkled eyes revealed that he was about fifteen years older than I.

We sat in two chairs positioned in front of Mick's desk and began discussing the opportunity. Mick explained that the plant's major customer, an automobile company, was concerned about Mick's organization's ability to meet the customer's growing expectations.

"They have introduced a new program called 'Q1' . . . you've seen their commercials saying 'At our company, quality is job 1,' haven't you?"

"I have," I replied.

"Well, quality and the Q1 program are becoming a big thing with our customer, and a major part of the Q1 program is auditing."

"Auditing?"

"Yes, they are going to audit us in a few weeks. It's a huge deal for us, and I'm worried we're not ready. I've been unable to get our people to understand that this is a titanic change for us."

Mick went on to explain that I would be helping him enroll his managers and employees in the importance of quality and customer service.

"The world is changing, Cort. Quality is going to become the driving force in business. This is a chance for someone like you to get in at the early stages and ride that wave into the future."

"Sounds exciting," I said. "Can I ask you a couple of questions?"

"Certainly. Shoot."

I hesitated, then asked, "Why me? I mean, you and I have always seemed to be at odds. Until today, every conversation we've had has been argumentative. I've always assumed you thought I was a major pain in the ass."

Mick chuckled. "I agree we've had our heated discussions, but I never saw them as argumentative. I've always seen you as the only person on-site who will stand up to me, who lets me know when I'm out of line or about to do something that's wrong, or worse, stupid."

"Really? So you appreciate when I push back?"

"Well, to be truthful, not always, at least not at the time. You've probably noticed I'm a guy who knows what he wants and is aggressive about getting it. This has served me well up to now. But like I said, the world is changing. I'm going to have to change the way I operate, and I need someone to help me make that shift."

"And you want me to help you?" I asked.

"Yes, but not just me. I want you to help me help my entire organization make a shift to a quality culture and a high focus on customer satisfaction."

"How do you see me helping you do that? Can you give me an idea of what that might look like?"

"Oh, I guess it would look something like what we're doing right now. You'd be in my office, asking me questions just like this."

"That'd be it?" I asked, puzzled. "I'd just be asking questions?"

"Of course, you'd do more than ask questions. You'd advise me. Tell me what I need to be saying to my people. Give me feedback on my behaviors. You'd observe me in meetings and debrief with me afterwards. You'd keep your fingers on the pulse of my staff and employees and let me know if I'm making the changes in their mind-sets and culture that I want."

I did not know it then, but Mick was inviting me to take on my first executive coaching position, a role I would play with my clients for the next three decades.

"I could do that," I replied. "I've never done it officially as a job before, but I agree I would be good at playing that role. But how will you convince the company to pay me to merely advise you?"

"Let me deal with that. Your main focus will be to help us earn Q1 quality status."

"Very well. But what is Q1 quality status?"

"Q1 status is what we will earn if we pass the upcoming audit and achieve a high-enough grade. If we don't pass, which I fear is likely, one of your first tasks will be to somehow get my staff to accept you as the person who will help us lead the plant's successful reaudit. We only get one chance to pass a reaudit. If we fail again, we will lose our customer, which means losing about 60 percent of our business. If that happens, the company would likely shut the plant down."

"Yikes! We can't let that happen. When do I start?"

"Don't you need some time to think it over?"

"What's to think over? You're offering me the opportunity to do something I think I'm very good at while helping save a lot of people's jobs. Why would I say no to that?"

"Outstanding!" said Mick. "I knew I'd picked the right person. I'll speak with Stanley and Paul today. Let's plan on you starting early next week, after I've informed my staff."

"That reminds me," I said. "What do you think your staff will think of me joining their team? Are they aware of the role you want me to play?"

"All I can tell you is whenever I've mentioned I'm impressed with you and would like to somehow get you on our team, they've agreed and been supportive. You'll begin in the role of advising me, and we'll have to look for the opportunity for you to advise them as well."

"I'm glad they think of me positively, but that's a long way from them accepting me as their advisor."

"Agreed. We'll just have to address that when the opportunity presents itself. I've seen you in action. I have confidence you'll find a way."

"I'll trust your judgment on this," I said. "I'll check in with you on Friday to see where we stand and plan on attending your Monday morning staff meeting."

I shook Mick's hand, left his office, and smiled to myself.

Mick was right about the plant's unreadiness. Shortly after I joined his staff, we failed the audit. As the customer's lead auditor, Evelyn, informed Mick, his staff, and me of the audit results, I could feel the frustration of my associates. What was disappointing to me, however, was that their irritation was focused at Evelyn and her audit team and not on us and our failure to do what was necessary to meet our largest customer's expectations. Mick's staff vigorously challenged Evelyn on several audit findings and generally behaved in a disrespectful manner.

Evelyn informed us that the Q1 program allowed for a reaudit within nine months and it was up to us to contact her to schedule it. She thanked us for our cooperation during the audit and left the room to debrief elsewhere with her team.

As I sat there with my associates, I pondered how I might use this obvious failure to help them prepare for the reaudit. We sat there silently for several minutes. Then Mick finally spoke.

"Gentlemen," he said, "this is a humiliating failure for which we are responsible. I don't want to hear any excuses or explanations. I want to hear what we're going to do about passing a reaudit as soon as possible and which one of you is going to lead that effort."

I realized that Mick had set me up well to propose the role he had envisioned for me, but something in me said I should let my teammates speak first. In turn, each spoke, breaking Mick's ground rules by doing a lot of excusing and justifying.

Then, Russ, the strongest leader of the group, said, "We failed the customer's audit. We need to accept that and move on."

"I agree," Mick said. "Which of you is the best person to lead us out of this mess? We must focus our attention on passing the reaudit as soon as we can. The organization needs a person they can relate to as the leader of that effort. Obviously, my inclination is that it should be one of you."

I looked around the table, wondering who would talk first, but all of my teammates were looking down. It was as if none of them wanted to risk making eye contact with Mick and, in doing so, be selected. I waited for someone to speak, but the room remained silent except for the creaking of chairs as the team shifted in their seats.

Finally, I said, "This staff and our employees are, by far, the best I've ever worked with. You guys are the most technically competent and passionate team of managers I've known, and your people love working for you and in this plant. You love everything about making that sheet of glue, and you take great pride in being the best in the world at what you do. I've only been here a few weeks, and from day one I've been impressed with each of you and what this organization pulls off every day." I paused, watching expressions relax. "Having said all that, I have a question for this team: how did we not pass this audit?"

"What do you mean?" Russ said. "You were here; you saw what happened."

"I mean, how did a group of such great managers and people not pass this audit?" I replied. "Is it because what the customer now expects is beyond our capability? Is it because we didn't give the audit the attention it required? Or is it something else? In other words, what's missing that, if we put it in place, we would pass this audit with flying colors?

We explored those questions for the next few minutes. The team started to open up to the possibility that four things were missing: leadership, coordination, collaboration, and a strong relationship with the customer's lead auditor, Evelyn. The group agreed that if these four things had been present, we would have likely passed the audit.

It was at this moment that I proposed that they empower me to help them lead and direct our preparation for the reaudit.

"I can help you and Mick lead and manage the response to this audit in a way that not only makes people forget this failure but builds the quality culture all of our customers are going to expect going forward," I said. "I can drive the overall coordination, encourage collaboration, and manage the relationship with Evelyn, but the leadership must come from you. If we come together on this plan, I see no reason why we can't pass a reaudit within six months. And on that day, we will hoist that big blue Q1 flag that Evelyn will present to us, while our people pop champagne corks in celebration."

At this, heads began nodding, and the team members shared approving glances.

"It seems the group thinks you're our man," Mick said. "Do we all agree?" There was a burst of agreement from the team members as they weighed in with their yeses.

After Mick and his staff accepted my offer, we adjourned until our next staff meeting. I immediately headed for the conference room where Evelyn was debriefing her audit team and waited until they finished. When they did, I informed Evelyn that I was officially requesting a reaudit in six months. She smiled.

"Somehow I figured you'd be the one coming to me with this request, Cort," she said. "I just didn't expect it to be today. Can I assume you're my main contact going forward?"

"You can," I replied.

Six months later, Evelyn handed Mick and his staff the big blue Q1 flag as our employees popped champagne corks in celebration. The only place where my prediction fell short was the champagne was alcohol-free due to policies prohibiting alcoholic beverages on company property. I could say it was my great coordination and advisement that made the difference, but in reality, I learned more from Mick and his staff than they did from me. Never had I worked with a team of such committed, hardworking, and smart persons who enjoyed their work so much and took such pride in their accomplishments. All they needed to pass the audit was a little leadership guidance.

I was impressed with Evelyn, the lead auditor, from the day I met her. She was the consummate professional, knew her stuff, and cared deeply about her company's mission to "transform U.S. industry." I thoroughly enjoyed working with her in preparation for our reaudit as she continually taught me about quality, auditing, and professionalism. What I was not aware of was that she was also impressed with me.

A few months after our successful reaudit, Evelyn called and invited me to a weeklong quality summit her company was holding at its world headquarters. She informed me all of the company's senior executives would be in attendance and that she had been given permission to invite a few select suppliers, of which I was one. Evelyn also let me know that the summit would be facilitated by "the distinguished Dr. Edwards Deming."

I eagerly accepted the invitation, even though I had no idea who Dr. Edwards Deming was. The idea that I would get to spend another week with Evelyn at the company's world headquarters learning about quality was more than enough for me to say yes.

I arrived at the customer's world headquarters a few months later, greatly anticipating the first day of the four-day event. As I entered the auditorium that first day, I was struck to see nearly five hundred executives from around the globe, all who would be sharing the experience with me. I suddenly felt the weight of being the sole representative of my company with such an important customer.

Evelyn greeted me and showed me to our seats. She was seated to my left in the very center back row of the enormous auditorium. As we waited for the session to begin, I joked to Evelyn, "I hope the good doctor doesn't do his famous disappearing dime trick."

Evelyn laughed. Then, looking past me, she gasped and whispered, "There he is."

I turned to see an elderly man being escorted down the aisle to the front of the auditorium. Dr. Deming appeared to be at least eighty years old. While the executives in the room wore expensive, tailored suits, his looked of the department store off-the-rack variety. He walked with a slight bend in his slender body but still looked to be a head taller than the two young women who were helping him make the long journey to the stage. As they proceeded down the aisle, more and more of the attendees noticed him, and as they did, the room became quieter until it was nearly silent.

Then, out of nowhere, a thundering round of applause and cheers rose from the crowd, and I found myself standing with Evelyn and the other five hundred attendees, welcoming "the doctor" to his summit. Evelyn wore adoration on her face, thrilled to be in his presence. I was immediately curious of who this man was and why he demanded such respect.

The doctor's guides led him to a small stage at the center of the auditorium. He eased into a simple metal chair with a cushioned seat, and next to him was a little folding table that held an old-fashioned chrome microphone, a tray of drinking glasses, a pitcher of ice water, and a copy of his book, *Out of the Crisis*. As the doctor sat and his helpers retreated, he drew a flask from his pocket and placed it on the table.

He sat there silently for a few moments. As the room became equally silent, he looked around at his audience, cleared his throat, and then said in a low, soft voice, "I'm Edwards Deming. Thank you for inviting me to be with you this week. Let's get down to business."

The first day of the summit was rather uneventful. The doctor spent most of the time introducing us to his ideas and theories, mostly through reading from his book and storytelling. Despite not being blown away by the first day, I was intrigued by this man who kept five hundred executives engaged as he explained why their foreign competitors were beating them at their own game. Something told me I had only seen the first act in a four-act play, and knowing that act two is usually where the suspense begins, I was looking forward to the next day.

The morning of the second day began just like the previous, with Dr. Deming being walked down the aisle to booming applause. Again, the doctor had only a microphone, his book, a pitcher of water and drinking glasses, and his flask, from which he took a sip from time to time. But just as the doctor was leaning into the mic to speak, a young "eager beaver" exec sitting in the second row rose and said, "Dr. Deming, I was so excited after hearing you speak yesterday that I couldn't wait to do something to improve our quality. But then I realized I didn't know what to do. If there's just one thing, one thing, that I could do starting today that would help my people improve our quality, what might that be?"

As the young man spoke, I couldn't help but notice the reaction of the other executives in the room. Most were shaking their heads in disapproval of this person interrupting Dr. Deming and asking such a question without prompting. Then I noticed that the doctor was leaning toward the mic to give his response. The entire room must have noticed the same, since all eyes shifted to the doctor, and the room was quiet with expectant silence.

Dr. Deming leaned closer to the mic, and I saw hundreds of bodies lean slightly forward. After a moment, the doctor said, "Stay home."

To my surprise, the entire room broke into hilarious laughter and applause. I assumed the other execs felt that he had put the young man in his place. But as the laughing and applause died out, the doctor leaned into the mic once again.

"Obviously, you think I was speaking to this enthusiastic young man," he said, "but actually, I was speaking to every person in this room. The answer to all your questions about why you are losing your business to the Japanese—why you can't compete in the global markets, why you can't produce a quality product that rivals your competitors—the answer to all your questions is in this room. You, ladies and gentlemen, are the primary source of variation in your organizations and, therefore, in your products. You, management, not your people, are the source of and solution to the problems you face. Most of you don't believe that today, but I promise you, you will by the time you leave this summit."

At that moment, I knew I was in the presence of someone special. I was looking directly at the person I wanted to be someday. I wanted to have so much conviction in my ideas and confidence in my abilities that I could sit in front of a room of hundreds of top executives and help them realize they are the solution to their problems. Or as I put it today when working with my clients, "The most effective tool you have for creating business results is sitting in your chair."

Later, during a break at the summit, I approached the doctor.

After shaking his hand and thanking him for his contribution to U.S. industry, I asked, "How do I measure the things you're talking about? I mean, they're so touchy-feely. If you can't measure it, you can't manage it, can you?"

The doctor looked at me with a slight grin. "Young man, you seem to assume that anything of value must be measurable," he said. "I'll tell you this: as you gain experience and mature, you're going to find that the things most important to quality, safety, productivity, or any human endeavor cannot be quantified."

He hadn't answered my questions. He'd done better. He'd challenged my assumptions in a way that made me reconsider my manner of thinking, something I came to learn is a key leadership skill.

I left the summit not knowing exactly what it was that Dr. Deming was doing with my customer's company. I had no idea what it was called, but I knew I would be doing it eventually.

Someday, I would find myself sharing my ideas and principles with hundreds of executives who would be eager to hear what I had to say. I didn't know how I would get there, but I committed to start on that path as soon as possible.

Chapter 8:
He's a Witch!

"If at first the idea is not absurd, then there is no hope for it."
—Albert Einstein

"In the 21st century, organizations have to achieve peak performance by creating conditions that allow them to unleash the power of their people—not leading them, not by managing them, but by co-inspiring them."
—Kevin Roberts, executive chairman, Saatchi & Saatchi

"In a room where people unanimously maintain a conspiracy of silence, one word of truth sounds like a pistol shot."
—Czesław Miłosz

After our successful reaudit, I didn't see a further role for me in the company. I continued on Mick's staff, helping establish a quality culture and put into place the systems necessary to support it. I challenged him when he needed it. As he put it, I helped him understand himself.

"It's like having a conscience that can get me to listen and act on the feedback," he explained.

But looking forward, I knew there weren't a lot of managers like him who saw the value in having someone play that role. When I raised this concern to Mick, he replied without hesitating.

"Make the role, Cort," he said. "Find another manager like me who could benefit from your advice and is willing to create a position for you. I bet there are more out there than you think."

I left that discussion with Mick, contemplating how I might find another manager like him who would want me to be his or her advisor. I couldn't yet articulate the value of such a role in a way that made the business case. Mick understood that I had helped him save his plant and secure its future; he realized the worth of my role in dollars and cents. But demonstrating that to another manager was, at that time, beyond my capability.

Then, one morning, I received a call from the company's global director of health and safety. Vance explained that he was on the corporate staff and reported to the CEO.

"We're looking for some 'out of the box' thinkers to come speak at our Global Health and Safety Conference, and your name was offered as a possibility," he continued.

"Really?" I said. "Who offered my name?"

"I was having dinner with your human resources manager, whom I've known for years. He shared about this young fellow at his plant who is from a different mold and has ideas well ahead of the curve. When Stanley told me that, I knew I wanted to check you out."

"I'll have to thank him for the recommendation. How do we proceed?"

"I was hoping to convince you to come speak at our conference. You'd only have about twenty minutes on the agenda, but I want

She's a Witch! | 75

someone who is willing to shake up our thinking about how we approach health and safety. According to Stanley, you have some strong views, some of which have gotten you into hot water with Paul. But Stanley tells me you stood your ground. That's exactly what I'm looking for, someone who is willing to say what he thinks in the face of strong opposition."

"What exactly would you have me say to your group?"

"The attendees will be plant managers and health and safety professionals from all over the world, about six hundred attendees. What you say will be totally up to you—maybe say what you've always wanted Paul to hear or what you think the audience needs to learn. Are you in?"

I realized this was my opportunity to be Dr. Deming, to get in front of a large group of executives and share my ideas. The thought of doing so was both exhilarating and terrifying.

"Yes, sir, I'm in," I replied. "Just say when and where, and I'll be there."

I hung up and immediately proceeded to Mick's office to share my conversation with Vance and gain Mick's support for speaking at the conference. He was pleased to hear that I had accepted the invitation.

"This is your chance to find the next person to advise," he added. "Maybe it will end up that Vance is the guy."

"I hadn't considered that, but you may be right. Maybe I'll find someone there."

"You will if you look hard enough."

Four months later, I was on a flight to the company world headquarters with my speaking notes in my briefcase. I'd taken Vance's advice and designed my talk as if I was chatting with Paul, or any other manager, and sharing my ideas about how we might better approach health and safety and performance in general.

As promised, Vance had set twenty minutes aside for me early in the morning of the conference's first day. When he introduced my talk, he simply said, "I've asked Cort to share his ideas on performance management with an emphasis on health and safety, which I predict will be different than most of ours. That's why I've brought him here: to shake up the way we think, get us to think outside our boxes, and consider new ways to do what we do. Cort has a reputation in the company as being an unconventional character who sees the world a little bit differently than most, and I think he's the perfect person to kick off this conference. Please welcome Cort."

As I stepped onto the stage, I looked out at the convention room full of six hundred executives. I thought to myself, Well, dude, you asked for it. Here you are, exactly where you had hoped to be. Don't blow it.

I took a sip of water and peered around the room, studying the eyes of the audience. I could tell from the anticipation on their faces that Vance had set them up well for my talk.

Over the next fifteen minutes, I made three assertions.

First, it is unacceptable to harm people in the pursuit of business results. I explained our current "injury and incident targets" were an admission that we believe people must be harmed for us to do business. I warned that the day was coming where society would no longer allow us to harm people in order to produce business results. We had better figure out soon how to produce those same results without harm to anyone or anything, or the public was going to revoke our right to operate.

Second, numerical injury goals have no place in the management of health and safety. I detailed how health and safety are different than any other aspect of business. It's about people, and the moment we start talking about numbers, we're not talking about people; even worse, we're objectifying sacred, living beings.

Third, you can't measure what is most important to performance. I concluded by explaining that health and safety professionals, as well as most of the managers in our company, are entirely too focused on the technical side of management. Instead, they must shift their focus to the human side. In the near future, health and safety, and performance management in general, would be much less about equipment, systems, and processes and much more about leading and inspiring people. Those executives who were unwilling or unable to make this shift would soon find themselves redundant.

I spent about five minutes on each of these points, giving brief examples to demonstrate why our current way of being and acting was limiting our performance. Finally, I said, "I very much appreciate the opportunity to speak with such a distinguished group of leaders. Thank you for listening to my ideas. I have five minutes left for questions."

I looked eagerly to the crowd. There were no questions.

For several moments, I stood there looking into hundreds of blank faces. Every time a person shifted in her seat, I looked in that direction, hoping to see a hand shoot up or someone stand. Neither happened.

If there had been crickets in the room, I would have heard them. I thought, I wonder if Deming ever experienced this?

Still, I remained confident in my assertions—not that I was right and the audience was wrong but that I could see a new way of attacking our performance challenges. From my perspective, lives and our company were at stake in this conversation, so I had no qualms about standing for those people who would be harmed if we didn't change our ways. I was ready and willing to take whatever response the group gave me.

My thoughts were interrupted when I noticed a person in the audience, about halfway back and to my left, standing. I smiled in his direction.

The man cupped his hands around his mouth and yelled, "He's a witch! Burn him!" The audience responded by laughing loudly, cheering, and giving the man a standing ovation.

I'm the young, enthusiastic exec the rest of the crowd is ridiculing, I thought. This is an interesting development.

Before I could even consider how to respond, I realized Vance had joined me on the stage. He was walking toward me, carrying a microphone. This got the attention of the audience, who stopped cheering and retook their seats. When the audience had settled down, Vance turned to me.

"I have to say, I don't agree with a single thing you've said here today," he said, drawing laughs and a few claps from the audience. "I have only one question for you, and that's this: would you be interested in joining my staff?"

This comment drew a collective gasp from the crowd.

"We need more people like you," he continued, "people who are willing to stand up and challenge the status quo, even in the face of strong resistance. I asked you to come here and shake up this group and you far exceeded my expectations. In fact, you've shaken me up to the point that I want you to help me see what I can't see and hopefully do the same for my staff. Thank you for coming here and sharing your ideas at our conference."

"You're very welcome, sir," I replied. "It was my privilege."

As I turned to leave the stage, there was very little applause for me. It was obvious Vance was one of the few attendees who appreciated my talk.

I returned home that afternoon, and the next day Mick asked me to brief him on how my talk was received. He listened, nodding thoughtfully.

"Sounds like you've found your next job," he finally said. "I think Vance wants you to play a similar role as you've played for me and my staff. Why don't you call him next week and explore that possibility with him?"

I didn't have to wait until the next week to speak to Vance. That Friday morning, Vance called and thanked me again for my talk.

"My offer for you to join my team was genuine," he said. "I need someone like you to help us get out of our ruts and think differently. Are you open to discussing the position?"

"I'd like that," I replied.

"Outstanding! How 'bout you fly up next week and we'll discuss what you might do for me and my team?"

Early the next week, Vance and I met for breakfast and then made our way to the world headquarters campus. As we drove onto the grounds, I took in the hilly woodland setting, beautifully complemented with dozens of marble and glass buildings and stunning landscaping. Finally, we stopped off at the cafeteria for some coffee.

"I prefer to meet here," he explained. "We're less likely to be interrupted."

We found a table and sat down. Vance, like me, came from Indian stock, but unlike me, he was dark skinned with bright silver hair. Prior to taking on the most senior health and safety position in the company, he'd served as plant manager in several of the company's largest and best performing plants. I felt honored that such an experienced and successful businessperson valued my ideas. Vance shared with me that he had spent a couple of hours on the phone, discussing with Mick the role I was playing with him and his staff and what my role might be for Vance.

"You're a unique guy, and I have a very unique role for you," he explained. "I'd like you to take a new position in our group that has two main functions. First, to help us understand and be as effective managing on the human side, as you put it in your talk, as the technical side. Second, to explore the latest, greatest thinking in business, find the new ideas, bring them back to us, and help us apply them to what we do. In a sense, I want you to help me and my staff lead the three shifts you talked about at the conference, while exploring even more ideas that we can apply."

"I'm very interested in that role," I replied. "Have you talked to your staff about this yet?"

"My staff will think I'm nuts when I tell them you're joining us. They'd probably have been first in line to burn you at the stake," he said, chuckling. "But that's exactly why I need you on my team.

"If you come, I promise to support you 100 percent in this role. You'll only have to answer to me. You won't be expected to manage the skeptics; that'll be my role. You've got some important things to say, and I will help make sure you get the chance to say it to as many people as possible."

"Consider me in," I replied.

Vance clapped his hands together. "Excellent."

With that, we spent the next half hour talking through my transition plan, dreaming up the impact I could have on the company.

I left that meeting with Vance, knowing I had found my next manager to serve. But unlike Mick, who wanted me to help him and his staff, Vance had a grander mission for me. I would impact a much larger audience and get to share my ideas, not merely my advice. I couldn't wait to get started.

Chapter 9:
You're an Executive Coach

"Choose a job you love, and you will never have to work a day in your life."

—Confucius

"Understanding variation is the key to success in quality and business."

—W. Edwards Deming

Vance kept his promise. I spent the next couple of years in his group introducing and, where possible, executing my ideas. At the same time, I sought out the greatest thinkers in the world, studying their concepts and bringing them back to Vance and his team.

My primary role was research and learning for the first year. Vance also arranged for me to give talks throughout the company, sharing my ideas with virtually every business unit and discipline.

"I want you to reach as many people as possible," he told me. "You need to learn how to enroll people in your ideas, not just share them."

During one of the first talks Vance arranged, I was severely challenged by a group of PhD researchers who felt my limited education disqualified me from having any useful ideas. Afterwards, as Vance and I were leaving, he put his arm around my shoulders.

"Don't let those eggheads discourage you," he said. "They're too smart to see past their turned-up noses. They attacked you because you're a threat, and it pisses them off that someone with less education thought of something they haven't. Just keep talking and sharing your thoughts. That's your gift, and you're getting very good at it."

I went on to conduct nearly seventy talks throughout the company during my first year and a half on Vance's team.

Then, in the middle of my second year, Vance walked into my office. I looked up from my desk.

"I just heard some news," he said. "You've been selected as a candidate for a new role in the company."

"What role would that be?" I asked.

"They're calling it 'internal consultant.' I'm not sure of the details. All I know is that if you're interested, you need to get back to this person"—Vance handed me a piece of paper—"and attend the orientation session planned for next month."

I looked over the paper before speaking. "How'd I get chosen?"

"You've developed quite a reputation within the company. It doesn't surprise me at all that they thought of you. It sounds like a great opportunity. It's your decision, but I suggest you check it out."

That afternoon, I made my way to the office of the corporate director of human resources, Mary. She explained that I was one of fifteen candidates, from which five would be selected and trained as internal consultants. The role would involve consulting executives and managers throughout the company in change leadership, culture building, negotiations, and other issues and challenges.

A month later, I found myself in a room with the other candidates, undergoing a number of verbal, written, and role-play scenario tests. At the end of the process, only three of us were selected. Apparently, none of the other candidates passed the threshold of the program.

Over the next three months, the other two selectees and I participated in an extensive training process taught by subject matter experts. We spent hours practicing to fulfill our new role. Two months in, one of the trainees decided she was no longer interested in the consulting role; a few weeks after completing the training, the other resigned from the company. So, at the end of all this effort, there was only one trained internal consultant standing: me.

Based on the poor outcome of the selection and training process, human resources canceled the entire program, and I was left trained but with no official role. Fortunately, Vance was more than willing to have me rejoin his team.

Vance was smart enough to realize that he now had a resource with an entirely new skill set on his staff, and he decided to start "farming me out" to executives who were looking for the type of support I was now able to offer. He suggested, however, that I not refer to myself as a consultant.

"People expect a consultant to be a subject matter expert who tells people what to do," he advised, "and you're not that."

"If I'm not a consultant, then what is it that I do?" I asked.

"I don't really have a name for it," he said. He paused in thought before continuing. "You provoke novel thinking but without teaching. You help people see with new eyes, giving them new perspectives but without showing them the solution. And you cause people to look inwardly at how they're contributing to a situation but without making them feel wrong.

"On the other hand, you tell people what they need to hear. You can be extremely blunt but only when they need it and are ready to hear it. And you do these things in a way that causes people to be more effective and get better results out of themselves and their people. That's what I see you doing, but I can't think of a name that captures it. I guess I'll just tell people, 'I'm sending you Cort, and he will help you solve your problem or turn around whatever you're struggling with.'" He nodded once, pleased with his solution.

"That works for me," I replied. "Got any idea what my first project might be?"

"Why don't you spend a few weeks writing an article discussing the points you made at last year's Health and Safety Conference? I'd like to get it published in the company magazine so that the message sent last year is heard once again."

"Great. That gives me the chance to build on some of the points and really land them."

A few months later, my article, "Incident-Focused Managers, Obstacles to Safety Performance," was published in both the company magazine and a leading business periodical. No surprise to Vance and me, it received a reaction similar to my talk at the Health and Safety Conference. The reader commentary was 90 percent negative, but there were a few who were intrigued and said it was "enlightening."

A couple of months later, I received a phone call from an operations manager within a major oil company. He explained that he was the chair of a committee planning the company's annual Operation Managers Conference, and they were interested in me being the keynote speaker. He told me his committee had read my article and were fascinated by my ideas.

"The committee is meeting in Houston for two days," he said. "I'd like you to sit in and help us plan the conference around your article."

I told him I was intrigued by his invitation and would get back to him in a couple of days.

Before we hung up, he added, "If you agree to come, just sent me a confirmation email and be sure to state your fees for the visit. And of course, we'll reimburse all your expenses." At that moment, it dawned on me that he was offering to hire me and pay me to work with his team.

Hours later, I sat in Vance's office, sharing what had occurred.

"What are you going to charge them?" he asked.

"Well, if I go . . ."

"If you go! Of course you will go. This is an enormous opportunity for you. This is what you have been working towards for the last several years."

"I know, but I'm surprised you're encouraging me to do work outside the company."

"I never expected you to stay long with us. You know as well as I do that there are only a few managers here who get what you offer and see its value. If you stay here, there will be limited opportunities for you to do what you do. It's time for you to branch out and find a place where you get exposed to more people and have more opportunities to do your thing. I'm just glad I've had access to you for as long as I have."

"I guess I just always assumed that my entire career would be here. But maybe you're right. Maybe it's time to move on."

"If you're going to move on, you need to know what you're worth. What do you plan on charging that committee? You know, people who do that type of work base what they charge on a daily fee."

"Oh yeah?"

"Do you remember the consultant we had in earlier this year? Her fee was $7,000 a day."

"Seven thousand a day! Are you kidding me?"

"No joke. And she was worth every penny," he said. "You won't be able to command a fee like that because you don't yet have her credentials or experience. But someday you will command that type of fee . . . maybe more."

"Given that, I'll say $4,000."

"That sounds reasonable. Send out the email, and let's see if you have your first client."

In less than a day, I had secured my first client. The operations manager I'd spoken with accepted my fees and made arrangements for us to have breakfast the morning before my first day with his committee.

Several weeks later, I was in Houston meeting with the conference committee. I proposed a three-pronged approach. First, my article would be sent to the fifty conference attendees as a pre-read. Second, at the dinner the evening prior to the conference, I would enroll four of the senior-most participants in an exercise that I would lead on the following day. And third, on the first day of the conference, I would give a two-hour talk, building on my article's key points and including the exercise. The committee seemed to love my proposal, and the chair said he'd recommend it to senior management. I was certain I would play a major role in their upcoming conference.

However, a week later, the chair called to inform me that his management felt my article was too controversial for their conference. He thanked me for the time I had spent with his committee and promised to pay my invoice as soon as he received it.

As I shared my disappointment with Vance, he told me, "Cort, they're just not ready for your message. You're better off not working with them or any other group until they are ready. Don't let yourself dwell on this. Another opportunity will come your way soon—I'm sure of it."

Vance was right, because a little less than a year later, a consulting firm from the West Coast that had read my article approached me. They invited me to visit their headquarters and explore the possibility of joining them. During that trip, I learned that the company was just recently formed and was comprised of MD and PhD psychologists, all from academia. None had worked a single day in business or industry, which concerned me. When I expressed my concern, I was assured that the reason they were interested in me was because I could bring a business and industry perspective to the company.

Around the same time, I was contacted by the same committee chair from the Houston oil company.

"We're planning our annual conference again," he said, "and we're interested in you visiting Houston a second time to explore playing a key role."

"Are you sure your management is up to what I proposed last time?" I asked. "I need that assurance before I come, and you need to understand that I am not willing to deviate significantly from the plan we agreed to last year. I want to be sure that what I do for your conference makes a real difference."

He assured me that he had the approval of his management and said they were happy to pay my previous rate and reimburse all my expenses. I accepted his invitation.

When I brought this up to the consulting firm, they promised that if the opportunity arose to work with the oil company, they would support me working independently.

Less than two months later, I said good-bye to Vance, thanked him for his guidance and support, and started my new life as a consultant. Within a few weeks with my new company, I realized I had made a mistake. Like the group of research PhDs I had attempted to speak with a few years earlier, I found that my associates, with a couple of exceptions, were not interested in my ideas. It became painfully obvious that unless you had the prefix "Dr." in front of your name, your input was not valued.

Worst of all was the company founder, Kirk, who was a classic narcissist. Before I became aware of his true nature, I gifted him a copy of one of my favorite business books, Peter Senge's *The Fifth Discipline*. To my amazement, Kirk brought the book back to me a few days later and hurled it onto my desk.

"Don't ever give me a book like this!" he screeched. "I couldn't stand to read more than one chapter. I hate that new age bull crap." With that, he turned and stormed out of the room.

There were several staff who observed Kirk's behavior, and their pensive reaction to his outburst told me he was disliked, disrespected, and feared by his own people. Little did I know, that would not be our last confrontation, nor did I realize how closedminded and married to one's paradigms a so-called thought leader could be.

As I was getting ready to leave for Houston to keynote the conference for the oil company, Kirk got wind that I was planning to visit them. He fast-walked to my desk and asked what I was planning for the conference. When I began explaining my concept, he interrupted me.

"You'll do what we do. I'll give you the presentation you'll give," he said.

"That's not what we agreed to when I started here, and I expect the company to keep its promise to me," I replied. "I'll be presenting what I and the preparation committee have already decided on."

The look on Kirk's face told me my future in the firm was probably over, but after learning what the company was really like, I wasn't concerned. I knew I was sharper than these people, despite their advanced education, and I could do much better somewhere else. And anyway, I had a conference to prepare for.

The conference was attended by about fifty refinery managers and operations executives. At the dinner prior to the conference, the company president spoke briefly. He welcomed the attendees, thanked them for their attendance, and shared with them the plan for the next few days. Near the end of his comments, he referenced my article.

"I read this pre-read article on data-focused managers," as he waved my article in the air, "and to be honest, I'm not sure what to think about it," he said. "I will try to keep an open mind tomorrow."

The planning committee was sitting at my table, and upon hearing the president's comments, they nervously suggested we change our plans for the next day. I assured them our plan was solid, and they needed to trust that their leaders were capable of seeing what they had come to recognize. The committee settled down, and with the chair's reassurance, they agreed to stay the course.

After dinner, I approached four of the senior-most executives in the room, each a VP. I enrolled them in making a short presentation to the attendees the next morning. I handed them each a chart of year-to-date performance and said I needed them to make this presentation "as if your job is on the line." The VPs, to my surprise, willingly accepted their assignment.

The next morning, I spent about thirty minutes speaking to the key points in my article. During the interactive presentation, I told stories and used humor to relieve the tension, since some of my points were controversial to the audience.

When I came to a main point of the article where I discussed how overly dependent many managers are on data and how misinterpreted data can lead to poor decisions and counterproductive action, I introduced the exercise.

"Each of these four managers is going to present his performance over the last year. I want you, the audience, to assume you're the boss of these managers," I explained. "Also, due to a company-wide restructuring, you must eliminate one of the four managerial positions. Of course, you want to make that decision based on their performance.

"After all four managers present, I'll ask you as a group to make three decisions: which of the managers, if any, you will give a raise based on their performance; which of the managers you'll not give a raise but allow to keep their jobs; and which manager must be let go." As I said these words, I could sense the tension in the room rising.

After everyone was clear how the exercise was to work, I invited the first VP to make his presentation. The VP presented in the exact manner I had requested. He was serious about his presentation, as if his job really was on the line. He went out of his way to emphasize the months where his performance was good and minimize where it was not. He gave creative and persuasive arguments for each of his negative variances, and the attendees nodded their heads in recognition and even grinned and nodded because they had used the same explanations themselves.

Then the other three VPs made their presentations in a similar manner with similar reactions from the audience. It was obvious the presenters and audience were thoroughly enjoying the exercise because it was applicable to how performance was presented and assessed in their company.

After the last presenter was finished, the group quickly decided to give one a raise, allow two to keep their jobs, and terminate the other. I thanked the presenters for their participation, and the group gave them a cheerful round of applause. I then informed the group that we would take a fifteen-minute break, and upon our return, we would debrief the exercise.

My typical debriefing method is to ask three simple questions: What happened? What did you learn? How can you apply what you learned to improve your performance? However, for this exercise, a different approach would be more effective.

When the conference attendees returned, I waited until they had quieted down. I took a good look around the room to get their attention and then turned on the projector to display the four sets of data used by the VPs during their presentations.

Finally, I said, "You know, a good question to ask when anyone gives you data is, 'Where did this data come from?'" I paused for a long period, but there was no response from the group.

"As I said," I continued, "a good question to ask whenever you're given data is, 'Where did this data come from?'" Again, I paused, and again, there was no response from the crowd.

So, I said, "Anytime you are given data, I encourage you to ask this question: 'Where did this data come from?'" Another pause.

Finally, the president, who was seated at a front row table, said, "OK, I'll play along. Where did this data come from?"

"That's a great question, sir, and one I encourage you to ask anytime you are presented data." This got a light chuckle from the president and audience. "This data came from a computer random number generator program. I had my computer create twenty-six samples of data, with an average of 87 percent, which by no coincidence is the performance of your company the previous year. Did you notice that all four charts had an average of 87 percent?" I looked around the room, but nothing but blank stares were looking back at me.

I continued, "I also asked the computer to give me samples that were within statistical control, assuming three-sigma control limits. Did you notice that all the data points on all four of the charts fell within the same range of variation?" Again, I saw a room of stunned and blank faces staring back at me, including the president.

"Finally, I labeled the samples A through Z, threw them up in the air in my living room and asked my three-year-old daughter, Katy, to bring me four of them. In other words, they were randomly selected. Did you notice that each of the four charts was labeled with a different letter—samples C, J, K, and T?"

After saying this, I said nothing more. I wanted the group to have time for the ramifications of what I'd revealed to sink in or for someone who didn't get the meaning to ask. To my surprise, after what seemed more than a minute, the president was the first to chime in.

"I'm not sure what all this means, young man," he said. "In fact, looking around the room, I'm not sure any of us do. What's your point?"

"With all due respect, you just made my point. This group of executives just decided to give one manager a raise, let two others keep their jobs, and terminate the other, all based on data you don't understand. If you did, you would have realized that all four charts contained essentially the same data and were representative of the equivalent performance."

"Huh? W-what? What did you say?" said the president, shaking his head in total befuddlement, which triggered a round of laughter from the audience.

"In other words, instead of being informed by the data, you were fooled by the very creative and persuasive explanations offered by the presenters. I asked them to present as if their jobs were on the line, and because of your inability to accurately interpret performance data, it was the quality of their rationalizations, not their performance, that influenced your decisions as to who to keep and let go."

"But I still don't see what you're asking us to see. The charts are different. His performance was worse than the others," the president said, pointing at the manager chosen to be terminated.

"Don't you see, sir, they appeared different to you because of your lack of understanding of variation? Your inability to separate the noise in the data from the true signal blinded you to what the data was really saying. Each of the charts was saying the same thing, but you couldn't hear it."

"And that was?"

I turned off the projector and stepped toward the president's table.

"That this organization's performance is averaging 87 percent, and that the capability of this organization is to perform somewhere between 82 and 90 percent. All four of these charts are saying this, and therefore, all four managers, for all intents and purposes, are producing the same performance."

"But there is a difference in those charts," he replied. "Put them up on the screen again. They're not the same."

I displayed the charts again, giving the president time to study them. Finally, I spoke.

"Again, there's no meaningful difference in these four sets of performance data, and therefore, there is no meaningful difference in the performance of any of these four managers. But if we don't learn how to better interpret data, charts and presentations like these can fool us into seeing differences that aren't there. Those who do understand know that before looking at any data, the first step is to separate the noise in the data from the true signal present. When I said earlier that I'd asked the computer to produce charts in statistical control, to anyone who understands variation, that would tell them that the charts represent the performance average and present capability of the organization. And most of the visible ups and downs that people pay so much attention to are insignificant noise that can be ignored."

"Ignored?" asked the president. "But we use data like this all the time. Those ups and downs are what drive our business. Are you saying all our charts are straight lines?"

"I'm not saying that at all."

"Then what the hell are you saying, son?" The president's hands went up in frustration.

"I realize this is a difficult concept to grasp. But I promise you, if you stick with me, I'll give you insight that few of your competitors have, and that insight will give you a competitive advantage over them. Are you interested in gaining that insight?"

"Proceed," he said in a resigned tone, his face relaxing. "I'll stick with you as long as you need."

"Thank you," I replied. "It can be frustrating and exhausting, but I promise you there is a big payoff at the end.

"Here are the key takeaways from this exercise. First, data is, at best, worthless and, at worst, dangerous, until statistical rules and tools have been applied to remove the noise so that the true signal is clearly visible. This is simple to do if you know how. I did this with these twenty-six samples using my home computer, which is significantly less powerful than the ones you have access to. Here's what the data looks like when the noise is removed and all that remains is the signal."

The audience sat in stunned silence as I showed charts that appeared extremely similar, comprised of lines with minimal variation that rose no higher than 90 percent and not lower than 82 percent. The inference was clear: all four managers were producing performance that averaged 87 percent and could be expected to fluctuate somewhere between 82 and 90 percent at any given time.

"The second takeaway is that if you're not applying this simple statistical tool to your data, you are bound to make well-intentioned but misguided decisions and take nonproductive actions, as you did here today when you decided to fire a manager who had the same performance as his three counterparts.

"The third takeaway will be the hardest for you to swallow, especially if you are one of the most senior executives in this room: many of the members of this audience got the meaning of this exercise almost immediately. That's not because they're smarter but because they live it every day. There are people in this room who have to defend their performance all the time, and like the four presenters this morning, they are forced to conjure up bullshit explanations for their variances, in the hope that their management will buy it and they can get by another quarter. They do this because the only explanation possible has to be bullshit, since they are usually explaining meaningless noise that hasn't been removed from the data; again, just as the four presenters did

this morning. And their managers tend to accept these explanations because they don't have any better answers. But again, how
could they? Everyone is trying to explain what's not there—it's just
noise in the data!"

I paused and allowed the reality of what I had just said sink in.

"We are all playing this insane game," I continued. "You play it,
and I did when I was in a company like yours. It's as if, deep down,
we all know it's a game, and we all accept that's the way the game
is played, but no one will admit to it. Well, I, for one, will admit
it, because this game is a huge impediment to performance. The
good news is that with some simple training and changes in our
paradigms associated with data and how to interpret it, we can
start making better decisions and take more productive actions—
actions based on the true signal within our data.

"Am I making any sense at all?" I asked the room. "Is this
landing with anyone?"

A young refinery manager sitting at the rear of the room was
the first person to speak. He nervously stood and said, "I'll be the
first to admit it. I play this game. I make up bullshit explanations
for our performance all the time, in the hope that my manager
will be fooled into believing them. I even leave those meetings
sometime saying to myself, 'I can't believe they bought it.'"

This last comment got a great laugh from the room, and the
group gave the young manager a loud round of applause.

"Is there anyone else who understands the points I'm trying to
make?" I asked.

The next person to speak was one of the VPs who had presented
during the exercise—the one the group had decided to terminate.
He turned to the president.

"Tom, I can see that you are struggling with this, and I would
have too if I hadn't presented this morning," he said. Then, facing
me, he added, "I'm glad I was one of the presenters. It forced me to

experience what being in the shoes of the refinery managers is like. I've not worn those boots for a long time, and I'd forgotten what it was like to defend performance data like this."

The VP then turned toward the room. "And yes, I will admit that my explanations of my variances this morning were total bullshit. But did you have to fire my ass?"

At this moment, the room exploded with laughter and applause. When it died down, the VP turned back to the president.

"We may not completely understand what Cort's trying to help us see, but it's obvious most of the people in this room do. We owe it to them to do whatever it takes to learn how to use our data in a more useful way. If not, we'll make foolish decisions like we did during this exercise."

The VP sat down, and there was a long pause. All eyes were on the president. After a few moments, he rose, walked to the front of the room, and stood next to me. To my astonishment, he put his left arm around my shoulders and pointed at me with his right.

"You know, I think this kid has shined a bright light on a major problem in our company," he said. "I didn't realize it until this morning, but this conversation has helped me see that we are making decisions in this company every day based on nothing but bullshit." The room burst into laughter and applause.

The president then stuck out his hand and, while shaking mine, said, "I underestimated you. I'm not sure why. Maybe it's because you're so young or maybe because you're so cocksure of yourself. Regardless, I want you to know I'm sorry for not giving you the respect you deserve. I want you to know that you, sir, are welcome in my company anytime."

The president then turned to the committee chairperson. "Your committee outdid itself this time. Well done. I'm not sure what your committee has planned, but if Cort is available, I'd like for him to stay with us all week. I think he can add insight to much of what we'll be discussing in this conference."

"And Cort"—he stepped back slightly to meet my eyes—"if you can, I'd like you to stay through Friday morning. I have my weekly staff meeting that morning, and I'd enjoy having you sit in and see what you can contribute."

"I'll be there, sir."

"One last thing," he said. "You can call me Tom."

The president then suggested we take a break, which we did. During the break, several members of the group approached me, thanking me for exposing "one of the biggest problems I have to deal with."

I remained at the conference for the rest of the week, contributing when asked or when I thought I could add value. It was a pleasure to see the impact that one simple but powerful insight could have on an organization and the positive energy it could inject into a group. After the conference, the planning committee debriefed. My presentation and exercise were cited as the highlight of the week, and the group declared the conference their best ever.

On Friday morning, I entered the president's conference room on the top floor of a Houston skyscraper. Also present were Tom's executive administrator, his staff, and a woman who had been at the conference, and who I had assumed was an operations executive. The woman introduced herself as Debra, Tom's "executive coach," and she had been interacting with Tom throughout the conference.

As the meeting progressed, Debra and Tom kept turning my way, asking, "What do you think, Cort?" and "Have you dealt with this before, Cort?"

When asked, I shared my thoughts as best I knew how. On a few occasions, Debra went out of her way to acknowledge my insights. She seemed intent on making sure I was consulted and my thoughts were expressed.

Participating in Tom's staff meeting was an experience I guess many must go through in their lives. I kept thinking, How did I get here? I'm not supposed to be in the president's office. A refinery manager's office, yes, but not the big guy's.

Eventually, there was a break in the meeting. Debra approached me during the break.

"You're wondering how you got here, am I correct?" she asked.

"How did you know?" I replied.

"All coaches go through that."

"We do?"

"Sure. It usually happens when you coach up a level from what you're used to. You've never coached at this level before, have you?"

"Is it that obvious?"

"Actually, it isn't," Debra answered. "At least not to Tom and his team. But I've been where you are, and I know how it feels."

She glanced at the group beginning to regather around the conference room table. "Relax. You're doing great, and you're completely worthy of sitting in this room and coaching the president of a large firm. I've been watching you this week, and you are an amazing thought leader and coach. You've got some un-conventional ideas and the guts to stand behind them. I shudder to think how good you'll be when you have more experience."

I'll never be able to thank Debra enough for giving me that encouragement. If someone of her status thought I had what it took, I decided it must be true. Vance had been telling me that for a couple of years, but until that day, I had my doubts.

That experience in Tom's office and interaction with Debra created a defining moment in my development as a coach. For the first time, I had a name for what I'd been for the last several years: executive coach. And I had confirmation from a person skilled in the craft that I was worthy of that title.

The following week, I attended the quarterly consultants' meeting at my employer's home offices. I was sitting with the coaches early one morning, waiting for the session to begin, when Kirk, the founder, entered the room.

"Mr. Dial, I understand you were at the Houston oil company last week," he said, his expression hard.

"Yes, it was a blast," I replied. "I was even invited to sit in on the president's staff meeting."

"Where the hell do you get off visiting our client without my permission?"

"Well, first of all, it was my client I was working with. They engaged me for that conference before your company hired me. And, you will recall, you approved me delivering on my commitment to speak at that conference when I interviewed."

"You get one thing straight," Kirk said as he pounded the table. "You have no clients. I have clients, I will decide where you go, and I will decide what you do. I checked up on what you did there; you did that new age bullshit with them, didn't you?"

"I don't do and never have done bullshit. I did what the conference committee and I agreed on months ago. The plan was approved by the president."

"And where do you get off talking to company presidents?" Kirk squawked. "I talk to presidents, not you consultants." He pointed to the others in the room. "No president wants to hear what you have to say."

Just as I was about to tell Kirk that I was no longer interested in dealing with a raging narcissist, the company's marketing director barged into the room.

"Cort, I don't know what you did over at the oil company last week," he said, "but I just got off the phone with them, and they're raving about it. They told me the president gave you a hug in front of the whole group, and he had you come to his staff meeting!"

Tim, the director, had already been one of my favorite people in the company, but after what he did for me in that moment, he was my favorite person on the planet. Before anyone could respond to what Tim said, he turned to Kirk.

"Kirk, whatever Cort did over there, we need to bottle it and give it to every consultant. I've never seen a response like this before."

The room sat in total shock and silence. The consultants said nothing, although I'm sure, like me, inside they were jumping for joy and high-fiving. Tim stood there with a grin on his face as big as Texas. Kirk remained motionless, his face turning the deep red of rage. After a few moments, Tim recognized that something was amiss.

"What's going on here?" Tim asked.

"We're taking a break," Kirk replied and bolted for the door.

As he was leaving, I said, "Are you not man enough to admit when you're wrong and offer me your apology?"

Kirk ignored me and proceeded out the door. Once he was beyond earshot, the consultants explained to Tim what had occurred. It was the one time I saw them enjoying themselves that entire week.

Tim turned to me and said, "I'm sorry for putting you in that situation, Cort."

"No worries," I said. "It was nice to have someone in this company appreciate what I bring to the party."

Twenty minutes later, Kirk returned and acted as if nothing had happened—a common characteristic of narcissists, I later learned. I spent the remainder of the day planning how I was to inform my manager that I was quitting the company. He was not present at the meeting, but a counterpart of his, Kyle, was. As we adjourned for lunch, I looked in his direction.

Kyle was about twenty years my senior, with a six-foot eight-inch, slender frame and kind face. For my money, Kyle was the smartest PhD on the staff. He was not only academically intelligent, but he also possessed the emotional intelligence that many of his peers lacked.

During the lunch break, Kyle took me aside and whispered, "Cort, I'm sorry about Kirk. But you need to understand that this is a company of dogmatic behaviorists. We see everything through one lens, the behavior lens, and that works for us. I mean, you see the results we produce, you know it works."

"It works, but there's a lot more to performance than behavior," I replied.

"Yes, there is, and you're unique in that you seem comfortable playing in any arena. You don't seem to be committed to any theory or model."

"I'm not. All I care about is that the model gets performance while caring for people."

"I know you do. We are extremely dogmatic where you are pragmatic," Kyle continued. "Kirk and those who run this company are only interested in consultants who buy into the behavioral model of the world. They expect total devotion to that and won't tolerate anything else. You, on the other hand, are an explorer. You're constantly looking to find and pioneer the next model, the new paradigm. For example, you keep asking questions about things like commitment, caring, and purposefulness, and we behaviorists don't like those types of questions."

"Why not? If the answers lead to better performance, why wouldn't you want the questions asked?"

"Because our model of the world, the behavioral model, can't answer such questions. Our theories are robust in that they hold up under most circumstances. But they fall apart in other circumstances. Every theory or model is useful, but none is perfect or applies to all situations. So when you ask questions like, 'What about the person who doesn't give a damn about the antecedents and consequences, and who does what he wants only because he wants to?'—you are asking a question that does not compute with Kirk. You're asking about an area of psychology that has to do with intention, and that's a completely different ball game than behavior."

"I'm tired of behavior being the answer to every question I ask. I've only been here a short while, but I know in my gut that there's more, something better. Where can I learn about intention?"

"I'd be happy to teach you what I can about intention. We can discuss that later, but I'm not sure you're getting the message I'm trying to convey here."

"I think I do. What I hear you trying to say is that I don't fit in here . . . and that I never will."

Kyle paused thoughtfully. "Yes, I am telling you that, but I'm also telling you that there's not much left here for you to learn. You've learned all there is to learn about antecedents, behavior, and consequences, wouldn't you agree?

"I would. And no offense, but you guys sometimes act as if your stuff is the greatest thing since sliced bread, when in reality, it's basic behavioral theory."

Kyle laughed. "I guess we deserve that because of the way we sometimes behave around here."

"Some of you deserve a lot worse, but we won't go there."

"No, we won't," Kyle responded. "There's no cheese at the end of that rat hole."

"Agreed."

It was time for me to leave the company for good. I soon departed and moved on to the next stage of my journey—this time, as an executive coach.

Part 2:

My Journey to
All-In Leadership

Chapter 10:
Paying Penance

"A human being is a deciding being."

—Viktor Frankl

"Every advance, every conceptual achievement of mankind, has been connected with an advance in self-awareness."

—C. G. Jung

About a month after leaving Kirk's company, I received a call from a former associate of mine, Alsaf. He urged me to visit his facility—a chemical plant in Louisiana. He'd gotten my personal phone number from Vance.

"You ought to come see the 'coaching workshops' that we're doing with our people; we're teaching them how to coach one another," he said. "The guy who's leading the workshops reminds me of you. He's doing things with our employees that I never thought possible. It makes me think of some of the work you did while in corporate. Vance told me you are on your own now. I think you and this guy would really hit it off."

Given that I had plenty of free time on my hands and was always looking for something else to improve performance, I traveled to New Orleans to see what Alsaf was describing. The workshop I observed was like none other I'd ever seen. The facilitator, George, was one of the oddest characters I'd ever met.

On day one of the workshop, George entered the room looking like he'd slept in his clothes. His thick, bushy hair was unkempt, and his cotton shirt and corduroy pants were wrinkled—a look that didn't match his position as CEO of his own consulting company. George stepped up on the slightly elevated stage and immediately invited the seventy-five participants to come up and view pictures of his newborn daughter, which we all did.

Then George proceeded to train and entertain us for two days as we learned how to give and receive coaching feedback. None of the actual coaching techniques George taught was earth shattering, but what was extraordinary was the way he made the training so much fun and cultivated a personal connection with every participant.

I'd never witnessed anyone who experienced so much joy as George did while practicing his craft. It was as if he was completely comfortable in his skin and perfectly alright with the participants accepting or rejecting what he had to offer. He wasn't there to sell us on the training and his ideas; rather, he wanted us to freely choose whether we embraced them.

In the middle of the first day of training, George was reinforcing a coaching concept. I noticed a woman in the back corner of the room stand. She proceeded to disagree with one of George's premises, sharing her point of view in detail. He thanked her for her thoughts and proceeded to move on. She interrupted him.

"Aren't you going to counter my point?" she asked.

"No, I'm not," George replied with a slight grin, "but thanks for checking." He chuckled and again proceeded to move on. When he did, the woman interrupted a second time.

"Why aren't you addressing my argument? Your behavior is insulting."

"I choose not to," George responded, looking directly at the woman with a tender smile. "I said at the beginning that this workshop is about choice, and each of us has the unique human ability to choose who we are, how we feel, and what we do and say. I heard your point of view, thanked you for it, and chose to move on with the training. It appears you're choosing not to move on and instead be 'insulted.'"

A third time, George attempted to continue, but the woman again interrupted.

"Your behavior is totally unacceptable," she said. "Either apologize to me right now, or I'm leaving."

George walked over to the woman and stood in front of her.

"I will say once again, this workshop is all about choice—that thing about us that makes us human. Only we, of all species, have the ability to decide whom we choose to be and how we choose to interpret and respond to any circumstance. I encourage you to choose whatever interpretation and response to this circumstance you feel best serve you and your teammates in this room."

As the woman opened her mouth to respond, one of the participants said, "Don't you get it, Latanya? George hasn't insulted you; you're choosing to interpret what he did as an insult. That's a basic premise of the coaching training. If you don't get that, you're missing the entire point of the workshop."

"No, I don't get it. I've been insulted. I want an apology, or I'm out of here."

"Then you're out of here," the entire room responded, almost in unison.

Latanya stood. "Fine, I'm leaving," she said, grabbing her bag. "I'm not going to sit here and be insulted."

"Latanya, no one is insulting you but you," the participant from earlier said. "If you can't get that, then you're right; you need to leave. Because without that awareness, you can neither give nor receive coaching."

Latanya left and did not return.

I sat in awe as I observed George during the entire conversation. Like Dr. Deming, he was sure of himself and his ideas. But unlike Deming, his key teaching tools were not his knowledge and experiences but rather his personal connection with everyone in the room. It was as if he was having a one-on-one conversation with seventy-five people. His ability to allow the participants to express their free will and choose to participate was inspiring. I later learned from George that this is a key aspect of "enrollment." As I watched George that day, I realized although I possessed what Dr. Deming had—knowledge, ideas, and experiences— I was nowhere near as developed as George when it came to "enrollment skills."

At the end of the workshop, I approached George and shared how much I enjoyed his interaction and facilitation abilities.

"I was fascinated watching how you worked with these folks," I said. "These are hard-core union employees, but somehow you've convinced them to volunteer their own time to help facilitate this training. I've never seen that at a union plant."

"Thanks, but actually we haven't convinced anyone. I'll let you in on a little secret. This work we are doing here is about much more than coaching skills. The skills come after what we are really working on."

"What's that?"

"Enrollment."

"Enrollment into what?"

"Enrollment into the possibility that people, even in a hard-core union plant as you call it, can work together for the greater good.

That people can choose to change who they are, what they think, and how they act. You missed the workshop prior to this skills training. In that workshop, union and management leadership placed that possibility in front of these people, who then explored that possibility and chose whether to sign up for it."

"Fascinating. Where did you learn how to do all this?"

"Help me pack up my things, and we can go have coffee and chat if you'd like."

George and I developed a business relationship over the next year where we would call each other with a question or thought, or just to "shoot the bull." I suggested a few books to George and he suggested a few to me, and we often discussed them during our calls.

One day, George called me with his entire senior staff on the line. He wanted my thoughts on a consulting engagement they were struggling with. I offered my consultation and the call ended. Over the next several months, we had a number of these types of conversations.

Then, one morning, George called, but this time he seemed hesitant to reveal what he wanted to discuss. The small talk lingered a little too long, and finally there was a thick pause.

Eventually, I said, "George, why did you call?"

"Well, I was sitting here with my staff discussing another engagement, and someone said, 'Why don't we call Cort?'" he said, then paused again before continuing. "It dawned on me that we've called you several times, and I said to my staff, 'Instead of calling Cort all the time, why don't we just hire him?' So . . . I guess I'm calling to see if you'd be interested in visiting Texas and exploring joining our firm."

The line was silent while I thought for a moment. I recalled Kirk and what it was like being employed by a narcissist. But George wasn't that way, and it wouldn't hurt to explore the opportunity. I was almost certain I'd find no "Kirks" in George's company.

"I'd like that, George," I said.

Julie and I did visit Texas, and a few months later, we relocated our family. Upon joining the firm, I was assigned to a project team that included George and a few of the other senior players in the company. The project's objective was to figure out how to apply the company's methodology to eliminating injury from the workplace. Up to that point, the company had only consulted in the areas of improving efficiency, productivity, and cost. George, however, had recently become preoccupied with the possibility of eliminating worker injuries from the workplace and was committed to developing what he called "a safety practice" in his company. Since his intention and my commitment to the health, safety, and well-being of working men and women were compatible, I was eager to assist in any way I could. Regardless of the performance area on which we focused, I was going to get to learn from George.

Within about six months, our project team felt we had something ready to take to clients. At the same time, we were approached by a major petrochemical company and asked to support performance on a sizable capital project in the Middle East. The company planned to build a large, complex plant and was concerned about how to achieve the performance they were capable of in North America using Middle Eastern workers. We accepted the engagement and soon afterwards, I was on my way to Bahrain to attend a meeting of the project's investment partners.

The investment partners meeting was held in a large hotel room with an enormous round conference table that seated about two dozen partner representatives, each with their own stake in the project. The meeting was scheduled to last three days.

I was seated by one of my company's senior managers, Rob, who led our consulting team and was my immediate supervisor. Stacked on the table in front of each of the meeting attendees were mounds of project documentation in big, four-inch binders. I stared at the binder in front of me, thinking of the one Bud had knocked me out with while exploring how we had killed Harry.

The first day of the meeting involved high-level project scoping, approval of schedules and budgets, and the like. It was more like a U.N. meeting than a project meeting, with people from all over the world in attendance. One of the processes used during the meeting was for each representative to declare whether they accepted or rejected whatever was being considered whenever a consensus decision needed to be made.

On the second day, I was feeling a bit drowsy after lunch. To help prevent myself from dozing, I began browsing the different binders on the table. In one binder, I came across a section entitled "Project Safety Performance Calculations." As I read the section, I came to a table that predicted the number of fatalities and serious, potentially disabling injuries that would occur during the project's execution. I was shocked to see a prediction of two fatalities and one hundred serious injuries. I pointed the table out to Rob.

"That's one of the main reasons we're here," Rob said, his expression confident. And then to my surprise, he added, "I have to leave for a moment. You represent us while I'm gone."

Not two minutes after Rob left, I heard the meeting facilitator say, "Now, let's talk about project safety performance."

The group then proceeded to hear from several of the petrochemical company's safety professionals, including their corporate safety director, about the highly hazardous work this project would entail and the poorly skilled workers they would have to employ. They projected the table from the binder onto the wall, talking dispassionately through the numbers. The reality, they asserted, was that the investors would have to accept poorer safety performance than they were accustomed to.

Once the presentations were finished, with the table from the binder still on the wall, the facilitator invoked the consensus decision process and started polling the representatives. I was seated about eight chairs to the left of the facilitator, who turned to the representative immediately to his right.

"Can you accept this performance?" he asked.

The rep replied apathetically, "Yes, we can."

I sat there stunned as I observed rep after rep casually respond affirmatively, as if they were approving something as mundane as a budget. I was taken back to the meeting with Bud, where he asked each participant, "How did we kill this man?" I thought, My God, I'm in the same damn meeting! Only this time, there are hundreds of lives at stake.

I was in a room full of people who were willing to let these people suffer and die, simply because they saw it as the price of doing business in the Middle East.

As the facilitator proceeded around the table, I kept looking over my shoulder at the door, hoping Rob would return and answer for our company, but he never appeared. Finally, it was my turn.

"Can you accept this performance?" the facilitator asked.

I looked around the room. Virtually no one was observing me. They had given their answers and were distracted by other concerns. It was up to me to wake up this group; if I failed, hundreds of people and their families would suffer immensely.

I took a deep breath and said, "No, we cannot."

The facilitator began to ask the person to my right the same question and then suddenly realized I had not responded affirmatively. He paused and got his bearings before speaking.

"Am I to understand this performance is unacceptable to your company?" he asked.

"It is," I replied.

"May I inquire as to why?"

"It's very simple. My company is not interested in participating in any endeavor that is planning to harm anyone, let alone knowingly kill or seriously injure them."

"That's a nice sentiment," said the petrochemical company's corporate safety director. "But surely you must face the reality of the situation in the Middle East. This is not the U.S. They don't have the systems or the skilled workforce we have, so it's unreasonable to expect the same level of performance."

"I don't expect the same level of performance as we see in the U.S.," I said. "We still kill and hurt people in the U.S. on projects similar to this one. I expect to harm no one, and I can't support a project that expects anything less. I encourage all of you to do the same."

"That's just totally unreasonable," said the safety director. "You have to face facts."

"Then I'm choosing to be unreasonable and ignore the facts, because if I don't, we're going to kill two men and seriously hurt a hundred others just to build a plant. To me, that's unreasonable, and I want nothing to do with any project with that as part of their plan. If that's unacceptable to this group, then I think it best that our company withdraw from this project."

"I'm with Cort," I heard someone behind me say. I turned to see who had spoken and was surprised to see that Rob had reentered the room sometime earlier and was now supporting my stance.

"We're willing to be part of this project," Rob continued, "if this group is willing to commit to harming no one in the process of building the plant. We're inviting you to join us in making that the key goal of this project—to figure out how to build a plant like this and harm no one in the process."

Rob then turned to the facilitator. "I request that you put a question before this meeting: can your company be responsible for us building this plant free of injuries? I want to hear from each representative whether they can make that commitment."

Rob asked the question around 2:00 in the afternoon. That conversation ended around 6:00 that evening. Much like the meeting with Bud, there was yelling, arguing, and even a few tears.

But around 5:30, the gentleman who would be the construc- tion manager for the petrochemical company rose. He turned to the project manager and said, "Hank, if you can't stand and say yes to this question, then I want off this project. I never saw it this way before, and I never saw myself this way before, but these people are right. The world doesn't need another goddamn chemical plant bad enough that it's worth even the tip of a worker's finger, let alone his life."

"I can say yes," Hank replied. "I was a yes an hour ago. I just didn't want to say so because I wanted everyone else to be free to make their choice."

"I think it's time to take another turn around the table and see who's agreeable and who might still be struggling with this commitment," Rob said.

I quietly exhaled in satisfaction as I heard the last yes. Everyone was in. And in that moment, I somehow felt I had paid my penance for my sins against Harry and his family, at least as much as a person can do such a thing.

As I looked around the room, I realized that what George had emphasized during the coaching training in Louisiana, choice and free will, was at play in that meeting. I saw how important intention was to enrolling people in a lofty goal such as a project free of injury.

About half an hour later, as Rob and I walked out of the meeting, I looked over at him.

"You, sir, were unbelievable," I said.

I went on to share how impressed I was with his mastery of the conversation I had just witnessed. He was every bit as skilled as George, and for the same reasons: because of who he was in the conversation and for his ability to make a human connection with the participants. It was completely clear to everyone in the room that Rob would accept nothing less than the goal of harming no one, and if the group decided otherwise, he would choose to withdraw from the project.

"Well, you set them up. I just knocked them down," he said. "Anyway, they're enrolled. Now the even tougher work begins. Now we have to help them figure out how to do what they've never done before. I'm not sure yet how we'll do that, but there's one thing I am sure of."

"What's that?" I asked.

"We're the right people for the job."

"That we are."

"We'll be back here tomorrow for the last day of this meeting," he said. "Now that the team shares a common commitment, tomorrow should go smoothly. But in a month, we're going to be back with this project team, starting the process of translating the commitment that they generated today into concrete actions. Let's get something to eat and discuss how we might go about that."

Chapter 11:
Falling in Love

"Man becomes great exactly in the degree in which he works for the welfare of his fellow-men."

—Mahatma Gandhi

"The Waste Land is a world where people live not out of their own initiative, but out of what they think they're supposed to do."

—Joseph Campbell

"To love what you do and feel that it matters—how could anything be more fun?"

—Katharine Graham

A couple of weeks after Rob and I returned from Bahrain, we were sitting on George's home patio, discussing the next trip to the Middle East.

"You'll be first to go back," George said to me. Rob nodded.

"Me? Why?" I asked.

"You embody the commitment we're asking the people in this project to make. I want them to meet you first and experience what we've experienced as we've gotten to know you."

"OK, I guess. But what will be the objectives of my visit?"

"I want you to get to know these people and fall in love with them."

"Fall in love with them?"

"Yes. You and Rob will be literally fighting for these people's lives over the next few years. You need to develop an intimate relationship with them, as if each person is one of your own. That will help you stand for them when the need arises."

"Cort, just go over there, and be who you are with us," Rob added. "Do what you do. Stand for the well-being of working men and women. You do that, and you'll meet our objectives for your visit."

"I'm going to spend three weeks over there doing that?" I asked.

"No, you're going to spend a few years doing that," George said. "That's why we have you on this project, to embody the possibility we're all going to help them embrace and then turn into reality."

A few days later, I was on a jet headed for the Middle East. The trip from the airport in Bahrain to the project site was a four-hour drive involving a number of military security checks. Young men pointed automatic rifles at me, fumbled through my belongings, and asked a lot of accusatory questions. Somehow, with help from my driver, I made it to the project's front entrance.

The security guards waved our vehicle through the main gate onto the project site, which at that time was no more than acres of desert surrounded by a ten-foot security fence and several large construction trailers.

As we approached the trailers, I noticed the project had built carports for all the vehicles. As we drew closer, I saw dark shapes beneath each vehicle. I squinted my eyes, but I still couldn't make out what the masses were. Suddenly, I flashed back to the dark shapes I had observed as I walked towards the site of Harry's accident. I blinked my eyes, trying to remove the vision from my head.

As we approached an empty port reserved for our vehicle, I saw one of the shapes move. I leaned out of the car window, expecting to see an animal, and recoiled upon realizing what it was.

The shapes were human beings resting under the vehicles.

We had arrived at lunchtime. The men were getting out of the hot sun the only way they could by crawling under the sole shade provided on the entire job site. Shade not for men but for cars.

The driver escorted me to our consulting team's office, my mind still on the men. I spent the next hour settling in. I was in the process of writing an email to George and Rob, letting them know I'd arrived safely, when in walked Hank, the project manager.

Hank was the epitome of a "long, tall Texan" with a personality as large as the Lone Star state and a way of smiling that let you know he enjoyed what he did and the people he worked with. I'd been looking forward to seeing Hank again and was glad he'd found the time to drop by.

After shooting the bull for a moment, Hank said, "I hope you're here to keep the conversation from the investor's meeting going. I'm worried we might lose momentum and drift backwards."

"Well, then, you'll be pleased to know that's exactly why I'm here," I responded. "When do we start?"

"Outstanding! We have our daily project leadership team meeting at 3:00. Why don't you sit in?"

I entered the meeting later that afternoon and introduced myself to the eight senior-most managers on the project. Each represented a different company associated with the project: the

American petrochemical company who would own and operate the plant; a Japanese engineering firm; a Greek construction firm; and contracting companies specializing in accounting, human resources, and other key functions.

After introductions, the team reviewed the minutes from the previous meeting, discussed a few issues of the day, and debriefed. After the debrief, the engineering team manager, a sharp-looking young executive named Kadomo-san, turned to me.

"Cort, do you have anything you wish to ask us?" he said.

"Thank you, yes, I do," I replied. I turned to the group. "I couldn't help but notice as I drove onto the project site that you've managed to get all your vehicles into the shade."

The group laughed. The construction team manager, Mohamad, added above the laughter, "We have got our priorities straight around here, do we not, gentlemen?"

Once the noise died down, Kadomo-san looked at me.

"That was not a question," he said. "Something tells me that you have one."

"I do. As I was saying, we've managed to get our vehicles in the shade. My question is, when and how are we going to get our people in the shade?"

No one spoke for several moments. I looked around at the men, waiting for a response.

"What point are you trying to make? Surely you do not think we are going to construct a shade roof over the project," Mohamad said. "I realize you are from Texas, but we have no plans of building another Astrodome."

Mohamad's comment solicited another round of hysterics, with the exception of Hank and Kadomo-san. But before I could ask either of them to talk, the project safety manager, Donny, leaned forward in his chair.

"I heard from Dick, our corporate safety manager, that you guys were nuts, but come on now. You don't really expect us to build shade for all these hands, do you?" Donny said.

"That's for you, the leaders of this project, to decide," I responded. "I'm here merely to coach you. On the projects I've coached that experience the best performance, leadership treats its people at least as well as it does its equipment. I'm simply advising that this leadership team do the same."

Again the room was silent for a long period. Then Kadomo-san spoke.

"I should have recognized this myself," he said. "Thanks for helping me see that we are mistreating our people."

"I do not think we are mistreating anyone," Mohamad argued. "That is just the way business is done here."

Hank finally chimed in. "What I think Cort is trying to help us recognize is that the way we treat our people impacts our performance. I agree."

Hank's tone became serious as he continued. "Gentlemen, I committed at the investors' meeting that we are going to build this project without harming anyone. And on the first day he's here, the first thing Cort sees is us doing just that. I don't care what it costs or how we do it, we will provide our people shade and do everything humanly possible to care for their well-being. I want providing shade to be a standard practice on this project, and I want anyone who can't meet that expectation to get my approval before allowing his people to work in the sun. Can I get each of you to support that?"

"Absolutely," declared Kadomo-san. No one else spoke.

"How 'bout the rest of you? Can I get your assurance that you will make sure our people are afforded shade? If not, speak now."

"You have my assurance, Hank," said Mohamad. "I do not yet see why this is necessary or how such a thing is even possible, but if it is that important to you—"

"It is."

"Then, yes, I will do what you wish."

The others agreed to support Hank's new policy, and the meeting adjourned.

After the meeting, Hank invited me into his office, an office in which I would spend hundreds of hours over the next few years. I entered the room, and he closed the door behind me.

"Cort, these people, the ones who come to the Middle East every day to sacrifice their lives for their families back home, well, they've been waiting for someone like you and Rob to lead this change," Hank said. "We're going to do some history-making stuff on this project; I can feel it. I can't tell you how excited I am to have you guys here."

"Thank you, Hank," I said. "I'm excited about working with you, as well, and demonstrating what performance is possible when people are well led."

After we discussed the next day's plans, I left Hank's office. The driver took me to my hotel, which would be my home away from home for the duration of the project.

The next morning, the driver picked me up at 5:00. I was to interview about a dozen of the "hands" on the project at 6:00, and I had decided to bring them a gift. I arranged for the hotel to prepare a boxed breakfast for each of the interviewees. Inside each of the gold paper boxes were plastic utensils, a purple paper napkin, one hard-boiled egg, tiny plastic salt and pepper shakers, a breakfast biscuit, and a small helping of orange marmalade jelly in a round, glass jar with a golden metal lid. I didn't get Hank's prior approval for these boxes, but something in me said he'd approve.

Prior to the interview, I was introduced to the interpreter, Patel, who would be assisting me. Patel was approximately ten years older than I. He was short and thin, with copper skin and a white, crooked smile, and sported well-groomed, ashen hair. As I got to know him, I sensed a deep wisdom and peacefulness in him I had not experienced in anyone since my mom. In addition to being one of the project's interpreters, Patel was also the project's medic. I later learned he was a medical doctor, educated and licensed in the U.S., who had found his life in the States unfulfilling.

Although people on the project were from Egypt, Jordon, Saudi Arabia, Greece, Japan, Britain, France, Germany, the Philippines, and many other countries, the group I was to interview were the lowest on the Middle East caste ladder—Indian and Pakistani laborers.

As Patel and I approached the conference room where the interview was to occur, I saw men lined up on both sides of the hall, standing with their backs against the wall, as if at military attention. As I approached, I realized there was barely enough room for my American frame to pass between the two rows of men. I motioned for the men to go into the room ahead of me, but Patel grabbed my wrist and said, "No, Mr. Cort. You go first."

As best as I could, I squeezed through the human tunnel. The hallway was poorly lit, so as I passed through the group, I could not make out much about these men; however, I could smell them. Having supervised laborers all over North America and having done labor myself in the Texas sun, I had a good idea what a hot, sweaty laborer smelled like. These men smelled nothing like that. To me, an American, it was as if they had never bathed in their lives. I was to learn later this was not far from the truth.

Patel and I entered the room, and I stood at the head of the long conference table. Patel ushered the men past me to their seats and then drew a chair up to my right. As each man passed me, he smiled and bowed to me. Patel later explained that they understood that I was a teacher, and that in their countries, teachers were held in high regard.

The conference room was much better lit than the hallway, and for the first time I could see these men's clothing, hands, and faces. I was surprised to see they were not wearing the company uniforms I was accustomed to seeing on projects in the U.S. These men were obviously wearing their personal clothing, which for most, was cheap men's slacks—some without underwear—a long-sleeved nylon shirt, no socks, and sandals.

The men's faces told the stories of their lives. There were a few who must have been no older than thirteen; they appeared terrified and sat looking down at their waists. Most of the others appeared to be in their thirties and forties; they were extremely thin and, again, looked ill at ease. And then, finally, there were a few who looked to be about one hundred years old, their faces dark from the sun and full of cracks and wear. Their hands looked like old, cracked catcher's mitts. Patel informed me afterwards that none of the men was younger than twenty or over forty-five, and none weighed more than ninety pounds.

Once the men were seated, I asked Patel to introduce each of them to me. "Please tell these gentlemen my name, my role, and that I welcome them to the project," I said. "Also, please ask them to honor me by sharing their names. And finally, please tell them that this"—I held up one of the breakfast boxes—"is a gift to them from Hank, the project manager."

Patel did a fantastic job following the introduction process I'd requested. I had, for the most part, no idea what he or the men were saying, but I could tell the process was making them more comfortable.

As the men examined their breakfast boxes, it was as if someone had handed them a box of real gold. Each took a few minutes appreciating the box itself. They kept looking at Patel and me, as if to ask, "This is for me?"

Then, as they opened the boxes, their eyes got as big as a child's on Christmas morning. Slowly, almost as if in slow motion, they retrieved each item from the box and examined it with amazement. After a while, each had his egg, biscuit, and jelly sitting in front of him on the table. I asked Patel to tell the men to go ahead and enjoy their breakfast.

"That would not be proper," he replied. He then turned to the men and said something I didn't understand. To my surprise, all the men stood, brought their hands together in front of their chests as if in prayer, and bowed to me. Afterwards, each sat back down, replaced his items back into the box, and placed the gift on his lap.

I turned to Patel and said, "What was that?"

"I will explain later," he replied. "It is time to move on to the interview."

I nodded. After each man shared his name and home country, I asked Patel, "Please ask these men why they chose to come to the Middle East and work on this project."

"Sir, they will not understand the question."

"Why not?"

"It will make no sense to them. They are not like you."

"I don't see what you mean," I responded. "Why won't they understand?"

"It is hard to explain to someone like you," Patel said. "I am not sure how to say it in a way you will understand. But I promise you if you ask these men your question, all you will get back are puzzled looks."

"Will the question offend or embarrass them? Will it hurt their feelings?"

"No, it will not harm them. They just will not understand what you are asking."

"If it won't harm them, then I want you to ask it," I replied. "Please ask them why they chose to come work here."

As Patel asked the question, I observed the men closely. They reacted as he had predicted. Some shook their heads, others wrinkled their brows, a few hunched their shoulders, and all started to speak to one another as if they were inquiring if the other understood the question. It was obvious Patel was right—these men had no idea what I was asking.

Patel looked at me and smiled as if to say, "See, I told you so." I must have looked lost because he quickly made a suggestion.

"Why not ask them how they plan to use the money they will make while working here," he offered. "That might give you some insight into why they are here."

"That's a good idea, but I still want to get some idea of why they chose this project and not to work somewhere else."

"Sir, these men are not like you and the men you know," Patel said, his voice edged with frustration. "Many were probably sitting on the side of the road a couple of months ago when a truck pulled into the village and someone jumped out and said, 'Who would like to make $2,000 in two years?' These men would make a small fraction of that if they stayed in their village for decades.

"To them, this is an opportunity to contribute to their families. They are all the eldest in their families, and it is their role to provide for the future of their brothers and sisters. Today, that often means going off to some foreign land and laboring so their siblings can get a decent education."

Patel looked at me for a moment before continuing. "You see, it is not a choice they made—they have no choice. It is simply their role in life, as they see it. None of these men chose to come here in the way you think you have; they are here simply because it is what they are meant to do."

"I'm sorry," I said, "but I still don't see what you mean."

"Always remember when you look in these men's faces, Mr. Cort, that you are looking into the face of conscious contribution. These men are the eldest males, and they willingly give their bodies, their lives, in service of the well-being of their younger brothers and sisters, many who become doctors and lawyers. And they are completely content in playing that role."

I sat in deep thought before speaking. "I will remember that. But still, you must have had a choice. Didn't you choose to come to the U.S. to receive your medical education?"

"I come from a very large family, and I am one of the middle children. I had plenty of older siblings to provide for our family, so I was sent to university. Like these men, my older brothers and sisters made it possible for me to go to university. But I did not choose to go; if anyone chose, it was my family who chose to send me. However, I do not relate to it as a choice. It is just what we do. Middle children go to university or do something else to contribute to the family."

"I think I'm starting to understand. It's hard for me to put myself in your place and see the world the way you do."

"It is hard for me to understand you too," he said. "I have the advantage of having experienced both sides. When I was studying in the U.S., my mother and sisters came to visit. While they were there, I took them to the supermarket. When we entered the store, my mother began to weep. She was overcome by the abundance."

"Did she think she was in heaven?" I asked. Patel laughed.

"Only an American would equate a supermarket to heaven," he said, looking down and laughing while shaking his head. Patel took a deep breath then looked back up at me. "No, I think that for the first time in her life, she experienced unlimited choice— genuine freedom to choose whatever she wanted. You see, you and your family experience more choice in a single trip down the market aisle than my mother had in her whole life. I think she realized how much choice there was at that moment, and it overwhelmed her. She understood the gift that choice was and she was overwhelmed by being in the presence of so much of that gift. She could not handle it, so she wept."

At that moment, I realized Patel and I were ignoring our guests. I turned to them.

"I'm sorry. We've been ignoring you," I said, but then I realized they had no idea what I was saying.

Patel jumped in and said something that caused them all to smile, snicker, and nod their heads.

I asked Patel, "What did you say?'

"I said, 'Please bear with me while I try to explain to this American our way.' And they indicated, 'Good luck with that.'"

I laughed, and Patel and the men laughed as well.

"We can continue to talk," Patel said. "These are very patient men, and they are enjoying watching us talk. They are glad to see one of you taking an interest in them. Up to now, no one ever has."

"It pains me to hear that. But if you say it's OK to talk in front of them, then very well. I'm still not entirely clear what you are trying to teach me."

"Take me, for example," Patel replied. "I have a medical degree from the U.S., which could provide me with many material things. But I came here instead to work with these men, not because it was the right thing to do, or because I had to, but because it is who I am—I have committed myself to the welfare of men like these. Can you not relate to that?"

"That," I said, "I can relate to."

"If I had instead stayed in the U.S., I would have been a lot more comfortable, but I would have forfeited my life by doing so. Here, although I have very few in the way of things, I have my bliss, and I am very content."

"Your mother raised a wise son."

Patel grinned in reply. "Shall I now ask the men how they plan to use the money they will make on this project?"

"Please do."

As each man answered Patel's question, I became more and more astounded. Several of the younger men said they would give their money to a sister as a dowry for her wedding. A few others spoke of helping send their little brothers or sisters to a university in England or the U.S. One of the older men said he was the mayor of his village, and the money was needed to help decontaminate the water supply.

What impressed me most, however, was that as the men spoke of what I considered great sacrifice, each was smiling, almost glowing in the knowledge he was making a contribution to his family or community. None seemed to consider his situation a burden but rather saw it as a privilege. In fact, I'm not sure the word sacrifice or anything like it was in their vocabulary. They were completely content just to serve—to make a meaningful contribution.

Later, after the interview, I shared my feelings with Patel.

"I've never been in the presence of such generous people," I said. "Those men were completely unselfish."

"They are neither generous nor unselfish," Patel replied. "They are just being who they are; they are doing what our men do. And they are content doing it. You see, my friend, when one does not have choice, one does not have to deal with the dilemma it creates. One just does what one does. But introduce choice into the mix, and problems can arise."

"What do you mean?" I replied. "What problems? Are you saying choice is wrong?"

"No. It is neither bad nor good. I am just saying if you were to introduce choice into this culture, these men would now have to deal with something that they are free of, namely choosing. When I first left India, I struggled with having to make all the choices people like you must make. I never got comfortable with it. That is one reason I returned home and came to work with these men."

"Because you didn't want choices?"

"Let me explain. Growing up in America, you have had to deal with an abundance of choice your entire life, to the point where you do not even realize when you are and are not choosing. When in the U.S., I saw people who thought they were choosing but were actually allowing others or their circumstances to choose for them. At the same time, I saw people who thought they had no choice when they actually did."

"You're confusing me now. Do I choose, or don't I choose?'

"Did you choose to come to the Middle East and work on this project?"

"What?" I replied. Patel really caught me off guard with that question.

"Did you choose to come work here?" he asked again.

"Well, no, not really," I said. "It was the next assignment my company wanted me to take."

"So, you had no choice in the matter?"

"No, not really, I guess."

"Are you happy working here on this project?" he asked.

"Yeah, sure," I answered. "It pays the bills, and I'm the breadwinner, as we say in America. I have to come here to provide for my family. I guess I'm like these men we're interviewing. I don't have a choice; it's what I do."

"For your own good, I am going to tell you something that you will not like hearing," Patel said with concern. "Do you want me to say it? If not, I will not."

"I want to hear what you have to say," I replied. "Please say it."

"I have two things to tell you," Patel replied. "First, you are not happy here. Second, you are not like these men."

"OK, I admit it. I don't like working overseas. I like working with these men and having conversations with people like you, but I miss my family. My kids are growing up, and I don't get to see them as much as I'd like. I'm not here by choice. I'm here because I don't feel that I have a choice."

"And that is why you are not content, my friend. You are a person who has more choice than most people on the planet, and like most Americans, you do not exercise that choice."

"But I can't choose where my company sends me, can I?" I responded. "I have to go where my boss tells me to go. It's either go to the Middle East or quit."

Patel folded his hands on the table in front of him, leaning toward me as he spoke.

"You have more choice than most," he said. "You just do not see it anymore. It has disappeared into the background of your consciousness. All I am trying to do is awaken you to that."

"So, you're saying I'm unhappy being here, not because I'm in the Middle East but because I am not choosing to be in the Middle East—because I am not exercising the choice that I have been given. Is that what you're trying to get me to wake up to?"

"Yes, and that is why I say you are not like the men we interviewed. These men are doing what they do. Choice does not even enter into the equation. For them, there is no equation, they do not weigh options, there is no choice—there is just what they are to do.

"You, on the other hand, are doing what others have chosen for you to do—your company, your boss, your concept as a 'breadwinner,' and your financial obligations are doing the choosing. Is it not ironic that those without choice are the ones who are content, and those with all the choice often are not?"

"It is. I've learned a lot today, even though it was difficult to hear. Thanks for being so patient and generous with me."

"My friend," Patel replied with a grin, "it is what I do."

As the interview ended, I stood and walked to the door to say good-bye to the men. As each passed me, he once again smiled, clasped his hands, and bowed.

I looked at Patel and said, "You were right; they really do appreciate teachers."

After the last man had exited, Patel replied, "Mr. Cort, those men were not bowing to you because you are a teacher."

"No? Then why?"

"They were acknowledging the 'divinity' in you."

"You mean they think I'm a god?"

Patel shook his head and laughed to himself. "No. They know we all are."

As we exited the room, Patel paused for a moment, turned to me, and said, "May I take you to lunch today? I will come around at noon."

I accepted his invitation, and Patel left me with my thoughts until lunchtime. As I walked to my office, I contemplated what he'd said. I came to realize that despite the fact that I had not chosen the Middle East, my company's decision gave me the opportunity to live the commitment I'd made years prior with Bud. Where else did the men and women who design, build, operate, and maintain the world need more of a champion for their health, safety, and well-being than here, on this project?

As I pondered the morning, I recognized I had already met the objective George had given me for my visit: I had fallen in love with these men. For the first time, I chose to be on the project—not out of guilt or obligation but simply because I wanted to be there and serve these men. I was well aware this choice would mean less time with my family, but at that moment I chose to give that up, at least for a few years. I also realized that I had a great wife who would support my choice and give my children all the love and parenting they needed when I was not home.

Exercising that choice gave me a sense of purpose and contentment I had not experienced since accepting the assignment to work on this project. All the resentment I'd felt toward my company for taking me away from my family evaporated. What remained was my appreciation for my wife's support and the opportunity my company had given me to do whatever it took to ensure the welfare of these men.

And it's a good thing I came to that place, because my first opportunity to fulfill this purpose was only a few hours away.

Chapter 12:
The Grand Tour

"From a certain point onward there is no longer any turning back. That is the point that must be reached."

—Franz Kafka

"The price of greatness is responsibility."

—Winston Churchill

As promised, Patel arrived at my office just before noon to take me to lunch. When I asked where we would be eating, he replied, "It is a surprise."

We procured a project vehicle and headed toward the rear of the property. I was confused as to why we weren't leaving by the main entrance, but I assumed Patel knew what he was doing.

As we approached the rear boundary security gate, I noticed a long line of about twenty school busses exiting. Each was full to capacity of men like those Patel and I had interviewed that morning.

"Where are they all going?" I asked.

"They are heading to their camps for lunch," Patel responded.

"I just assumed they brought their lunch to work like construction workers do in the U.S. I never considered they don't live nearby and go home every day. Where do they live?"

"You will soon find out. We are going to eat lunch in a camp where about five hundred of these men live. There are presently two camps for the project. As the project grows, there will be other camps added. We will be going to the camp where the men you interviewed this morning live. It is the camp where mostly Indian workers stay."

"Great. I'll enjoy seeing them again. So, half of these busses will be going our direction, and the other half is going to the other camp?"

"Yes, approximately. But I want to prepare you for what you are going to see. When I say camp, it is not what you think of in America. Do you understand what I am saying?"

"I think I do," I said, doubting that I did.

"Just prepare yourself. You may see some things that can be quite overwhelming."

"I appreciate you looking out for me, Patel."

"You are welcome, Mr. Cort."

We followed the long row of busses for several minutes, when it dawned on me that although we were in an air-conditioned project vehicle, the men's busses were not cooled. I pointed it out to Patel.

"I was wondering if you would notice that," he answered. "I have taken measurements; it can reach 130 degrees in those busses on a day like this."

"My God! Have you told anyone about this?"

"I have brought it up to Donny, the safety director, several times, but he has declined to take it to management. Donny is not like you. He is only interested in getting his inspections done and completing his paperwork. The people do not even register with him."

"I've noticed that about him. I'll talk to Hank about the busses when we return. That"—I pointed at the bus in front of us—"is unacceptable."

Soon, about half of the busses turned onto another road toward their camp while our line of busses continued straight ahead. About fifteen minutes later, we reached the camp. Like the project, it was surrounded by a tall security fence with barbed wire along the top.

Then I saw something I will never forget. As the busses were rolling to a stop at the main entrance, men began flowing out of every window and door. It was as if the men were wet clay being squeezed out of every opening. I sat in our vehicle, observing the scene.

"Look at that, Patel!" I exclaimed. "Look at those men!"

Before Patel could speak, I added, "Oh, my God! They're going over the fence!"

As the men flowed out of the busses, some ran through the main entrance gate, which was about twenty feet wide. The rest climbed over the fence, somehow avoiding the barbed wire, and dropped to the ground on the other side. It was as if the clay became a herd of gazelles. I had never seen anything like it before and was amazed that human beings were capable of such a feat. The wave of humans was both beautiful and horrifying.

As they landed on the other side of the fence, each and every one of the five hundred men began sprinting into the camp, heading for a building they referred to as the canteen. I turned to Patel.

"Why are they doing this? Why jump the fence and run?"

"It took us fifteen minutes to get here, and it will take fifteen to get back to the project," Patel replied. "The lunch break is one hour. That means all five hundred of these men must be fed in thirty minutes. That is impossible and these men know it. They run because they know only the first half in line will be fed."

"Surely we wait until everyone has had time to eat," I replied. Patel smiled sympathetically at my naïveté.

"No. The order is to leave the canteen twenty minutes before 1:00, so there is time to board the busses and return to the project. About half the men will return with an empty stomach."

"Not today, Patel. Today we stay until everyone is fed."

"With all due respect, sir, you do not have the authority to make that decision. If you gave that order unilaterally, you would only create enemies within the project, and that would hamper what you are here to do. But I am hopeful that after this visit, you will go back and influence those who do have the authority."

"You know I will," I replied. "This is unbelievable."

We exited our vehicle and proceeded to follow the cloud of dust stirred up by the men running to lunch. The canteen was a large, rectangular metal building painted white. As we entered, I was pleased to see that it was air-conditioned and relatively clean and modern. Inside, the white metal walls contrasted the green tile floor. Scattered throughout the large room were laminated bench tables much like you would see in any American school lunchroom. In the rear of the building was the kitchen. There were no walls separating the kitchen from the eating area, and I could see the cooks preparing the meal.

Between the kitchen and the eating area was a long table from which the men were served. A queue of men circled the entire inside walls of the building, waiting to be fed. The queue was about five men thick at any location along its length. Yet there was no pushing or shoving—in fact, the men were extremely docile given that many would not be eating.

"Are you sure many of these guys won't get to eat?" I asked Patel. "I'm surprised there isn't more competition to get to the front of the line."

"Such a thing is not in these men's nature," he replied. "They all know that tomorrow they could be the one at the front of the line."

At that instant, I recognized men from the morning interview, distinguishable because they were still holding the breakfast boxes we'd given them.

"Why are they still holding the boxes? I assumed they'd have finished them by now."

"Mr. Cort, to you, those are just breakfast boxes. But to these men, those boxes are precious."

"Precious?"

"First of all, they were a gift from you. These men got to know you this morning, as you did them. They like you and can see that you are different than the managers who have preceded you."

"That's nice to hear."

"But the larger reason they consider the boxes precious is that they were given by one of the bosses. That never happens here. You are the first boss who has ever acknowledged that these men exist as more than just tools to dig holes, erect steel, and clean bathrooms. By giving them that box, you have declared that they matter, that they are much more than a tool, that they are like you, a man, a human being. That is why the box is so precious to them."

As Patel was speaking, I couldn't help but notice that every man in the room was looking at me.

"Why are they all looking at me?"

"Because to them you represent hope. In fact, we have a word for it, *asha*, which means a wish or hope. That is my sister's name, Asha."

"Me? I represent hope? But most of these men don't even know me."

"They have not met you, but they know of you. They know that you and your friends, your consulting teammates, are here. So do the men at the other camp. They know what you stand for, and they are hopeful that you can help make things better for them."

It was difficult to maintain my composure when Patel said this to me. There was something completely overwhelming about being the object of hope for a thousand suffering men. As I looked around the room, every man smiled in my direction.

"This is too much to take," I said. "I'd better sit down before I lose it."

Patel signaled to a couple of the men, who helped me to one of the tables. For a moment, I thought I was going to collapse, and I think I might have if they had not been holding each arm. At least at that moment, the burden of those men's suffering was too much for me to carry. While this was going on, a few other men brought me a large bottle of cold water.

"Drink, Mr. Cort," said Patel. "Soon you will eat." Two other men placed plates with a hamburger and French fries in front of Patel and me.

"What's this?" I asked Patel.

"It is your lunch," he answered. "Eat. You are going to need your strength."

"No, no, no. We will eat what these men are eating." I had noticed earlier that the men were eating what appeared to be stew and flatbread.

"You cannot eat what these men are eating. You will get violently ill if you do. That is why they have brought you bottled water. Please, eat your lunch, or you will offend these men and me."

"I'm sorry. I didn't realize."

"No need to apologize for your ignorance, Mr. Cort," said Patel. "Eat."

As I ate my lunch, Patel left. Two of the men stayed behind, sitting across from me, ready to serve me at a moment's notice, smiling anytime our eyes met. I gazed around the room and was glad to see that many of the men were eating and no longer staring at me.

Just as I was feeling more relaxed, Patel returned with two men. From my years of working in union plants, I could sense that the two men were leaders within their community.

"Is this the union committee?" I joked. Patel's blank face told me he had no idea what I was talking about. He ignored my comment.

"If you are up to it, these men would like to take you on a tour of the camp," Patel said.

"Don't we need to leave in a few minutes? I mean, it's almost twenty minutes to 1:00."

"Normally, yes, but I just called the project guard, and he informed me that all the bosses have just left the project to eat lunch. That means we can stay an extra thirty minutes. They will not get back until well after we return."

It was at that moment that I realized the significant role Patel played on the project. Unknown to management, he was doing what he could to assure the well-being of the workers. I was impressed with not only his commitment but his savvy, as well.

"You really look out for these men, don't you?"

"I do. And I am glad that you and your friends have come to help me."

Patel then went on to explain that he had arranged for the two men to secretly escort me out of the canteen to tour the camp. This was something that was highly forbidden. The men were not allowed during lunch to go anywhere but to and from the canteen, the bathing and showering facility, and the busses. Patel turned to the two men and spoke to them in Hindi.

"What did you say to them?" I asked.

"I told them I would go distract the camp bosses, and as soon as I have, you three should sneak out the door for the tour." A few minutes later, we did exactly that.

My escorts were pleased for the opportunity to show me the camp, but at the same time they were obviously concerned about being caught outside the canteen. I was told later they had risked, at best, losing privileges—of which there were few—or at worst, being beaten by the camp bosses. As we walked, both of the men's heads were on a swivel, behaving as would any prey on the lookout for predators.

The first stop on the tour was the barracks, the buildings in which the men slept. The barracks were two-story wooden buildings painted dark red. I wondered who in the world would paint a building red in the desert. The stairways and hallways were not air-conditioned, and the heat was unbearable.

I was led to a room down one of the halls. As we traveled down the hall, my guides pointed out the smoke alarms, which were either missing or physically damaged. I surveyed the hall, noticing absent fire hoses, standpipes with no water, and fire extinguisher hooks without extinguishers.

One of the guides knocked on a room door. A tiny Indian man, who could not have been any taller than four feet and must have weighed about fifty pounds, opened the door. He smiled at us, speaking in Hindi as he opened the door wide in welcome and motioned for us to enter, clearly grateful to show us his room.

As I entered, I was shocked to find the room no cooler than the hallway. I was also surprised to see that there were five other men in the room as well, all equally small and frail and eager to show me their concerns. All at once, they began tugging at me, wanting to show me their needs.

The old man who had first welcomed us into the room pulled my arm and dragged me over to the room's one tiny window, which had a small air conditioner installed. He turned on the unit, but only dusty, sandy, hot air blew out. He opened the unit to show me that it was clogged full of sand. He looked up at me as if to say, "Please, let someone know about this."

The others then showed me their beds, of which there were four. One held up six fingers and then tapped several of the beds.

"Are you saying there are only four beds for six people?" I asked, holding up four and then six fingers.

He smiled and nodded with relief at me and the other men, as if to say, "Yes, he understands."

The man then motioned for me to lie on the bed. As I did, I was almost overpowered by the odor of the mattress, but I didn't show any discomfort. I didn't want to insult the men, and I realized that my discomfort was momentary—theirs was permanent.

As I lay on the mattress, I understood why I had been asked to experience it. It was like lying on a burlap bag full of large, hard sticks.

The last thing the men showed me was their lockers. Like the beds, there were only four. Two of the lockers had been damaged, making them unable to lock. Someone had obviously broken into them and, in doing so, damaged the units. One of the men gestured toward a padlock that had been cut. His message was clear: "We have no place to safely store our valuables."

Then one of the men opened the one locker that was padlocked. He did so without concealing the combination, which indicated to me that he either trusted the other men or they all shared this one small locker. The man opened the door and very gently and carefully pulled from it one of the golden lunch boxes from the morning's interview. I realized he must have attended the interview and had placed his box in the locker for protection.

As the man pulled the box free of the locker, he lifted it up to me and smiled an enormous smile of yellow, decayed teeth, many of which were missing. It was clear that, as Patel had told me, the box was a most precious possession. The other men gazed at the box as if it were the Hope Diamond.

This experience, on top of my experience in the canteen, was too much for me. I sat on one of the beds and began to weep. I was overtaken by a host of emotions but mostly pity, anger, and guilt. I thought to myself, I'm in a slave labor camp. These men are prisoners, and their only hope is me.

The men did their best to console me, and after a moment, I composed myself, thanked them for their hospitality, and my escorts and I moved on. As we were leaving the barracks building, my hosts once again became concerned of being caught and quickly whisked me off to the "Recreation Building." As we arrived, one of the guides slid open a large door panel, revealing that the building was full of mechanical supplies and equipment. It was obviously being used as storage for the project.

My guides then proceeded to show me a basketball court with no hoops or balls, a soccer field with no goals or equipment, and a swimming pool that was empty except for a dark, disgusting liquid at the bottom of the deep end. Their message was clear: there was no recreation going on in this camp.

The last stop on the tour was the bathing and showering area. The facility was no more than a concrete area about the size of a basketball court, covered by a corrugated metal roof attached to a steel pipe frame. As we approached the area, I was overcome by the stench of urine and feces. It was so disgusting that I fell to my knees gagging and coughing. My tour guides helped me to my feet and, covering my mouth and nose with my hands, we approached the large shed. I peered inside and then immediately recoiled, sprinting away while vomiting my lunch. My guides helped me steady myself; they were apparently prepared for my reaction because they immediately offered me a new bottle of water.

What I had seen were men in the room urinating and defecating into holes and drains in the concrete floor. The men were standing in pools of urine and feces as they went about their business, with the liquid and solids flowing over their sandals and between their toes. The stench was beyond description. Moreover, the excrement was flowing into the shower area, across the floor, and down the drains. Most of the drains were plugged with feces, causing large pools of urine and waste to form everywhere. Not that anyone could have showered, anyway, since all the shower heads and faucet handles were missing.

As I was sitting on the dirt regaining my bearings, I was reminded of the milking rooms on my grandfather's dairy farm. When milking the cows, the men had to stand in cow urine and feces, but they wore protective clothing and boots. I never imagined that there were men who had to stand in human excrement as a normal course of using the bathroom after lunch.

"Where do the men wash their feet?" I asked my guides, motioning with my hands the act of washing my foot. I assumed they hadn't understood me, because they lifted me to stand, and we proceeded to walk back in the direction of the canteen. As we approached the front entrance, they diverted me to the side of the building, where I observed several men washing their sandals, feet, faces, and bodies in the long cast iron trough intended for canteen visitors to wash their hands. This was where they bathed.

Before I could speak, I heard a voice behind me ask, "So, how did you enjoy your tour?"

I spun around and saw Patel. He was smiling but at the same time dead serious to hear my response.

"I would not associate joy with what I just experienced," I replied. "What I observed was nothing short of human suffering—totally unnecessary and entirely irresponsible. Who on this project is accountable for this camp?"

"Mr. Kadomo-san," he replied. "This is his company's camp."

"Do they stay here? I mean, Kadomo and his staff?"

"No. They stay at the management camp, where all the managers and professionals stay. This is a labor camp."

"That it is," I answered. "Let's get back to the project. I need to speak with Kadomo-san right away."

Patel and I thanked our servers and guides. By this time, all the busses had either left or were leaving. As we drove away from the main gate, I looked at Patel.

"You set me up, didn't you?" I asked, still shaken from the experience. "You arranged this whole visit for my benefit and the benefit of these men. Am I right?"

"Yes, you are right," he replied. "I am sorry—"

"You're sorry?" I interrupted. "You have nothing to be sorry about. What you are doing here for these men is Mother Teresa stuff, Patel. Thank you."

"I do what I can."

"You do a lot more than most. You're an amazing person. I don't think I've ever met anyone as selfless."

"Again, I do what I can," he answered. "But now that you and your friends are here, I think together we will do a lot more."

"You can bank on that, my friend. And the first step is a chat with Kadomo-san."

Chapter 13:
I'm So Ashamed

"I've observed many a cow in the pastures of Ireland, and not once have I ever sensed that one was contemplating her inner calf."

—Father John O'Donohue

"They are our pilots. It was our aircraft. The aircraft should not have been on that runway. We accept full responsibility."

—Cheong Choong Kong, CEO, Singapore Airlines

"Heaven knows we need never be ashamed of our tears, for they are rain upon the blinding dust of earth, overlying our hard hearts."

—Charles Dickens

"But the Kingdom of the Father is spread out over the earth and men do not see it."

—Jesus of Nazareth

Upon returning to the project, I immediately sought out Kadomo-san. Kadomo's company was located in one of the larger project trailers, and his office was just inside the main door.

As his executive administrator ushered me in, Kadomo said, "Hello, Cort. You missed a good lunch with the leadership. We looked for you, but we were told you had already left with Patel for the camp." Kadomo spoke very good English, but few of his team spoke any at all.

"I'm sorry I missed that," I replied. "Maybe next time."

"I will make sure we inform you earlier next week."

"I appreciate that," I responded. "I'm here now because I need to set up a time to share with you some of my observations at the camp. I feel it's urgent. When might you have time to meet?"

"I have time right now. Sit and tell me about your visit."

"I will. But I want to tell you more than just what I saw. I want to tell it in a way that you can experience, as much as possible, what I experienced."

"Alright," Kadomo said. "Please begin."

I proceeded to describe in detail what I had seen, heard, and felt that morning. Kadomo sat quietly as the story poured out of me. Not once did he interrupt or ask a question. He just sat there, listening intently and staring at me.

I must have spoken for ten minutes, and as I finished, I looked up to see Kadomo's reaction. He was sitting slouched in his chair, and his head had fallen so that his chin was resting on his chest. I leaned toward him and noticed that his eyes were closed. He was perfectly still as if in a state of meditation or deep sleep. I leaned closer.

"Kadomo?" I said, my voice soft. "Kadomo?"

But he did not respond. I thought, Oh, my God! I killed the guy.

I stood from my chair and said louder, "Kadomo, are you OK?"

Again, he didn't respond. He didn't show any sign that he could hear me. He just sat there motionless. For a moment, I considered reaching over his desk and shaking him, but instead I decided to go for help.

I darted out his office, but Kadomo's administrator was not at his desk. I ran down the hallway, frantically sticking my head into each office, asking, "English, do any of you speak English?" Everyone shook his head. Finally, down at the end of the hall, a man stepped out of his office.

"I speak English," he said.

"Come quickly!" I yelled. "I think there's something wrong with Kadomo-san."

We both dashed down the hall and entered Kadomo's office. I let the other gentleman go ahead of me, assuming he would rush to Kadomo's aid. But as we entered, the man stopped dead in his tracks, grabbed a chair, and sat down. I was dumbfounded that he was not attempting to revive Kadomo or in some way assure that he was all right.

The man said nothing, turned to me, and directed me to sit in the other chair to his left. I sat but remained confounded as to why we were not aiding Kadomo. We waited silently for what seemed forever, until I could stand it no more.

I opened my mouth and started to speak, "Kadom—"

The man's hand went up in rebuke, and I was wordlessly directed to sit back and keep quiet. Kadomo remained still.

We sat there, completely noiseless for another minute or so. Then, without forewarning, Kadomo took a deep breath, slowly raised his head, and looked directly at me through soulful eyes.

"I am so ashamed," he said.

Kadomo's workmate then dropped his head, and they both sat there, unspeaking, for what seemed an eternity: Kadomo looking at me with his sorrowful eyes as the other man kept his eyes closed and head bowed. It was as if time stopped. I can't recall ever being so still, and all I could think was, My goodness, this is the first time in my life I have been in the presence of genuine shame. These guys are not offering excuses or justifications. They are baring their souls to me.

It became clear that Kadomo's teammate had recognized what was going on the instant we entered the office. I was grateful he had forced me to give Kadomo the space he needed to pray, meditate, or do whatever it was he needed to do, before he could express his shame to me.

Kadomo's teammate then rose and, as he was leaving the room, Kadomo said something to him in Japanese. The man turned back to Kadomo, bowed silently, and left the room. I had no idea what their interaction meant, but my assumption was that Kadomo thanked the man, and the man's bow meant something like, "It was my honor, sir." I thought, What wonderful people.

As I turned my attention back to Kadomo, I noticed his face was no longer full of shame but rather resolve.

"What do we need to do first?" he asked. "You tell me what needs to get done, and I will make sure it is done."

The two of us proceeded to make and prioritize a list of actions necessary at the camp. The top priorities were anything that threatened the lives of the men. First on our list were the smoke alarms and fire equipment in the barracks. If a fire was to break out that night, dozens, if not hundreds, of men could die.

Kadomo called an emergency meeting of the project leadership team. At the meeting, he asked me to share, exactly how I had with him, my experience at the camp. As I was telling my story for the second time in front of a larger audience, for some reason, I broke down and started sobbing. I was surprised I wasn't able to keep my emotions in check.

Hank, the project manager, asked the group to take a ten-minute break and guided me into his office. He put his large arm around my shoulders.

"Cort, you've got a big heart, and that's going to be a problem for you over here," he said. "You need to realize you're going to see some terrible things here. Like this morning, I was in town, and there was a ragged old woman sitting on the street curb, begging with her blind daughter; the girl was no more than six or seven years old. Her daughter was missing both eyes, and there were flies moving in and out of her eye sockets. I learned a long time ago that you just have to look the other way and not let it bother you."

"What do you mean?" I replied. "What did you do for the girl?"

"I can't take care of every beggar I see over here," he replied, removing his arm from my shoulders and turning toward his desk, "and neither can you."

"So you did nothing for her?"

"No, I didn't, and you won't either after you've been here for a while."

"Then why were you there?"

"What? What do you mean, why was I there?"

"I mean, each of us is here and there for a reason, at least I believe we are. So I'm asking, why were you there with that woman and her daughter at that time?"

Hank looked at me with total befuddlement. "I wasn't there for that woman. I was there to buy a watch. She was outside of the jewelry store I was shopping in. I'd heard they have some good deals on Rolex watches, and I've always wanted one."

"Hank, I just shared my experiences at a camp for which two different managers are responsible: you and Kadomo-san. After hearing about the deplorable conditions, one manager took several minutes to compose himself and then said to me, 'I am so ashamed.' The other brought me into his office and told me about shopping for a Rolex watch. I think one of those managers has gotten so good at looking the other way, he can no longer see."

I didn't like saying those words to Hank, but I knew he was a wonderful person—too good for me not to open his eyes to who he was being. If it hadn't been for Hank's accepting Rob's challenge at the investors' meeting, I wouldn't be standing in his office. However, I was his coach, and it was my responsibility to tell him the truth and help him see his blind spots, even if it hurt.

Hank stood there, towering over me with a stunned look on his face for several moments. Then he turned, walked around his desk, sat down, and turned away from me. He just sat there, staring ahead into infinity. After a while, with his back still to me, he finally spoke.

"Tell the team I'll rejoin them in a few minutes," he said.

I returned to the team meeting and finished sharing my experiences at the camp. Just as I was finishing, Hank entered the room and took his customary seat at the head of the table. He sat there for several moments, looking down while the team sat silently, waiting for Hank to speak.

Hank lifted his head. "Gentlemen, as of this moment, this project is shut down," he said. "I want all our attention and resources directed at our two camps, and I don't want this project to restart until all of Cort's and Kadomo's concerns are addressed."

"Hank, that'll take us weeks," one of the team members responded. "It's going to throw off the entire project schedule."

"We have equipment showing up next week that we need to be ready for," another added.

"And that equipment can sit in the sand and rot until we fix our camps. That is this team's only priority. Nothing else matters; nothing else takes precedence. Have I made myself clear?"

"Yes, sir," the team replied.

"Can I ask a clarifying question?" one member asked.

"Always."

"How will we know when the camps are good enough? I'm not clear as to the standard we're shooting for."

"Good question. I'll make that very easy for you," Hank responded. "When you're completely comfortable having your daughter or son stay in our camps, then you will have met our standard."

The meeting ended, and for the next several weeks, the project focused its entire attention on improving the camps. Patel and I visited both camps regularly and reported back to Hank and his leadership team. Ultimately, Hank established a process whereby he and the leadership team personally inspected each camp monthly; they maintained that frequency for the duration of the project.

It was so gratifying to visit the camps a month later and see swimming pools with men swimming, new mattresses on every bed, sanitary bathrooms and shower facilities, and even a new Laundromat where the men could wash their clothes. On these visits, Patel and I no longer drove in a project vehicle but rather rode with the men in air-conditioned busses.

And when work on the project restarted, Hank applied the same standard. As he put it to the supervisors, "If you're comfortable with your son or daughter working here and doing what you are asking these men to do, then you've done your job. If not, you have more work to do."

The men worked in the shade whenever possible. Cooling stations were installed all over the property, and the men were allowed to use them as often and for as long as they saw fit. Every couple of hours, work was stopped, and the men were brought bottles of water or, if they preferred, a sports drink. Each man was given a phone credit card and vouchers for the local businesses, and the busses made daily trips into town so they could shop and call home. And rooms were set up for the men to pray during prayer call.

For our part, Rob and I brought treats and goodies from the States each trip, based on the feedback and special requests we received. A favorite of Hank's was Ro*Tel brand tomato and chili peppers, Velveeta cheese, and Doritos tortilla chips. At the project's peak, I was traveling with one suitcase for my clothes and three for the goodies.

There were many Filipino men working in administrative positions, and I learned that they loved American baseball. On our next visit, Rob and I brought each the official MLB cap of his favorite team; for some reason, most of them requested the Phillies. We did similar things for all the different groups on the project. The main intention was to demonstrate to all the men that they were much more to us than just tools to get work done—we valued them intrinsically as human beings, as well as instrumentally.

In short, Hank's standard was applied to every single aspect of the project, including the camps, transportation, work schedules, and working conditions. After about six months, the leadership started to realize there was a corresponding increase in productivity, quality, and even safety. Despite all the time spent fixing the camps, the project was ahead of schedule, under budget, and accident-free. Contrary to the corporate safety director's prediction, these unskilled workers, without any sophisticated equipment or systems training, were somehow outperforming their U.S. counterparts.

However, a threat to this extraordinary performance soon arose when one of the project's largest contractors, a company that would oversee the foundation and steelwork, arrived on-site. It became immediately apparent this company and its leadership and supervision were not aligned with Hank's standard.

In response to this threat, Rob and I began making more frequent visits to the project and focused all our attention on these new arrivals.

"I'll take on their managers," Rob said to me. "Your job is to enroll the supervisors."

Like many of the tasks during this project, this one would turn out to be monumental. And in working with the supervisors, I would come to love them as much as I did their workers.

Chapter 14:
Inshallah

"I am looking for a lot of men who have an infinite capacity to not know what can't be done."

—Henry Ford

"God changes not what is in a people, until they change what is in themselves."

—Koran

Before my next visit to the Middle East project, Rob and George invited me to support them with a two-day performance workshop with a large chemical company. Participating in the workshop were about fifty plant managers and a few of their corporate executives.

During the afternoon of the first day, the group addressed the subject of safety performance. George used this opportunity to share our assertion that there is only one appropriate performance goal when it came to safety: harming no one.

One plant manager in particular, Jerry, was extremely unreceptive to George's assertion and spent several minutes attempting to disprove George's theory. Jerry stated such a goal was impractical and injuries were a normal course of high-hazard work.

As he put it, "We hope to not hurt anyone, but at the same time, we know it's impossible."

As he and George when back and forth in a point-counterpoint interaction, I could sense the conversation was becoming tiresome for the other participants. I wanted to jump in and help George out, but I couldn't ascertain how. Then an opening presented itself.

As Jerry finished telling a story, it was apparent from his demeanor he felt he'd put George in his place. I stood and, stepping forward, asked George if I might interject. George nodded and stepped back, allowing me to "own the room." I walked over to Jerry's table.

"Jerry, you make a strong case, and it's obvious you're committed to the safety of your people," I said. "Would you permit me to ask you a few questions I think might help us all better understand where George is coming from?"

"Ask away," Jerry responded, his tone confident but welcoming.

"You just told a powerful story. Are you aware that you used the words 'recordable' five times while telling it?" (The term "recordable" is used in industry to refer to an injury so severe it is required by law to be reported to the U.S. government's Occupational Health and Safety Administration.)

"I trust that I did, if you say so. But what's your point?"

"Before I make my point, may I ask you another question?"

"You may," Jerry replied, making lighthearted fun of my politeness.

"I want you to imagine you're back in your plant, sitting in your office, and there's a knock on the door. You say, 'Come in,' and a maintenance supervisor steps into your office and says, 'Jerry, we just had a man get burned.' Here's my question, and I'd like every manager in the room to ponder it as well: what's the first thing you're going to say?"

The room became impossibly still, and Jerry did not make eye contact with me or anyone else. He sat there for several minutes, looking down at the table and fidgeting with the meeting agenda.

Finally, without looking up, Jerry said almost inaudibly, "I'm ashamed to say it, but I'm gonna ask, 'Is it going to be recordable?'" As Jerry spoke those words, many of the refinery managers sat watching him. I could tell from their expressions they felt a lot of empathy for him.

"What's the first thing you're going to do?" I asked.

Jerry responded without hesitation, "I'm going to call my boss and let him know we've had another 'recordable.'"

"So, in other words, you're gonna cover your ass?"

"I guess you could put it that way."

"Would I be wrong if I put it that way?"

"No, no, you'd be right."

"Thanks for answering so honestly," I said. "May I ask you just a few more questions?"

"You may," Jerry said, again making light of my civility.

"Do you have any children?"

Jerry sat up in his chair, and his chest swelled with pride. "Yes. I have five sons."

"Five sons? Can I assume that you and the wife gave up on a little girl after the fifth boy?" This got a light chuckle from the room.

Jerry laughed and said, "That would be a safe assumption."

"Let me ask you this: I know you love all five of your boys, but is there one who's just a bit special in your eyes?"

Without hesitation, Jerry said, "Yes, my oldest, Jerry Junior."

"OK, then. I want you to now imagine you're sitting in your living room this weekend watching the football game, and there's a knock at your front door. A man opens the door, steps into your living room, and says, 'Jerry Junior's been burned.' My question is: what's the first thing you're going to say?"

"Where is he?" Jerry replied straightaway.

"And what's the first thing you're going to do?"

"Go to him and make sure he's OK."

"I have one last question for you. I want you to imagine you're back in your office at the plant next Monday, and someone enters and says, 'We've had a mechanic get burned.' No shit, Jerry, what're you going to say?"

"Where is he?" Jerry replied in a loud, assured voice.

"And what are you going to do?"

"Go to him and make sure he's OK."

At that instant, the other managers in the room began applauding. I looked at Jerry; he was choked up but at the same time smiling. I sensed that a burden of some sort had been lifted off his shoulders.

After the applause ended, George stepped forward and spent the next several minutes debriefing my conversation with Jerry. George asked the managers to explore two questions first: Who was Jerry being at the beginning of the conversation when he was covering his ass, and who was he being when he was rushing to the burned mechanic's aid? The third question he asked them to consider was, which leader is more likely to get the best performance out of his people, safety or otherwise?

A few weeks after the workshop, Rob informed me Jerry had signed his plant up for an engagement with our company, and one of the reasons he gave Rob was that I'd really nailed him at the workshop.

"It was not pleasant at the time," Jerry had said, "but it got me thinking that we need to make some changes in the way we think and go about getting performance. And that change starts with me." He was right, and I knew we'd be able to do a lot of good with his company, just like we were doing overseas.

I made my second visit to the Middle East a week after my interaction with Jerry. I was looking forward to meeting the supervisors Rob had assigned me, but I wasn't sure what to expect.

After taking the first day to get settled, I arranged to meet with all the supervisors as a group the afternoon of the second day. As I entered the same room in which I had interviewed the Indian laborers, I noticed the conference table had been replaced with classroom-type seating with individual desks, as one would find in any U.S. junior high school.

At each desk sat a crusty, old, battle-hardened foreman, each wondering who this guy was and why they were spending their precious time talking to me.

As I set my backpack down in the front of the room and withdrew some papers, I heard someone speak.

"Who are you, and why are you wasting our time?" one of the men asked. "We have work to do." I was taken back to the first time I entered the union office years prior. My success with the union gave me the confidence to be myself with this group.

"I'm Cort Dial," I said, looking around the room at each of the foremen. "I work with companies like yours to help them improve their performance. I've been asked by Hank and his leadership team to meet with you. And the question they've asked me to explore with you is this"—I wrote on the chalkboard as I spoke—"Can you join with the project leadership team in committing to build this project without harming anyone?"

I looked out at a room of expressionless stares.

"I'll be visiting the project monthly," I continued. "We'll be getting together from time to time to explore this question. I look forward to getting to know each of you much better, and I'm excited about all that you can teach me about your jobs and your lives.

"Oh, and one last thing. None of you has to be here today. And you don't have to attend any future sessions if you don't want to. I'll make sure each of you is always invited and welcome, but it will be your choice if you attend. The leadership team agrees.

"So, who'd like to introduce himself first? Just tell us your name, nationality, a little bit about your home and family, and your job here on the project." I had written these four items on a flip chart before the meeting and revealed them as I asked the men for their introductions.

"I am Sabir Kahn," said the first man to speak. Sabir, I would learn, was the senior-most supervisor of the group and was held in high regard. "I am from Jordan, where I live with my family. I have been a supervisor for forty-two years. My job is to get this plant built as fast as we possibly can."

I thanked Sabir for his introduction and then said, "Sabir, I love your name. Does it have a meaning?"

"It means me," he replied with a confused look. "I am Sabir." The other men in the room laughed.

"Yes, I'm sorry," I said, "I didn't make my question clear. I was asking if there is any meaning behind your name. For example, my name is an American Indian word. It means to be still and quiet, like a lake can be still and quiet. So, I was just wondering if your name, Sabir, has some meaning behind it."

"No, it just means me."

"Why do you like Sabir's name?" said the man sitting behind Sabir.

"It sounds really cool to me. It's a strong, powerful name. Reminds me of a superhero or something . . . like SABIR KAHN!" I yelled as I stood tall, thrusting my fists toward the ceiling.

"That is Sabir," the man said, which triggered laughter from the rest of the men, including Sabir.

"I think Mr. Cort has found the meaning of your name, Sabir," another man said. This gave the entire room a good, loud laugh. I could see the men admired and respected Sabir, and he enjoyed their attention. I knew I'd found the leader of this group, and if I could enroll him, many of the others would follow.

I met with Sabir and his men three times during that trip, each meeting lasting one to two hours. Every time, I wrote the "big question" on the chalkboard: can you join with the project leadership team in committing to build this project without harming anyone?

I began each conversation by asking each man to give his answer and then share the reasons behind it. The answer was always the same—no—as were the reasons. Many said this level of performance was simply not possible. As one man said, "I have worked on dozens of projects and, on each one, men died and were injured. Why should this one be any different?"

But the most common answer given was something they called *inshallah*. As they explained to me, inshallah meant something like "God willing" or "it is in God's hands."

Every time I would start to explore how this project could be different and how we might be able to do the work without harm, one of them, often Sabir, would bring up inshallah. As they did, they would assert there was no use having this conversation because life and death were "in God's hands." This became their default position whenever I challenged them.

This conversation was repeated over and over during each of my subsequent visits to the project. Whenever we would get close to breaking through the men's history and exploring a future different from their past, someone would insert inshallah into the discussion, and all the creative tension would evaporate from the room. These men had found a surefire way to get off the hook anytime I was making them uncomfortable, and they knew it. I realized that if I was ever to breakthrough this barrier, I would have to find a way to counter their inshallah argument. If not, I would be wasting these men's time.

Then, during one of my return trips home, my driver and I arrived in Bahrain late in the afternoon. As we came down a hill on our way to my hotel, I noticed a huge, beautiful, rectangular building off in the distance. Its white walls were simultaneously lit by bright spotlights and the setting sun, and the structure was glowing a vibrant yellow.

"What is that?" I said to my driver. "I can't believe I've never noticed it!"

"It is the Grand Mosque, one of the largest in the world," he replied. "But we are Christians, so we cannot visit there."

"Do you think there might be someone there who can explain inshallah to me?" I asked. "Someone like the Muslim equivalent to a priest or rabbi?"

"Why do you care about such things?" he responded, his tone fatherly. "You are Christian, not Muslim. They do not welcome you there."

"I'm not interested in converting. I just want some information on this thing, inshallah. The supervisors on the project talk about it all the time, and I want to understand it better."

"You are a funny young man. I will take you, but I will not go in with you."

We arrived at the mosque, and I proceeded toward what looked like one of the main entrances. As I stepped from the car, prayer call began to ring out from the mosque's powerful speakers, beckoning people to the mosque to pray. The voice of the man singing this prayer call was exceptionally beautiful, and the backdrop of late afternoon on the mosque and city made the walk to the door a spiritual experience.

As I approached the entrance, numbers of men where entering. I stood there, asking them as they passed, "English, does anyone speak English?"

Most looked at me, shaking their heads to indicate they did not, and some seemed to ignore me. Finally, one of the men approached me, saying, "I speak English."

I knew the man was in a hurry to get to prayer, so I quickly explained my desire to speak to someone who could teach me about inshallah. He listened to me intently and then said, "Wait here. I will return."

I sat at the mosque entrance for about twenty minutes, listening to the men inside praying and what sounded like a teacher speaking. The cool breeze off the gulf and the long shadows made the wait exceedingly comfortable, and I took the time to enjoy the view as the lights of Bahrain began to turn on.

All at once, the hundreds of men who had entered the mosque began leaving. I stood, hoping to see the man who had directed me to wait, but he was not to be found. After all the men exited, I waited another ten minutes or so, hoping he would appear, but he did not.

My driver, who could see me, started honking the horn and waving for me to return. As I started to leave for the car, I heard a man's voice say, "I understand you want to talk to a teacher . . . that you wish to learn about inshallah?"

"Yes, that would be me. My name is Cort."

"Welcome, Cort. My name is Jabir."

I proceed to tell Jabir, who I assumed was some official of the mosque, my story about Sabir and the supervisors. I explained how they had been using, in my opinion, inshallah as an excuse not to fully explore the possibility of doing hazardous work without harm. He smiled as he listened.

"They are only telling you part of the meaning. You were correct to come to learn the entire explanation," Jabir said. "When we speak of inshallah, we are, as you might say, putting our fate in Allah's hands. You see, we believe all is written by Allah, and the future we hope for will happen if it is in Allah's design for the world. That is the most common meaning, as best as I can explain it to you in a short period of time."

"So, are you saying a man's actions don't determine his future? That what Sabir and the other supervisors do and say on our project will not affect our performance? That it's all up to Allah?"

"No. I am not saying that at all, and we do not believe that. There is another part of inshallah Sabir and his friends are not sharing with you. Yes, we believe whatever happens must be in Allah's plan for what is best for the world, but we also believe nothing happens without the will and acts of men."

"I think I understand. How I might put it is, 'With my hard work and Allah willing, it will happen.'"

"Exactly!" he replied. "You understand very well."

I thanked Jabir for his help, returned to my car, and shared my experience with my driver. After hearing what had happened, he said, "I could have told you that."

As I flew back home, I sat on the plane, content in the knowledge that I now had the ammunition to break through the inshallah argument. I looked forward to the next time I would be with the supervisors.

But until then, my attention turned to a series of workshops I was scheduled to deliver in a few weeks at a microchip manufacturer in the Southwest. It would be my first visit to that industry—and my first experience learning the power of making a declaration, from the unlikeliest of persons.

Chapter 15:
Juliana's Declaration

"When I confront a human being as my Thou and speak the basic word I-Thou to him, then he is nothing among things nor does he consist of things. He is no longer He or She, limited by other Hes and Shes, a dot in the world grid of space and time, nor a condition to be experienced and described, a loose bundle of named qualities."

—Martin Buber

After returning to the U.S., I spent a week at home resting and recreating with my family. I had negotiated a more predictable schedule with Rob that gave me at least one week a month of quality time with my family. I enjoyed that time connecting with my wife and kids before heading out to my next task: leading two performance workshops at a microchip fabrication facility, or "fab."

While sitting on my plane waiting to depart Austin, I reviewed the materials for the workshops. I was subbing for another consultant, and although I was briefed before leaving, I wasn't exactly sure what to expect. One thing I felt sure of was that this week would be a lot less intense than my trips to the Middle East. I was wrong.

I arrived at my destination, rented my car, and proceeded to the fab. As I was enjoying the desert scenery, I came over a hill and there it was, the largest manufacturing facility in the world. Looking at that gray, metal monstrosity sitting in the pristine desert, all I could think was, I'm entering the Death Star.

The "Imperial March" from *Star Wars*—"da, da, da, da-ta-da, da-ta-da"—kept playing in my head as I approached the facility and drove into the enormous parking lot. I wasn't sure why I felt so apprehensive, but something told me working in this place was not going to be the cakewalk I'd anticipated. I parked my car and proceeded to the main entrance.

As I entered, dozens of people were coming and going. Inside the entrance doors, there was no lobby area, no representatives to greet me and direct me to my appointment. Instead, there were rows of security lines where people were undergoing security examinations that involved everything short of a body cavity search.

The people around me displayed all the pleasantness and vitality of people standing in an airport security line. I thought, Not only have I entered the Death Star but I'm surrounded by an army of Stormtroopers.

My host, Gavin, stepped forward from this multitude, introduced himself, and said, "Follow me, please."

I endured the intrusive security process, where I was given the unmistakable message I was not trusted. Then Gavin guided me through a maze of floors, mile-long hallways, and thousands of cubicles to the room where the fab leaders and I would discuss any last-minute prep for the workshops. In all, the trip to the meeting room took nearly thirty minutes. Fortunately, Gavin had requested I arrive thirty minutes early.

Gavin, as was true of all the others I passed in the halls, didn't say anything to me or anyone else the entire time we were walking. It was as if I was being escorted by an emotionally drained automaton. He dropped me off at the meeting room.

While walking out the door, he said, "You'd better hurry and get ready. They don't like starting late."

I quickly readied for my presentation, but I was not prepared for what was about to happen. Approximately one minute before the meeting was to start, several managers rushed into the room.

"Will I get any 'ARs' out of this meeting?" they asked me, almost in unison.

"I don't know. What's an 'AR'?" I replied. I later learned that AR was short for "action required."

They looked at me in amazement and said nothing. I chuckled inside as I thought, I guess that does not compute. These people have been making computer chips for so long they have become computer chips.

I introduced myself, however, and the managers only shared their first names and then immediately turned their focus to their day planners. We sat there silently for almost ten minutes while we waited for Gavin to return. I would soon learn that there was no greater sin in this organization than to waste time, and calling a meeting and then arriving late was one of the cardinal sins.

Finally, Gavin returned, and as I began to brief the two workshops, one of the managers, named Pat, interrupted.

"Who is this c---s---ker, and why are we pissing our time away listening to him?" he asked Gavin.

I immediately began packing my belongings into my backpack.

"What are you doing?" Gavin said.

"I'm leaving."

To my amazement, Gavin asked, "Why?"

"You are my host, Gavin," I replied. "I am your guest. Someone calls me what I was just called and you sit there and ask why I'm leaving? That's more than enough for any decent person to leave. Wouldn't you agree?"

Pat stood. "Look, what's the big deal? He's overreacting," he said, pointing at me like a spoiled child.

"Here's the deal," I said, stepping toward Pat. "If you apologize to me right now and agree to treat me in a civilized manner, I will unpack and complete this meeting. But if you don't, I'm leaving and never returning. It's your call."

"OK, OK," Pat replied. "I was out of line. I apologize."

"Thank you," I said. As I was unpacking, I added, "By the way, while I'm unpacking, you might want to have a chat with whomever you're upset with in this room."

"What?" Pat said.

"Well, I know it can't be me. You just met me. But you're obviously very upset with someone, and instead of directing that at me, you might consider sharing with that person why you're upset. Go ahead, say what you want to say, but in a civilized way."

"Are you upset with me, Pat?" Gavin asked, to my surprise.

"Yes, I am," replied Pat. "This is the third meeting of yours I've attended this month, and in all three, I've sat waiting here, wasting my time while you were late."

"I'm sorry," Gavin said, rubbing his hand once across his mouth, as if to control his emotions. "I was on the phone with my wife about a problem with my son. I didn't mean to make you wait."

"What's the issue at home? Is everything all right?" Pat asked.

"No, but that's OK. We need to get back to the meeting. My personal problems are mine to deal with."

"That's right," one of the other managers said. "Keep your home and business separate. Let's get back to why we're here."

We returned to the meeting. Before we began, the group informed me they had decided to change the workshop format. Four hours, instead of the full day planned, was sufficient for each workshop, at least according to them. This, they informed me, would allow them "to get twice as many people through this training as soon as possible."

"The idea is not to get people through the training," I responded. "It's to change the way they think and go about creating performance. If you insist on four hours, you'll need to negotiate that with my company and reschedule these workshops with another facilitator." After about ten minutes of quarreling among themselves, the managers agreed to provide an entire day for each workshop.

Before we ended the meeting, I reminded the group of their scheduled interviews with me that afternoon. I told them participation was optional, but that the interviews were their opportunity to help me best serve their intentions during the workshops. Only Gavin and Pat showed up.

The next morning, I arrived for the first workshop. The sessions would be held in training rooms and attended by about seventy-five fab employees from all levels of the organization.

As I conducted the workshops, I was happy to see both were well received. The participants engaged actively in the conversations and exercises and gave positive feedback about the workshop and me as a facilitator.

One conversation was particularly intriguing for the participants and generated the most discussion. We discussed how performance goals, when poorly thought out, can actually limit performance. During this conversation, I stated that when discussing safety and environmental performance, leaders needed to come at it from a new perspective.

"When it comes to assuring the welfare of our people and planet, we need to recognize these are not the same as other areas of our business," I said. We then discussed how to relate to these unique aspects of business and what goals might be appropriate to help drive the best performance.

Friday morning, the day after the second workshop, Gavin asked me to sit in on the fab's weekly senior management meeting. This meeting was attended by all department heads, nearly fifty in total. Also, to ensure that management was aware of the "technician's perspective," about six fab technicians and supervisors were invited, and they sat along the wall at the rear of the room. Most of the meeting attendees had participated in one of my workshops earlier in the week.

The last to enter the room was the fab manager, Russell. As Russ made his way into the room, his large frame seemed to tower over even those who were standing. He sat at the biggest chair at the center of the endlessly long conference table, opposite from Gavin and me. He acknowledged no one.

A millisecond after his hind end hit the seat, he said, "Before we start this meeting, I just learned we're spending an entire day on these performance workshops. Can anyone explain why?"

"Cort Dial is here, Russ," Gavin responded. "He's leading the workshops and can answer any questions you might have."

"Hello, Russ," I said. "You have a question about the workshop timing?"

"I do. Why is it that you damn consultants are always trying to squeeze as much money out of us as you can?"

"I assume you're referring to the workshops being one day instead of four hours?"

"Yes," Russ responded. "Where do you get off telling us how long our workshops will be?"

"I did no such thing. The workshops are one day because that's how long they were designed to be, and that's what your people requested and agreed to when they contracted us."

"Humph," Russ grunted as he stared at me, his freckled face a bright pink. He paused for a moment and then said to a man at the front of the room, "Let's get going."

The fab's senior-most operations manager kicked off the meeting by presenting a "performance briefing." As is customary in most manufacturing facilities, the first performance area discussed was safety performance. The operations manager projected onto an overhead screen summary after summary of every accident that had occurred since the last meeting. He then shared data intended to reflect the fab's performance relative to its "safety goals."

The operations manager's approach was completely inconsistent with what the attendees had learned in my workshops. I sat there asking myself, *Isn't anyone going to point out the discrepancy between what is going on in this meeting and what they learned this week?*

Then, out of the corner of my eye, I saw a hand go up. I looked to the rear of the room. Sitting against the wall was a tiny Hispanic woman with her hand in the air. I recalled her from one of the workshops. Her name was Juliana. She was a young technician who was fairly new to the fab.

The operations manager finally noticed her. "Yes? You have a question?"

"I do," Juliana responded as she stood. "I'm confused. I just sat through a workshop with Cort, and he helped us see how unproductive performance goals, like the one you're presenting, can be. He pointed out how it can be detrimental to use words like 'recordable' and present injury data as if it were production data. But I sit here, and we're doing just that. I think he has a much better way."

"You said you had a question," the operations manager interrupted in a stern, frustrated tone.

"I guess my question is, why are we sending our people to workshops where they're being shown a way to get better performance, and we're not using that way ourselves?"

"What is your name?" the operations manager responded.

"Juliana," she said, widening her shoulders and lifting her chin.

"Juliana, the way of approaching performance you're learning in those workshops makes sense in your world. It's OK for out there. But, in here, we have to deal with the real world, and in the real world, performance is talked about the way I've discussed it."

"Well, then, I now understand why nothing is changing out there. Don't you realize that however you think and talk in here is how we think and talk out there? If you don't change, we never will. I left that workshop excited about a new way, but all my supervisors who attended are no different. They went to the training, checked the box, and went back to business as usual."

Then Russ, the fab manager, spoke up. "I think you've made your point, Juliana," he said. He turned to the operations manager. "Let's move on."

"There's one more thing I want to say," Juliana said, stepping closer to the conference table. "The safety goals you've listed there, on the screen—why are you continuing to use goals like that when we've been shown how counterproductive they are?"

"What do you mean? What's wrong with a goal to reduce our injuries 20 percent this year?" the operations manager asked.

"A whole lot of things, based on the workshops you asked me to attend. Haven't you been attending the workshops?"

"No, I haven't. But I still don't see anything wrong with these performance goals."

Juliana and the operations manager went back and forth for a few minutes as she attempted to help him understand what she learned in my workshops. Across the room, Russ shifted in his seat, tapped his fingers on the conference table, brushed back his bright red hair, and looked around the room, clearly tiring of this conversation. He finally intervened.

"Juliana, let me see if I can explain this in terms you can understand," Russ said. "Performance is performance. Whether it's productivity, quality, or safety, they are all the same. And we use these goals to set our annual targets and then do our best to achieve them. It's business 101. Do you get my point?"

"I don't," Juliana answered. "But I'm listening. Please continue."

"Well, it's like this: last year, we achieved 90 percent defect-free in our silicone wafers, so we set our goal for this year at 92 percent. It's the same with safety performance. Last year, we had ten lost-time injuries, and so we set our goal for this year at 20 percent less than that—at eight lost times. Do you understand my analogy?"

There was no hesitation in her reply. "No, sir. I don't understand any analogy that equates a defect in a piece of silicone to an injury to a human being."

The room became totally still and remained so for what seemed an eternity. Russ said nothing. He just sat there looking at Juliana, then at the operations manager, then at the data projected on the screen, and then back to Juliana. He did this several times.

"You're right, Juliana," he finally said. "It is different, isn't it?"

"I say it is," she replied.

There was another long pause in which Russ sat contemplating Juliana's declaration. Then he turned to the operations manager.

"Maybe we need to learn a different way to talk about performance," Russ said.

"A good start would be to attend Cort's workshop," Juliana suggested, which solicited an uncomfortable round of laughter from the room.

The meeting soon ended, and Russ, the operations manager, and the other senior staff dashed to their next meeting. Some of the lower-level attendees huddled around Juliana for a few minutes before leaving. I heard them congratulating and teasing her, saying things like, "So, where do you think you'll be working next week?"

Later, Gavin told me, "In this company, you don't disagree with the fab manager like that. Fab managers are gods."

After the meeting attendees had dispersed, I approached Juliana. "Where did you get the guts to say something like that to the fab manager?" I asked.

"You asked us in that workshop if we could commit to thinking and operating in a new and more productive way," she said, her gaze steady. "I accepted your challenge and made a commitment then and there to change. After doing that, there was no way I could keep my mouth shut."

"You made more progress with your managers than I ever could have, even if they'd attended the workshop. I'm afraid my workshops aren't making a whole lot of difference."

"I disagree. Russ and some of these managers may never change, but don't let that discourage you. That workshop had a huge effect on me and many others. You've made a big contribution here, even if they never ask you back. I know I'll never see things the same."

"Thanks. Hearing that makes the whole week worthwhile."

I guess she could hear a bit of dejection in my tone, because she continued by saying, "Don't ever underestimate the influence someone like you can have. Some people may not be ready to hear what you have to offer. But that doesn't mean it's not worth offering. You might not always see the results of your work, so you just have to have faith that you're making a difference. My mom always told me, 'Juliana, you will create wakes that you might never see hit the shore, but they will hit the shore.'"

I thanked Juliana again for her wisdom and leadership in the meeting, and we parted ways. A few weeks later, I heard from Rob that Russ had made the decision to remove our company from his fab, and our engagement ended.

I was disappointed for our company and Russ's people, especially Juliana, but I took the bad news in stride and turned my attention back to Sabir Kahn and his inshallah defense. I was looking forward to my next trip to the Middle East to see if this time, I could break through the supervisors' resistance.

Chapter 16:
I Am a Father

"One of the great lies of organizational life is that jobs can be as big as the people who fill them. It's not true. Teams can never be as big as our families. Colleagues can never be as big as our friends. Companies can never be as rich, as wonderful, as the people in them. We are bigger than our organizations. We just are."

—William Gartner

I returned to the Middle East project the week after the fab workshops. Although it was difficult to leave my family after being home for a short stay, I was excited about the possible breakthrough with Sabir and the other supervisors.

Upon arrival at the project site, I realized quickly much had changed in the time I'd been gone. There were several new trailers on-site, representing new business partners on the project—and, of course, many new carports for their vehicles. Laborers had begun digging the trenches for foundations, laying the groundwork for the administrative buildings and production units.

I could also feel a difference in the attitudes of the people on the project, starting with the security guards who waved and yelled out our company name as I passed through the main gate.

Workers I passed in the hallways seemed to have a bounce in their step and went out of their way to welcome me back. I saw smiles on every face and heard laughter coming from the offices. Hank's leadership team meeting had a highly collaborative tone, more than just schedules and budgets were discussed, and the team members seemed to enjoy working together solving both technical and human challenges. I recalled my conversation with Juliana and thought, Hmm, I guess some of our wakes hit the shore while I was gone.

Sabir and the supervisors were unable to meet with me for several days. They were training newcomers to the project and needed a few days to catch up before they'd have time for me. Finally, one afternoon five days after I had arrived, we met.

The group entered the room, and it was obvious they'd had a long, hard day. Once they were all seated, I said, "Gentlemen, you look like, as we say in Texas, 'a horse that's been ridden hard and put away wet.' Would you be interested in being treated to a steak dinner at the hotel restaurant?" All of a sudden, the men perked up and nodded their heads.

"If you guys can get there this evening, there will be steak dinners waiting for you all," I said. "Just let me know what time you plan on arriving."

"I will arrange for a bus for transportation," Sabir replied. "We will be there at 7:00."

"Great. Enjoy the rest of your afternoon, and I'll see you at the hotel."

I left the room as the men talked enthusiastically among themselves. While I couldn't understand what they were saying, I could tell they were excited about dinner. Not only did dining at the hotel mean they would enjoy an evening outside of their camp, but they'd also get to dine on finer food and drinks.

I headed straight for Hank's office, stuck my head inside, and said, "I just invited the supervisors to a steak dinner at the hotel. If you'll pay for it, I promise they'll come back committed to building this project without hurting anyone. Do we have a deal?"

"Deal," said Hank with a big grin. "Have fun."

The supervisors' bus arrived at the hotel promptly at 7:00 as Sabir had promised. They were all dressed in fresh attire, smiling and exuberant. It was clear they considered the dinner a special occasion and were grateful to be invited.

I had arrived at the hotel early and had been able to convince the staff, whom I'd become very friendly with over the last few months, to give us a private room. In the reserved dining area was a long table that seated all thirty-two supervisors and me. Sabir insisted I sit at the head of the table. He sat in the chair closest to me on my left.

As the evening progressed, there was a consistent stream of laughter as the men enjoyed their night out. Each devoured his T-bone steak, and a few even had seconds. I couldn't understand most of what was said, but I enjoyed myself in knowing that, at least for a few hours, Hank and I had given these men a departure from everyday life.

Then, as dessert was being served, Sabir tapped his glass with his ring. I was surprised how quickly the men noticed the sound and gave him their full attention.

I assumed Sabir was going to thank me for the invitation. But instead he said to his associates, "Gentlemen, I think our host has a question he wants to ask us."

"No, no. Not tonight," I replied. "Tonight isn't about business. It's about being with friends and enjoying one another's company."

"Mr. Cort, you are our friend and teacher. We enjoy your company and discussing your questions. So, please, ask your question. But understand this: a steak dinner will not always buy you a yes." This solicited a hearty laugh from the supervisors.

"Very well. Sabir, can you join with the project leadership team in committing to build this project without harming anyone?"

"No, Mr. Cort, I cannot," Sabir replied without hesitation. "Despite my belly and heart being full, I cannot say yes to your question."

"And why do you say no?" I asked. I looked around the table, and all eyes were intensely focused on Sabir and me.

"For the same reasons we have given you before. What you are asking is simply not possible here. Men are going to be hurt on this project, and some may die . . . as they have on all projects we have worked on. That is not up to us. We do not determine who lives and dies. Why can you not see that?"

"It's not that I can't see it. I can. I just refuse to accept that answer because you—all of you at this table and all the other men on this project—matter too much to me."

"Ahh!" Sabir belched while tossing his napkin on the table. "You are a very stubborn man, Mr. Cort."

"Now you sound like my wife," I responded, which got a chuckle from Sabir and a good laugh from the supervisors. "Speaking of wives, I see you're wearing a wedding ring. Tell me, do you have any children?"

Sabir sat up straighter as he answered, "I have thirty-three children."

"What! Did you say thirty-three?"

"Yes."

"One wife?" I asked with alarm.

"Three wives," he said, shaking his head and wrinkling his brow to mock my ignorance.

Sabir and the supervisors explained that, in their world, a man can have multiple wives, so long as he can provide equally and adequately for them. When they were done educating me, I turned to Sabir.

"Don't be offended by this question, but can you name all your children?" I asked. "Can you remember all their birthdays?"

Sabir, who appeared almost insulted, rose and stood at attention. One by one, youngest to oldest, he recited each of his children's names and birth dates. When he was done, all the supervisors gave Sabir a boisterous standing ovation—which, I could tell, he thoroughly enjoyed.

The last name Sabir recited was his oldest, who was named Mohammed. This reminded me of the conversation I'd had a few weeks earlier with Jerry, the chemical plant manager, about his son Jerry Junior.

I said to Sabir, "I know you love all of your children. I can see and hear it in the way you speak about them. But is there one of your children who is extra special to you?"

Without an ounce of indecision, Sabir replied, "Of course, my firstborn, Mohammed."

"Can you imagine your son Mohammed working on a project like this?"

"Certainly. He is on a project in Kuwait right now."

"Wonderful. I know it's getting late, and all of you need to get back and get a good night's sleep, but can I ask you one last question before we leave?"

"Go ahead," said Sabir.

I turned to the supervisors. "I'm going to ask this question of Sabir and each of you as well," I said. "After I ask it, we'll say goodnight and leave. I want you to think about the question overnight and meet with me at 6:00 tomorrow morning in the training room, where you'll give me your answer. Do you agree to these terms?"

The men nodded and leaned forward, anticipating the question.

I turned to Sabir. "Do you agree to my terms?"

"Yes," he replied.

"Here's my question: what's the difference between your son Mohammed and all the sons who will be working on this project, the sons you say may be hurt or die?"

I then stood and said to the group, "Gentlemen, it has been my honor to share this meal with you. I had a wonderful time being in your presence, and I promise we will do this again soon. Have a safe and peaceful evening." I turned and exited the restaurant, headed toward my hotel room.

As I left, the men just sat there, stunned by my question. No one uttered a word as I exited the room. I had no idea what the men said or did after I left. I knew, however, that whatever response they gave me the next morning would be their final answer, which I would have to live with.

I arrived at the project the next morning around a quarter to 6:00 and proceeded directly to the training room. I was surprised to find Sabir and the supervisors already in their seats, waiting for me.

After a few pleasantries and comments about the wonderful dinner we had shared, Sabir asked, "Are you ready to hear our answer?"

"I am," I responded. "But first, I want to remind us of why we're having this conversation. Can I do that quickly before you give me your answers?"

"Yes," Sabir said, as the supervisors nodded their approval.

"We're having this conversation because the project leadership committed months ago, while this project was being planned, to find a way to execute it without harming anyone," I said. "It wasn't easy for them to make that commitment, and they knew they were taking on something no one had ever attempted before. But they cared enough for you and your men to make the commitment.

"As part of that commitment, they've asked me to invite you to join with them and commit yourselves to build this project without harming anyone. That's why we've spent these hours together over the last few months. Do you agree that's why we're together, having this conversation?" Every head in the room nodded yes.

"Excellent," I said. "Now, as Sabir pointed out, I asked each of you a question at dinner last night. That question was: what's the difference between your son Mohammed and all the sons who will be working on this project, the sons you say may be hurt or die?

"I'd prefer to have this conversation first with Sabir, if that is OK with everyone. But if you feel the need, don't hesitate to get involved." They agreed. I turned to Sabir.

"What's the difference between your son Mohammed and all the sons who will be working on this project, the sons you say may be hurt or die?" I asked.

"There is none," Sabir replied.

"There isn't?" I asked, feigning surprise.

"No, those sons are the same as my son," Sabir proclaimed as he pounded his knuckles once on his desk.

"Let me see if I understand you. Your son is the same as the men who will be working on this project, the ones you say may be hurt or die. Is that what you're saying?"

"Yes, they are the same."

"So, your son Mohammed, if he was working on this project, he might very well be one of the men you say has to be hurt or even killed to build this project. Is that what you're saying?"

Sabir hesitated and then said, "No! I am not saying that."

"If your son was on this project, he would not be hurt? He would not die?" I asked.

"No," Sabir replied.

"Why not? Why is your son any different from the sons that you, all of you"—I gestured at the supervisors—"have been telling me for months must get hurt and die on this project?"

"Mohammed would not be hurt," Sabir said.

"Why?" I replied in exasperation.

"I would look out for him. I would take care of him."

"I would teach him," one of the supervisors in the room added.

"So, all of you would do whatever it takes to make sure your sons are not injured, do not die?" I asked.

"Yes!" they said in unison, their heads nodding up and down. By now, a few of the supervisors were standing.

"Well then, again, I ask you, what's the difference between your son Mohammed and all the sons who will be working on this project, the sons you say may be hurt or die?"

The men were like statues, perfectly still, as if frozen in time.

"Come on, tell me!" I yelled. "What's the difference between your sons, who you say will not die, and these other men's sons, who you say will die! Come on, what's the difference?"

"There is no difference," one of the supervisors said.

"It seems there is," I replied. "You say your sons will live, but the other men's sons must die. I'd call that a pretty big difference."

One of the other supervisors, a Jordanian named Bobo, then said, "The moon does not care if it shines on Jordan or India."

"Apparently it does," I responded. "At least that's what you've all been telling me for months now. Essentially, what you've been saying every time we've met is that it's acceptable for other men's sons to die building this project, but it's not acceptable for yours. And all I want to know is this: is that who you really are? Are you not willing to do for other men's sons what you would do for your own?"

"No, sir!" one of the men shouted. "That is not who we are!" Several others agreed.

"Is there any reason you can't teach other men as if you would your sons?"

"No," the group replied.

"Is there any reason you can't look out for other men's sons as if they were your own?"

"No," the group again responded.

"Then why in God's name do you say your sons will be fine, but these other sons must be hurt and die?"

At that moment, Bobo stood and yelled out, "I no longer say that. I am not that person anymore."

"You're not?" I asked.

"No, I am not."

"Then who are you? What do you say now?"

"I say that these other men's sons will not be hurt. They will not die. They are no different than my sons."

"And why are they no different?"

"Because I will treat them as my sons. I will teach them and look over them as I would my sons. I will do whatever it takes to keep them from being hurt, keep them alive."

"Why?"

Bobo paused and then, taking a pose like a sentry at his post, said, "Because they are my sons. Because the moon does not care if it shines on Jordan or Pakistan."

"Thank you, Bobo. They are our sons indeed." I allowed for a long, silent pause before continuing.

"A long time ago, I held a man as he died," I said. "He died on my project. He died for one reason, because I didn't care enough about him to protect him. I didn't look out for his welfare the way I would have for my son. And so I put him in a situation that I would never have put my son, and he died. I'll never be cleansed of that shame.

"I've come here for the last three months to talk with you in the hope that you could learn this lesson without someone's son having to die. I know you are wonderful, loving men and great constructors and supervisors. But if we are to do as our leadership has invited us to do, if we are to join with them in their commitment to build this project without harming anyone, we must change. Our men can no longer be 'hands' or 'laborers.' We must see them and supervise them as we would our most precious children . . . as Sabir would Mohammad."

I looked around the room, meeting the men's eyes, finding each staring intently at me.

"I want to thank each of you for being so patient with me over the last few months," I said. "Many would have given up and stopped coming to these sessions. But you guys didn't; you just kept coming. And I know it was for more than just a steak dinner."

The group laughed. I smiled in response.

"I think it's because you are such good men. And although you've been saying no to my big question for months, I think, deep down, you very much wanted to say yes.

"I don't know what each of your answers are to that question, and that's OK because the only person you really owe an answer to is yourself. But I do know this: we don't need to have this conversation again, and unless one of you tells me otherwise, I'll assume your answer is yes and treat you as such.

"Going forward, when we meet, I'll do my best to help you deliver on the commitments made today. I'll share with you what I've learned about performance and how normal human beings like you and me can go about doing something as impossible as building this project without harming anyone."

"Thank you, Mr. Cort," Sabir said. This was the first time since our conversation at the beginning of the meeting that Sabir had spoken.

"You're welcome," I replied. Unspoken in that "you're welcome" was my gratefulness to Sabir for remaining silent and allowing me to lead his men. To me, that was the greatest expression of how much he cared for those supervisors.

"There's just one last thing I feel we must discuss before I end this session, and that is inshallah," I added. The men immediately shifted in their seats; those standing turned their bodies toward me. I could sense they were ill at ease.

"Last time we were together, you guys said you couldn't say yes to the big question because matters of life and death were in the hands of Allah, and you called that inshallah. Am I right about that?"

"Yes," the supervisors said in unison, their faces showing concern for what I might say next.

"Well, on my way back home last trip, I decided to drop in on the Grand Mosque in Bahrain to learn a bit more about inshallah. I spoke to a teacher there who told me you guys had been giving me only half the meaning. Are you interested in hearing what he said to me?"

Again, the answer was another concerned yes.

"He said that when Muslims speak of inshallah, they are putting their fate in Allah's hands," I continued. "He explained that Muslims believe all is written by Allah and the future they hope for will happen if it's in Allah's design for the world. Would you agree that's pretty much what you've been telling me about inshallah?"

A third yes came forth, but in this one, I sensed a bit of relief that their version of inshallah had matched that of the teacher.

"But," I said, pausing to make sure I made eye contact with each of the men, "the teacher also told me there's a second aspect to inshallah you hadn't shared with me. He said it's equally as important as the first."

"What did he teach you?" Sabir asked.

"That whatever happens must be in Allah's plan for what is best for the world, but at the same time, nothing happens without the will and acts of men. Or, the way I would say it, 'with my hard work and Allah willing, anything is possible.'"

"He taught you well, my friend," said Sabir.

I turned to the supervisors and said, "That is the last thought I wish to leave with you today: with our hard work and Allah willing, we will build this project without harming anyone."

The men smiled and nodded, a few even applauded, and the meeting ended.

Eighteen months passed, and the project construction was well along. Not one man had been harmed.

Of course, there were men who visited Patel, the medic, for slight pains and ailments, but none required anything more than basic care, and no one ever left the site for medical attention. Over four million man-hours into the project, we were ahead of schedule, under budget, and experiencing great quality. We did not even have a single weld fail a quality test.

On the other hand, other projects being funded by the same investment group were experiencing poor performance and multiple fatalities. In response, the investors sent an audit team to visit our project to determine why we were outperforming the others.

The audit team spent several days examining all aspects of the project, but they focused their attention, as most audits do, on the project's systems, processes, and compliance—and mostly ignored the people. After a week of inspections, examinations, and interviews, the audit team leader requested a meeting with the project leadership team. Hank agreed to the meeting but insisted that it include a lunch and that all the project supervision attend as well. The audit leader agreed.

The following day, the audit team, the project leadership team, and about thirty supervisors were dining in the very same canteen Patel had taken me to nearly two years before. After we had finished our meal, the audit leader stepped to the front of the room and declared that his team had failed to discover why our project was outperforming our counterparts.

"This project has the exact same business partners participating and the same policies and procedures," the audit leader said. "You have the same equipment and materials. Of course, we did notice a higher level of compliance from your people, and they seem to be a lot happier and friendlier than people on our other projects, but that doesn't explain the difference in performance. It's perplexing me and my team. Everything is the same, and yet somehow you're getting performance we've never seen before."

As the audit leader finished speaking, I noticed something moving in my peripheral vision. I turned to my left just in time to see Sabir Kahn rising to stand. He took a deep breath.

"My friend, you will never find your answer where you are looking," Sabir said. "As you say, none of that is different. It is all the same as every other project. You are looking in the wrong place."

"Where, then, should we be looking?" the audit leader replied. "What's different?"

"You should be looking at me. I am different. We are different." Sabir pointed to the other supervisors sitting near him.

"What's different about you?"

Sabir paused and then said, "I have been a constructor for forty years. I can build anything. And I have been a supervisor for over thirty years. I consider myself a great supervisor. But, on this project, I am much more than a constructor, much more than a supervisor. On this project, I am a father."

Sabir stood there facing the audit leader, proud of who he was, with an unbending stand for his men's welfare. His statement moved everyone in the room, some to tears. Hank and I were two of them.

The audit leader looked back at Sabir. His systems-minded intellect struggled with what Sabir was trying to tell him, and his face twisted and flinched as he attempted to process all that had just happened. And then, just when I had concluded he would not get it, he looked up at Sabir with clear, bright eyes and smiled.

"I think I might have found how you are pulling off this miracle," he said.

The project was completed a year and a half later, still without a single person leaving the site for serious medical attention. It set company records for quality, productivity, and cost.

During the final week of my last trip to the project, I asked Hank if I could spend my remaining couple of days just walking the project, saying good-bye to the men, and "enjoying what we've pulled off."

"Enjoy yourself, boy," he replied. "You've earned it."

For the next day and a half, I did nothing but tour the project with Patel, thanking the men for the opportunity to get to know and work with them. At times, the conversations were heartbreaking and at other times heartwarming.

The men must have known why I was touring—maybe Patel had told them—because they had written names and places on pieces of paper, which they gave to me. As they did, some of the men would grab my arms and hands and plead with me to go to a project on which their son or brother was working, to help protect him. Patel and I sat with them as they told us horrifying stories of worker exploitation and mistreatment.

On the other hand, just as many men said their good-byes by sharing their gratitude for what the project leadership had done for them and for the roles Rob and I had played. They too gave me pieces of paper with their names and home addresses, and told me that if we ever visited their country, we were welcome to stay with their families.

By the time I left, I had a cigar box half-full of various notes from the men, each with either the name of a suffering loved one or a home address. I kept that box in my dresser drawer for years and brought it out anytime I was feeling mistreated or unlucky. It helped me to stay grounded and reminded me of how fortunate I was.

Many of the men we visited with on the tour said they did not expect to ever work on another project where the leader cared so much for his men. During the conversations, I noticed the men were using a term that sounded like "pre-mee-kah-kay-peeta" when they referred to Hank.

"What does that mean, that phrase they use when speaking of Hank?" I asked Patel.

"The best I can translate it would be 'beloved father,'" Patel answered.

"Wow!" I said.

"Yes, my friend, wow," Patel said with a big smile.

That afternoon, about an hour before my driver was to pick me up, I stopped by Hank's office to say good-bye. I mentioned that the men had a nickname for him.

"Oh, God, what are they calling me?" he responded.

"You'd better sit down," I replied.

"It's that bad?"

"Just sit down." Hank sat.

"According to Patel," I said, "your nickname with the men translates to 'beloved father.'"

Hank stared right at me with surprise. His eyes opened wide and then began to tear up.

"That's about as cool as it gets, Hank."

"That it is. And you know, that's how we did this, Cort. That's why we outperformed all the other projects. Not because we had the best-trained people or the best systems or equipment. But because we had the best leaders and supervisors, who cared for their men and affirmed their value as human beings. That's why they performed their best for us."

"And it all started and ended with you," I said. "If you hadn't made this change in yourself, none of the others would have. Those men I spent the last day with, they know it was you. I just wanted you to know it too."

I said my farewells to Hank and left his office, the cigar box of notes tucked under my arm. As I drove off the property one last time, I turned around in my seat to watch the immense structure disappear in the distance. I had never felt prouder.

Chapter 17:
Baton Rouge—Part 1

"If any thing is sacred the human body is sacred."

—Walt Whitman

I returned from the Middle East eager for time off to regenerate myself and reacquaint with Julie, Katy, and Charlie. It had been a long absence, and I'd missed my family. I'd been looking forward to some quiet days at home and enjoyed waking up in my own bed for the first time in weeks.

But things at work were not so peaceful. Rob, my manager, had been promoted. I was now reporting to a new manager, Andy, who was not aligned with Rob's policy of allowing me to spend time with my family after a long trip overseas. He attempted to immediately allocate me to an engagement with a chemical plant in Baton Rouge that was experiencing the worst performance in its company. But I stood my ground and insisted that he stand behind the agreement. Andy was not pleased.

Partway through my short sabbatical, the coach leading the engagement in Baton Rouge called me. I liked Max, as did his associates and clients. This was his first time leading a consulting engagement. Max was extremely amiable, always in a positive mood with an engaging smile. Thirty-one and, at that time, the only person of color in the company, Max was extremely handsome, powerfully built, and dressed like an elite professional athlete. A former college receiver in the Southeastern Conference, he had set several receiving records during his career. I'd never experienced Max as anything but extremely confident until the day of that call.

"Cort," he began, his voice tense, "I hate to interrupt when you're taking time for family, but I need your help."

"No worries, Max," I replied. "What's going on?"

"Being black, I know some people are going to have issues with me until they get to know me. But I've never seen in people's eyes that they wouldn't hesitate to slit my throat. I'm seeing those eyes at this place."

"I'm so sorry to hear that. Tell me what's happened."

"I'm in the plant this week interviewing some of the management and touring around the facility. I can't believe what I'm seeing. Cort, they still have separate lunchrooms and restrooms for whites and blacks."

"For Christ's sake, it's the 1990s," I said, taking in a short breath. "You got to be kidding."

"No," he replied. "They're not labeled anymore, but the blacks and whites use separate eating and bathroom facilities. And get this, the makeup of the plant is over 80 percent black, but there is not a single black supervisor."

"You said something about people who would slit your throat."

"Yes, you may not know this, but Baton Rouge has its fair share of KKK members. This morning, while touring, a group of mechanics cornered me in the shop and let me know in no uncertain terms that I was not welcome and should leave and never come back. One of the more senior black operators in the plant told me they are all KKK."

"You don't have to tolerate that crap. Stop whatever you're doing, find the plant manager, and inform him of what's happened. Remind him that he's your host and responsible for your safety while on his site."

"I did that, and he just said that's the way things are and that he's too busy running his plant to work on race relations." Max's tone was even, but I could hear the tightness in his voice. I wasn't sure if it was anger or fear, but I knew he needed to get the hell out of that place.

"Did you inform Andy of what's going on?" I asked.

"I did," Max replied, "but he's pretty much taking the same position as the plant manager."

"OK, here's what you're going to do. Go to the plant manager and tell him you're leaving. Tell him you'll be happy to return when he can ensure your safety. Then head to the airport and leave. If the plant manager wants to talk to your manager, have him call me."

"But what's Andy going to think?"

"Max, you're telling me people who would be happy to slit your throat are openly threatening you, and the plant manager is doing nothing about it. Get your ass out of there."

"Thanks for having my back."

"Of course. In the meantime, I'll call Andy, Rob, and George and make sure they know what's going on."

After a number of tense phone calls between the plant manager and our company management, Max and I returned to Baton Rouge a couple of weeks later. We spent four days interviewing a sampling of the plant's population. Although all of our questions probed the issues affecting performance, one question we asked near the end of each interview was, "Is race a performance issue in this plant?" We explained that we were asking the question because anything that negatively affects relationships within a team will have a detrimental effect on performance. To my astonishment, everyone interviewed the first two days was adamant race was not an issue. Max was not surprised at all.

Then, on the morning of the final day of interviews, a young black man entered the small conference room where I was conducting my interviews. Jeff was eighteen and a plant laborer. His father and grandfather were laborers in the plant as well. Jeff worked in a unit that produced carbon black dust that was used in car tires, paints, and dyes. The unit was something right out of the eighteenth century.

Jeff was my last interview before lunch and was gracious enough to show me where he worked. He was a typical teenager—sporting an LSU Tigers cap, waiting to outgrow his acne, and trying to grow a respectable mustache. But as we strolled across the plant site, I noticed that while no whites would give him a second notice, every black person was eager to engage with Jeff. Despite his youth, he had built meaningful relationships with all his peers. Something told me Jeff was an emerging leader and possibly my only chance to learn if race was part of the plant's performance problem.

Jeff's workplace was a large, windowless redbrick building, which Jeff referred to as "the house." Inside was an enormous metal "frying pan," as the workers called it. The pan was approximately one-third the width of a football field and hovered about six feet off the ground. A worker would fill the pan with about eighteen inches of diesel fuel through a three-inch rubber hose with a steel nozzle—all while standing on a rickety wooden ladder. Once the pan was full, they would ignite a rolled up piece of newspaper and set the pan ablaze. The large brick building was designed so that the fuel would burn with insufficient oxygen and generate carbon black soot. The soot dust flowed through holes in the ceiling into a room next door called "Dante's Inferno." When I asked, "Why Dante's Inferno?" Jeff replied, "Let me show you."

We exited the pan room and walked around the outside of the building to a green metal door on the opposite side. The door was not labeled. Most people would never have taken notice of it or understood its significance. Jeff opened the door and we stepped in.

I observed six young men standing in a line, pulling in unison a forty-foot-wide rubber squeegee. The blade raked the knee-deep black soot into a twelve-inch unguarded screw conveyor sunk into the concrete floor. The screw conveyed the soot out of the building to the packaging unit next door. Each man wore plastic goggles and a scarf over his nose and mouth. Their entire bodies were coated in a thick layer of carbon dust.

The room was extremely dark with a thick fog of black soot everywhere. The only sources of light were the "explosion proof" lanterns the men wore on their belts and the sporadic flashes of flames coming from the holes in the ceiling connected to the pan room. How those men could breathe in that room—let alone work and avoid stepping into the screw conveyor, which would be a gruesome death—was beyond me. But somehow that unit had existed since the early 1900s, and Jeff told me he was not aware of any serious accidents.

When we returned outside, I asked Jeff the question, "Is race a performance issue here?"

He looked up at me with astonished eyes. "You see any white boys working in there?" he said, pointing to the green door.

"I have no idea what color those men are. They're all covered with black soot."

"Well, you can be sure none are white and none ever have been."

As Jeff and I were leaving, I noticed three fifty-five-gallon metal drums near the building's wall, each with a shower head above the drum. I asked, "What are those for?"

"That's where we shower after pulling a house." It was at that moment I noticed bars of soap and rough brushes on the ground.

"You mean after you do that horrifying job, you come out here, undress, and bathe in a drum? Isn't there a shower room on-site for that?"

"Not one we can use."

We walked back toward the administration building and my interview room, saying nothing more. When we reached the interview room, I closed the door and invited Jeff to sit down. I took a deep breath and asked, "What's it like for you to work here, Jeff? You're a young, bright man; help an old, white guy understand what it's like."

"Mr. Dial, do you like listening to your stereo in your car?" he replied.

"Yes. In fact, I have a small fortune invested in my car and home stereos. I guess you could call me a stereo nut."

"When you're alone in your car, listening to your music, do you have the volume high or low?"

"High, of course. I crank it up."

"And when you drive into a parking lot, one where there are lots of people around, do you still keep it cranked up?"

"Well, no. I turn it down. I'm not sure why."

"That's what it's like for me, Mr. Dial. When I'm on my way to this plant, I'm Jeff, a young black man, and I'm turned up all the way. But when I drive into the parking lot, I have to turn me down. I have to become someone who's not me, but who the world insists I must be. What's it like for me? It's hell, Mr. Dial. You get all excited seeing me and my friends working in Dante's Inferno, but that's nothing compared to being someone I'm not—and having to see my dad and grandpa do the same, that's much worse."

"I can see it is. Thanks for helping me understand that."

On Friday, Max and I made our report to the plant management staff. I shared my experience with Jeff without mentioning his name. Most of the staff reacted violently to our report and accused us of arriving with an agenda.

"Our only agenda is to help illuminate the source of your poor performance, and we've done that," Max insisted. "The fact that we're shining a light on something almost no one wants to admit exists, and everyone is terrified of mentioning, is not of our doing. We found the root of your performance problem. You're going to have to decide if you want to take it on or not. We stand ready to assist you if you decide you do."

With that, the plant manager, Oscar, ended the meeting by saying, "I've been plant manager here only a short while, but I can tell you we don't have a race problem, and even if we did, it has nothing to do with our poor performance. I asked your company to come in here and help us turn around our performance. And for some reason, you've made this process all about race. I see no further need for your company's services."

I was sad for Jeff and the others we could have helped, but we left as requested. Several years passed.

Then, one day, Max called to let me know the plant manager had telephoned him. He told Max he'd just returned from the funeral of one of the young black men who had died while working in Dante's Inferno.

I took some solace learning it had not been Jeff who'd died. But I quickly realized it was some other sacred being whose loved ones were now suffering, and only because he'd been seen as unworthy of his leader's concern.

"What else did the plant manager say?" I asked Max.

"He said, 'I have to stop this before someone else dies. I have no right to ask after how we treated you guys, but would you consider returning?'" Max was quiet, waiting for my response.

"Sounds like he's ready for your coaching. Let me know if there is any way I can support you. And remember, be fearless."

I hung up asking myself, Why can't people see the light before someone dies?

That's a question I'm still asking to this day.

Chapter 18:
No Shit

"If you were on your deathbed, I doubt you'd be complaining that you hadn't spent more time at the office."

—Dan Miller

I returned home from Baton Rouge the weekend before Thanksgiving, and I was looking forward to some uninterrupted time with my family. On Thanksgiving Day, Andy called and asked if I could meet him in the company offices the next morning. He said he was excited to tell me about the partners' meeting that had occurred earlier in the week.

"I appreciate that you're excited about updating me, but I'm declining your request," I said. "I've spent the last several years away from my family, and I don't want to miss my Thanksgiving Friday with them for something that can wait until next week." It was a formal practice in our company for members to make requests and for the recipient to either accept, decline, or negotiate an alternative. In fact, all employees were trained and expected to operate in this manner.

"This is not a request," Andy replied. "It's an order."

"Andy, as you know, giving orders is not our way. I'll be in the office Monday morning, and I'll be glad to speak with you then. Happy Thanksgiving." I hung up the phone.

I was not a big fan of Andy. He was hired into the company just as I began the project in the Middle East, and from my perspective, he operated completely outside the company's values. Andy had been a client of the company, and I felt he had used that relationship to get in good with the partners. I guess he must have convinced them he could help the company operate more efficiently, grow, and make more money. But his presence did just the opposite. Andy's leadership style was "command and control, take names and kick ass," which is appropriate under some extreme situations, but which, in most situations, severely limits engagement, effort, and performance.

While assigned to the Middle East project, I avoided visiting the company offices when home. Not because I didn't enjoy the people in the company but because all they seemed to do was complain about Andy and the direction the partners were leading the company.

I had become somewhat disenchanted with the partners over the previous year. One reason was they allowed Andy and others to behave so inconsistently with how the partners claimed the company functioned. The other was the way their focus had shifted from serving the client to a near obsession with billable days, profitability, and growth. This change was perplexing to me since, as far as I knew, the company was doing well financially. In fact, in each of the last few years, all employees had received a profit-sharing bonus, and I had received an additional cash "extraordinary performance" award. Consequently, I saw the introduction of old school managers like Andy as a desperate, profiteering move by the partners to take the company in a direction I wasn't interested in going.

The last straw for me was when Andy shared a rumor that the partners were considering voting "no confidence" in George's leadership and ousting him as CEO. I was shocked Andy would share such highly sensitive gossip with me, especially since I knew George considered Andy a loyal and trusted friend.

George believed the way to profitability was to have the best-skilled coaches in the business who were highly committed to the client and its business imperatives. I shared and benefited greatly from that philosophy. I strongly believed the wisdom I had received from Rob and George was one reason why I'd been so effective in the Middle East. Just being in George's presence and observing him practice his trade, I was able to see what great coaching looked like and learn from his tutelage.

But the scuttlebutt in the office was that some key managers and partners felt George was too focused on the client and consultant development at the expense of profit—which, I assumed, they felt could be going into their dividends. Even from as far away as the Middle East, I could feel the company and its leadership changing in ways that unsettled me. So, well before that Thanksgiving morning call from Andy, I had pretty much decided it was time for me to gracefully exit and was considering starting my own private coaching practice.

The next morning, Thanksgiving Friday, I took a walk with my wife, Julie. I shared my concerns about the company and the call I'd had the previous day with Andy.

"What do you think he's going to tell you on Monday?" she asked.

I replied, half-jokingly, "I hope he tells me he's letting me go so I can take my severance and move on."

"Well, you never know. Maybe you'll get your wish."

I arrived at the company offices early Monday morning and checked by Andy's office several times, but he was nowhere to be found. I hung around for a few hours, and at 10:00, I gave up on meeting with him. As I was packing to head back home and saying good-bye to some of my associates, I heard a stern voice from behind me say, "Cort, follow me."

I turned to see Andy briskly walking away from me toward his office. This inconsiderate behavior was not unusual for Andy, so I thought nothing of it. I followed him, and as we approached his office, we took an unexpected, abrupt right turn into the office next to his. In the office was a young, blond gentleman whom I'd never met, sitting at a desk. My first thought was that Andy wanted to introduce him to me. But instead, Andy told me to sit at a small table. He sat opposite of me and the young man was to my right.

Andy made no attempts at an introduction. He looked at me.

"As I told you in our call, Cort, the partners have met, and I have some news for you," he said. "The news is that the partners have taken a good look at the future of the company, and you're not in it."

"No shit?" I replied.

"No shit," Andy answered, with no emotion at all. I recalled the automatons with whom I'd engaged at the microprocessor fab and thought, I'm speaking with another computer chip. Why is it that the computer chips, and not the human beings, tend to rise to the top in so many companies?

"Actually, that's not what you said to me on the phone," I said. "But I'm not surprised that you would lure me in here under false pretenses to fire me. I've come to expect such things from you. By the way, when were you planning on introducing me to this gentleman to my right?"

"I'll get to him in a minute, but before I leave, I have a request."

"A request or an order?" I asked, snickering.

"It's something I expect you to say yes to. Before you leave us, I want you to take one more trip to the Middle East. There are a few loose ends that need to be completed. It's something Rob would normally do, but he's very busy right now, and I think you owe it to the company to make this one last trip."

I turned to the young man, who to this point had said nothing, and said, "Pardon me, but I'm Cort. Who are you, and why are you here?"

"We've hired his company to help us with the terminations," Andy interrupted. "After I leave, he's going to process you."

"Process me?" I chuckled. "Like link sausage?" I heard the young man snicker.

I turned to the young man again. "Well, Mr. Processor, do you have a name?"

"My name is Colin," he answered.

"Hello, Colin. Very nice to meet you," I said. We stood and shook hands.

"Can we get back to my request?" Andy interrupted. "Are you going back or not?"

I turned to Colin. "Will my answer to Andy's request in any way affect my severance or the process you'll take me through?"

Colin looked at me with a sly grin as if to say, "Go for it," but instead said, "No, it won't."

I looked down at Andy. "Andy, as of two minutes ago, I stopped working for you and this company. Please leave so Colin and I can get to work."

Andy stormed out of the room without a word. I closed the door behind him and turned to Colin. "Colin, what the hell is going on here?" I said.

Colin proceeded to tell me that from his point of view, there had been some major mismanagement of the company, and the firm was in dire financial shape.

"How can that be?" I responded. "My project has made a healthy profit. And we've all been receiving bonuses."

"Yes, but your project is one of the few that's turned a profit. And from what I've been able to determine, the bonuses were paid with borrowed money, some out of the partners' pockets." He went on to talk about partners mortgaging their homes, lawsuits, and other things that did not quite register, probably because I was in shock—not because of being fired, but that the partners could have allowed the company to get into this position.

"But if I'm one of the few consultants actually turning a profit, why let me go?" I finally asked.

Colin then informed me that dozens of employees, including all but a few of the lowest-paid consultants, were being terminated.

He leaned toward me and said in a quiet voice, "They're having to cut off their heads just to survive. Believe me, you're better off taking your severance and leaving." He glanced at the door and then whispered, "Even Andy will be terminated as soon as they no longer need him." I'd be less than honest if I said I didn't take some satisfaction from hearing that last piece of information.

I left the company office, walked to my car, and immediately called Julie.

"Guess what? I got my wish," I said.

"Oh, my God! They fired you?" she replied.

"From what I was told today, they're firing everyone but the cleaning lady."

"Well, come on home, and let's start thinking about what you might do next."

I drove out of the parking lot and headed home. I was on my own, starting a new adventure. And I was damn excited about it.

Part 3:

All-In Leaders
in Action

Chapter 19:
The Chicken-Shit Principle

"No one wants to come to work if it's work. You want great performance, find a way to make work fun."

—Roy Flores

"Remind yourself that when you die, your 'in basket' won't be empty."

—Richard Carlson, PhD

After my termination, I decided to take the summer off to get reacquainted with my family and make some decisions about my business future. For the first time in a long time, I was able to go to lunch with my wife or take the kids swimming. It was so restful to just sit at the pool under the shade of a Texas live oak, chat with Julie, and know I had no obligation to anyone else.

By the end of the summer, I was ready to start thinking about my business. I finally had space to invest in myself and consider my own distinct approach to coaching leaders. I had a lot of great experiences to draw from and had become very good at what I did, but I knew I needed to figure out what distinguished my methodology from my competition and how to brand it.

But before I got very far in that endeavor, I received a call from a consultant I'd worked with years previously. He was asking for my help. Roy was one of the most unique coaches I'd ever worked with. I knew of no one like Roy who could inspire and motivate people at all levels in an organization, and we shared the same values and coaching philosophy. He asked if we could meet for lunch to discuss partnering with him on a project. Although I knew that partnering with Roy would delay the creation of my own practice, I agreed to meet with him primarily because I was so fond of Roy, but also because, like Rob and George, Roy had wisdom and skills I wanted to add to my coaching toolbox.

Roy and I met at a Mexican restaurant in the neighborhood where he'd grown up. Roy's grandparents had emigrated from Mexico in the early 1900s. He had risen from meager beginnings to be a Marine pilot, a degreed psychologist, and an extremely talented motivational speaker. I could see Roy enjoyed returning to his old neighborhood, I think because he liked seeing old friends and being reminded of how far he'd come in life.

As we sat eating our Tex-Mex lunch specials, Roy informed me a large oil and gas firm was building a new unit in its refinery, and the primary constructor had approached him about coaching the firm's leadership and supervision. Moreover, the individual's organization was a former client of the company that had just terminated me. The constructor had told Roy, "We don't want them. We want you and Cort."

As Roy shared, "We'd be coaching one of the most committed and courageous leaders in the business. His name is Lamar, and he's the executive project manager. Lamar has recently seen the light and is very much aligned with our way of thinking. He wants us to help him enroll his people in our approach to performance."

I agreed to partner with Roy, assuming it would be a six-month engagement, or eighteen months at the most. A few weeks later, the two of us were sitting in a conference room with Lamar and his leadership team. Lamar was a native Texan with a Texas accent as substantial as his frame. He wore the same uniform as did his laborers, and it was clear after only a few minutes that he was a straight shooter who spoke softly and carried a big stick.

Roy had shared with me that, before Lamar's transformation, he was "as command and control as a leader could get." On previous projects, Lamar had closely timed breaks and lunchtimes, limited bathroom visits to ten minutes, and made people provide their own office supplies. But a serious health scare had "woken Lamar up," and he was rethinking his role as a leader.

Roy facilitated the meeting. It was obvious these leaders, especially Lamar, had a lot of respect for Roy and valued his counsel. Roy had a knack for making work fun, and we made a great team. He knew exactly when and how to use me during the meeting.

When the right moment presented itself, Roy said, "Lamar, I'm now going to ask Cort to lead us in a conversation I think you'll find illuminating."

At Roy's prompt, I turned toward Lamar. "Lamar, what are we going to build this time?" I asked.

Lamar replied in his low, soft Texas drawl, "Well, Cort, it's another unit just like the one we built a few years ago, a mirror image. Nothing that special, but given the economy, we have to take what we can get."

"Wow," I said, chuckling, "the way you describe this project, I can't wait to get going." A few members of the leadership team laughed. Lamar did not.

"What do you mean?" he asked.

"If you want to get the most out of your people, you're going to have to give them a bigger game to play than that. One of the things Roy and I have learned working with other leaders is the bigger the game you can invite your people to play, the more of themselves they will give you . . . and all that discretionary effort adds up to extraordinary performance.

"I have interviewed thousands of people around the world, and for years, I have asked them a question," I continued. "I draw a circle on a piece of paper. Then I say, 'I want you to assume that everything you have to offer to the world is in this circle. Everything you have to give as a human being—your time, energy, ingenuity, passion, even spirituality—is in this circle. Now, I want you to tell me, what percentage of that circle do you have to give your employer to keep your job and keep your boss happy?' If I averaged all the answers I received to that question over the years, what do you think the percentage would be?"

"Fifty percent," Lamar said.

"Not even close," I replied.

"Sixty percent."

"You're getting colder."

"Less than 50 percent?"

"Much less. In fact, at one time I did the math, and the average was 28 percent."

"I find that hard to imagine," Lamar said. "I spend more time at work than I do at home and so do my people."

"I'm sure you do," I said. "But I bet you have a lot more to offer the world than just your time, your physical presence, and effort. Would you agree?"

"I guess I would. But 28 percent? Man, we could never get a project off the ground with 28 percent."

Roy jumped into the conversation. "The point is," he said, "people only give a small percentage of what they have to offer to keep their jobs and make the boss happy. I'm sure you've heard it said in your company, 'I don't know what someone has to do to get fired,' have you not?"

"Yeah, I have," Lamar said with a chuckle.

"So, if the truth is people only have to give a small fraction of themselves to keep their jobs, how do we get them to give us more than that?" Roy asked. "They don't have to give it. It's their choice whether they do. They won't lose their jobs or their boss's approval if they don't, so what good reason can we offer to compel them to give us that optional part of themselves?"

"With all due respect, Lamar," I interjected, "the answer isn't by inviting them into the project you described a few moments ago."

"I see your point. I guess doing what's been done before isn't a very big game," Lamar replied.

"No, it's not, and especially not the way you described it," I said, then turned my attention from Lamar to address the entire leadership team. "You see, gentlemen, one of the key roles you play in an enterprise like this is to conjure up the game you'll invite your people to play—the mission you're asking them to execute. If that mission is, in their eyes, something worth giving more of themselves, they will give. But if it isn't, they won't.

"And it's not just the mission. It's also how you speak about that mission, whether you articulate it in a way that gets your people to say, 'I want to be part of that. In fact, I want so much to be part of that, I'm willing to give more than I normally do.' The mission you conjure up and how well you enroll your people in it, more than anything else, will determine the performance you get on this project."

"I see your point," Lamar replied. "But please don't tell me you're going to force us through one of those horrible mission writing exercises. I hate those things. I've never seen one produce anything of value."

"That's not our plan, and I promise we won't do that to you," I said. "But I do have another question."

"And that would be?" Lamar asked, clearly still suspicious that I was setting up a mission writing exercise.

"How many more projects like this do you have in you?"

"Well, actually . . . I haven't shared this with anyone, and I want it to stay in this room until I announce it. But this will be my last." The leaders around the table leaned forward with surprise at this news.

"Really?" I asked. "What do you plan on doing after this project?"

"My wife and I are going to retire in Hawaii."

"Wow! That sounds wonderful."

"We're really looking forward to it."

"OK, then. Given that this is your last project, your last time to make a difference, let me ask you this: Is there something you've always wanted to do, something you were never quite able to pull off? Do you have a legacy you want to leave behind that all of us can join with you to make happen on this project?"

Lamar sat and thought for a long time. No one said anything as he pondered my question.

Then he looked up and said, "You know, I've always hated the way we're treated—I mean, the way contractors and constructors are treated—like second-class citizens. It's always bothered me. If there's some way we could change that, if I could leave that as my legacy, then I would retire a happy man."

As Lamar spoke, I noticed all the other leaders in the room nodding in agreement. Each of them, like Lamar, had risen from the lowest laborer job to the senior positions they now held. They had felt the indignity of being banned from using the company restroom, having to park in the dusty and muddy contractor parking lot, and being seen as subhuman and unworthy of common decency.

As I observed these men's reaction to Lamar's words, I was taken back to my own dishonorable actions that contributed to Harry's electrocution. I thought, Here I go again. For some reason, God keeps putting me in these positions where I can atone for my sins and make a difference for people who will continue to suffer if I don't intervene.

Roy turned to Lamar and said, "Lamar, state exactly what you want to accomplish in as few words as you can. Say it in your own words. Say it with all the passion you can muster."

Lamar looked up at the ceiling, contemplating his words for a few moments. Then he looked back at his team.

"Gentlemen," he said, "I want to set a new standard for the quality of life of the construction worker, and I want to do it in a way that demonstrates to those sons of bitches in the home office that it's good for business."

Roy and I knew instantly that we had our big game. There was a loud cheer and applause from the leaders in the room, and Lamar smiled a big grin, which was not his nature. Lamar had crafted the perfect mission for that project, one which each of his leaders and workers would certainly see as worthwhile and give of themselves to accomplish. From a leadership standpoint, he was handed a lemon of a project, something they'd done a few years prior. But as my grandmother used to quote, "When life gives you lemons, make lemonade." And that's exactly what Lamar did.

Right then and there in that meeting, Lamar and his team made key decisions that would have a lasting impact on their people and the project's performance. Roy and I shared some of our learning from working with other clients; after we finished, the team decided to build shade for the workers, have cooling stations throughout the site, and assure high-quality food and facilities.

But Lamar and his team went even further. They built a paved parking lot with a car wash station for the project's employees.

"Porta-potties" were replaced with cooled and heated restroom trailers. As Lamar put it, "I want our people to have the dignity of washing their hands after doing their business."

Moreover, the team rented a circus tent with heating and air-conditioning. Inside the tent were about a hundred picnic tables where the workers could sit during meals and breaks. Along the walls were long tables with dozens of microwaves and vending machines, about five times the amount that would normally be provided. Lamar said, "I don't want my people spending their lunch break standing in line waiting to heat their meals."

In the mid-morning, which tended to be cool, supervisors would traverse the project in golf carts, delivering hot coffee, cocoa, water, and sports drinks to the workers. In the afternoons, which were normally warm, supervisors brought cool beverages. And at least once a week, all project employees met in the circus tent, where Lamar and his leadership team would update them on the project's performance, welcome newcomers to the project, and say good-bye and thank you to those who had completed their work. Lamar even had a large stage built at one end of the tent with lighting and a public address system to assure that even those in the back could see and hear what was being presented.

"If we want people to be interested in performance," Lamar told his leaders, "then we have to account for it weekly, let them know where we stand, and help them see how they're contributing to it. I also want them to know whom they're working with, what companies are on-site, and what each is doing to contribute. And I want every person welcomed when they arrive and thanked when they leave."

Lamar made it a practice to sit down face-to-face with each newcomer to the project on the person's first day. He would ask new workers to pull photos of their loved ones out of their wallets and place them on the table. He would then say, "I want you to know that my primary job as your project manager is to make sure you go home to those folks each day in good health and spirit. I will do my best to do that for you. Will you do your best to help me live up to that promise?"

Lamar would then ask the employees for their main contact person, normally a significant other. That same day, he would write that person a letter, making the same commitment and including his phone number. Lamar said in the letter that if the person saw anything more he could do to help his or her loved one show up for work ready for duty and arrive home healthy and in good spirits, the person was to call him immediately.

One day while I was touring the site, a supervisor who was new to the project pulled me aside.

"What happened to Lamar?" he asked. "I worked for him years ago, and he was the meanest, stingiest son of a bitch I'd ever seen."

"I don't know. I've never seen that Lamar," I responded. "I've heard stories, but I've never known the person some people say he used to be. I guess he decided to change."

The project started each day around 6:00. Every morning, Lamar was at the project entrance with three or four of his lieutenants passing out coffee, cocoa, water, and breakfast burritos. As they did, they would say good morning as each person passed by. I once asked Lamar why he was there every morning without fail.

"I know a few of those people had a rough night last night," he said. "Their kid was up sick all night or they had an argument with their girlfriend or husband. I know that each day, some of the people coming through those turnstiles had to bust their butts to get here on time. But I don't know which ones to thank, so the only way I can be sure to thank those few is to thank them all."

Whenever a project performance target or milestone was met, the leadership team would host a barbeque, crawfish boil, or other outdoor event, and the leaders would cook for and serve their people. At each celebration, everyone was given a "token of appreciation" by the leadership team, commemorating the accomplishment.

Lamar also created a new position with the sole purpose of tracking what it cost to treat his people well and correlating that to performance. Lamar told the person in this new role, "The only thing they respond to at the home office is figures, so I need you to give them figures that show that the investment we are making in our people is paying off in performance."

During this time, Roy and I helped Lamar and his leadership team develop some guiding principles for the project. They included the following:

Our vision is to set a new standard for the quality of life of the construction worker—and prove that doing so is good for business.

Our mission is to complete this project ahead of schedule, under budget, with great quality, without harming anyone, and have fun in the process.

The leadership team's role is to (a) embody the vision and mission; (b) enroll project management, supervision, and employees in the vision and mission; (c) ensure that they stay on mission; (d) eliminate anything that can distract them from the mission; and (e) have fun in the process.

Management's role is to (a) embody the vision and mission; (b) help supervision translate the vision and mission into tangible priorities, goals, behaviors, activities, and events; (c) account for progress and performance weekly—explaining and adjusting for any variances—and communicate the status to the entire project team; and (d) have fun in the process.

Supervision's role is to (a) provide their people, each day, clear expectations that serve the mission; (b) confirm that the expectations are understood and people have what they need to meet the expectations before work begins; (c) verify whether the work was completed satisfactorily and deliver appropriate acknowledgment and/or correction; and (d) have fun in the process.

Roy's and my role was to coach primarily Lamar and his leadership team as they went about making their vision, mission, and principles a reality. This was a daunting undertaking, given that this was a new way of operating for the thousand or so people on the project. It was a monumental change—something they had never attempted.

We first helped Lamar and his team design and deliver enrollment workshops where everyone on the project was invited to commit to the vision and mission. Most did. But as soon as they committed, their first question was, "Now that I'm in, what do I do differently?" Roy and I helped translate good intentions into specific ways of thinking, speaking, and acting that not only made sense to them but would help them deliver on the project's performance goals.

Specifically, we trained supervisors how to speak to and interact with their people in ways that solicited their discretionary effort. We taught them how to create crystal-clear expectations when assigning tasks to assure the work was completed as planned. And we trained them on how to reinforce behaviors favorable to performance and stop and redirect counterproductive behaviors.

About a third of the way through the project, Lamar was called to the home office to explain to his management the "large sum of money the project had spent on needless amenities." Lamar asked Roy and me to accompany him to the meeting. He also brought along the accountant who'd been working to demonstrate how this investment was paying off in performance.

At that time, the project was ahead of schedule, under budget, and had outstanding quality. Not a single person had been injured. Also, turnover was at record lows and attendance was at record highs. Lamar presented this data, but his managers seemed myopically focused on what they felt were "unnecessary, wasteful amenities." Lamar also attempted to explain the concept of discretionary energy and effort, but his managers were only interested in hearing clear justification of the cost of "luxuries," such as air-conditioned bathrooms, circus tents, and breakfast burritos.

Finally, Lamar pointed out that several other project managers had made a collective visit to his project to see how he was creating such extraordinary performance. Some had started to implement many of the same changes and were seeing a positive effect on performance. The accountant then presented data, comparing Lamar's project with all the other projects, which clearly demonstrated that those who were following Lamar's lead were significantly outperforming those who were still practicing the old paradigm.

"I don't see how anyone who looks at this data with an open mind can come to any conclusion other than what we're doing is working," Lamar said. "The money we're investing in what you call 'amenities' is paying off in performance I never thought possible. It's been—"

"I've heard all I can stand," interrupted Mark, the vice president and senior-most person in the room. "You will stop wasting the company's money on these luxuries. We're not running a country club here. You either stop, or I'll put someone in charge who will."

Lamar backed his chair away from the table. Looking down at his boots, he said, "Well, then, you'd better start looking for my replacement, because I'm not stopping. To stop would go against everything I stand for and everything this company says it stands for. Stopping would mean hurting people again and losing all the gains in performance we've worked so hard to achieve."

He stood and faced the room before continuing. "I realize that to you who sit in your leather chairs and eat in your fancy cafeteria each day that all this stuff is chicken shit. But to my people and me, it's not. I've learned from these guys"—he pointed at Roy and me—"it's the magic formula to extraordinary performance. I'm going to leave now. You obviously have a choice to make. Please let me know what you decide."

Lamar left the room with the accountant trailing closely behind. Roy and I began to follow, but Mark called us back.

"What load of horseshit have you sold my people?" he asked.

"Mark, I sympathize with you and the others in this room," Roy said. "It's hard to make the connection between what Lamar and his team are doing and the performance they're getting just by sitting in this conference room looking at a lot of slides and data. If you really want to understand what Lamar now understands and make an informed decision, I suggest you put on a pair of jeans and boots and walk his project for several hours. Talk to his leadership team, his managers, and his people. I think if you do, you might realize that we're not selling horseshit; we're selling performance."

To my disbelief, Mark replied, "I might just take you up on that."

Lamar, the accountant, Roy, and I stopped for lunch on our way back to the project. We all shared with Lamar how impressed we were with the stand he'd taken and how he had confronted, in a professional manner, his managers and their thinking. I told Lamar we needed to add another principle to the project's list.

"What would that be?" Lamar responded.

"The chicken-shit principle," I answered with a laugh. "Any time there is something that needs doing, and you say to yourself, 'What a load of chicken shit,' that thing, no matter what it is, rises to the top of your to-do list."

"I love it," said Lamar, chuckling. He turned to Roy. "Let's be sure to discuss the chicken-shit principle with the leadership team tomorrow morning."

Two days after Lamar's meeting at the home office, he called Roy and me into a conference room. "Guess who called me and is coming out to the project tomorrow?" he said.

"Don't tell me," I replied. "Not Mark, the VP?"

"Bingo," said Lamar.

224 | Heretics to Heroes

"We'll miss you, Lamar," Roy said, laughing.

"Very funny, amigo," replied Lamar. "Actually, I want him to tour the project with the two of you."

"Us? Why us?" responded Roy.

"I want him to experience you guys. To see how well received you are by my people. And I want you to guide him so he sees and hears what he was unable to sitting in the home office. I want Mark to understand how much our people love working here and how they're giving everything they've got for our mission and performance goals."

"Consider it done, Lamar," Roy said.

At 7:00 the next morning, Roy, Mark, and I began our project tour. Mark was instantly impressed by how everyone on the project approached us to say hello and meet our guest without prompting. We explained that each of us had regular one-on-one or group conversations with the employees and that they were aware we were the catalyst for the quality of life improvements.

"So you're buying their respect," he said, to which we did not respond.

Later in the tour, Mark commented on the cleanliness and orderliness of the site. "This place is immaculate; everything has a place and everything is in its place," he said.

We suggested that when people feel like they've built their workplace, that it's of their making, they look out for it and take care of it. He replied, "Makes sense."

At one stop, Mark spoke with a team of electricians about their work. He was impressed by how clearly they could recite their supervisor's expectations for that day. He was even more amazed when one of the electricians said, "Actually, sir, our supervisor is home sick today. We agreed on these expectations before starting this morning, since she wasn't here."

While Mark and the electricians were talking, a man began sweeping up the area and gathering the wires, cables, tape, and other scraps that electricians often create while doing their work. Mark walked over to him.

"You must be a helper," he said. "You're doing a great job keeping this project clean."

"No, sir," the man replied. "I'm a master welder, but we're ahead of schedule, and at yesterday's performance meeting, we were told these electricians were a bit behind. So, I asked my supervisor if I could spend the morning trying to help them catch up."

"Even though it's outside your craft?" replied Mark.

"It's not just outside his craft," one of the electricians interjected, "he works for a different company than us."

"On this project, there are no crafts or companies," the master welder added. "There's just a team of folks committed to completing this project ahead of schedule, under budget, with high quality, and without hurtin' no one."

"Don't forget the having fun part," one electrician added with a smile. Roy gave him a wink.

"I'm starting to realize people on this project mean what they say," Mark responded.

At that moment, two supervisors in a golf cart rolled up and offered us some refreshments. It was extra chilly that morning, so we all took coffee or cocoa.

"You wouldn't have any of those breakfast burritos I've heard about, would you?" Mark asked. Roy and I exchanged subtle grins.

"No, sir, we're fresh out of them," one supervisor replied. And then they reminded the group that there was a steak and potato cookout for lunch that day to celebrate the project completing one year without an injury or a failed quality test.

The last stop on our tour was the carpenters' shop. There were no carpenters present, only a carpenter helper—a tiny, middle-aged woman named Wilma. There was no special reason to visit the carpenters' shop, but I always made it a point to go by there in the hopes of running into Wilma. Wilma was a ray of sunshine who greeted everyone with a big, wide smile full of gold teeth. She was always good for a positive thought or piece of Southern wisdom. Something told me it would be a mistake to finish the tour without Mark meeting Wilma.

After a few minutes of pleasantries, Mark turned to her.

"Wilma," he said, "I've been giving Lamar and these two a hard time about all the money that's been spent on luxuries—things like the air-conditioned lunch tent, the cookouts, the breakfast burritos, and the nice facilities."

"You have?" said Wilma. "Now why would you go and do something like that?"

"Well, I have to explain to my bosses why we're spending all this money on luxuries for the workers, and they don't like hearing that unless it's impacting the bottom line," he replied. "What I want you to tell me is how all this, all these creature comforts, are helping you do a better job—impacting your productivity, your quality, your safety. Can you give me anything I can take back to my superiors?"

"Well, sir, I don't know anything about that kind of stuff," Wilma responded. "That's stuff people like you and all them bigwigs know about. But I do know this: I am fifty-seven years old. I've worked as a laborer my entire life, ever since I was fourteen years old."

A big smile broke across her face as she continued. "This is the first place I've ever worked where I wake up in the morning excited about coming to work. And when I get here, there are people waiting to greet me who are excited about being here too. And once I'm at my job, I want to work hard and do good quality work to do my part for the mission—for them, my managers. They've earned my respect, and I'm going to give them all I have as long as I am here. Now, I'm not sure how that calculates into all those numbers your superiors care about, but I do hope they're smart enough to see the obvious."

"And what is that?" Mark asked.

"That we're kicking every other project's butt, if you'll pardon my French."

"Yes, that's obvious even to a bean counter like me."

Mark didn't have a lot to say as we made our way back to the main project trailer and Lamar's office. He thanked us for the tour, spent about thirty minutes behind closed doors with Lamar, and then departed. Afterwards, Lamar found Roy and me.

"Well, boys, they're off our backs for now," Lamar said.

"And they will be, as long as we keep performing," replied Roy.

"Amen to that," said Lamar. "And while we're on that subject, let's round up the leadership team and continue our discussion of the chicken-shit principle." This got a hearty laugh from Roy and me.

About a month after the project completed, setting multiple performance records, Lamar invited Roy and me to a meeting with his managers back in the same conference room at the head office. As Roy and I entered the room, I realized it was the exact group we'd met with a year prior while helping Lamar defend his project.

But at this meeting, the managers were trying to convince Lamar to delay his retirement. They wanted him to develop a guide manual for project managers that captured what he'd done on his project.

One of the managers said, "Lamar, we want you to describe that magic formula you showed us last time we met and in a way it can be shared with other project managers. We don't want what you know to leave when you leave."

Lamar laughed. "Gentlemen, I don't know nothing other than what Roy and Cort have shared with me," he said. "It's them you need to talk to, not me. I'm going to be living in Hawaii in a few weeks."

"We can't afford to have an army of consultants on every project," Mark, the vice president, responded.

"What army?" Lamar said. "I had these two guys. They visited my people and me from time to time. They shared their wisdom and taught us 'a new way to think, speak, and act,' as Cort always puts it. There was no army. I spent a few hundred thousand dollars on these two, and they helped me and my team perform like we never thought possible and save millions."

Mark then turned to me. "What exactly is it that you do?" he said. "What did you do for Lamar?"

"I would not say we did anything for Lamar, but we did quite a lot to him," I replied.

"What does that mean?"

"It means we believe the most effective tool a leader has to improve performance is sitting right there"—I pointed at Lamar—"in his chair. We've worked with leaders like Lamar all over the world, and we've come to realize that the guy or gal at the top has more effect on performance than anyone in the organization. So, we helped Lamar get clear on the vision he had for his project . . . a vision that gave him and his people a good reason for getting up and wanting to come to work each morning. You saw that yourself, sir, when you spoke with Wilma, did you not?"

"I did."

"And then we helped his managers give their supervisors a clear mission, and we taught them how to keep them on mission and give their workers clear expectations for each day. You saw that as well when you spoke to the electricians. Do you recall that?"

"Yes, that was quite impressive. But what was even more impressive was the welder who worked for another company and was helping the electricians clean up."

"Do you want me to go on? It would take me about an hour to cover everything we've taught to Lamar and his team."

"Even if he did," Lamar interrupted, "a lot of it won't make sense to you. One thing they taught me is, as an early adopter, there will be little evidence to prove that this new way is the better way. That's why leaders must trust their gut and take a leap of faith. I trusted my intuition when it came to these two, and it paid off time after time."

"OK, I get all that," Mark said, "but help me understand why we need these two. I mean, we must have thousands of years of project management experience in this company. Why, in all those years, haven't we learned what they know?"

Lamar looked at Mark carefully. "Because in all those years, we've been building projects and getting better and better at that, and they've been building leaders and getting better and better at what they do. We know how to erect steel; they know how to grow leaders."

"I think I'm getting it, finally," Mark responded. "Thanks for putting up with my resistance for so long. It says a lot about you and the leader you are. I wish you all the best in your retirement in Hawaii. Please express my appreciation to your good wife for all the years of service you and she gave us."

"You are very welcome," Lamar replied.

There was a long pause, one of those pauses that lets everyone know the meeting has nearly ended. But then Lamar leaned forward.

"There is one last thing I want to emphasize before we end this meeting," he said. "I'm not sure you all fully understand what it takes from a person to lead the way Cort and Roy have helped me learn to lead. I can tell you it takes everything a man can give. It is a heavy, heavy burden to shoulder—the well-being of thousands of men and women, I mean—and to carry that for years is a demanding commitment."

Lamar stopped for a moment, let out a long sigh, and then continued. "I'll tell you this: I'm exhausted. I've never been so completely worn out after a project, and you guys know I've led my fair share. Don't get me wrong. This has been my favorite project, and I've never had so much fun or satisfaction in my work. But the emotional burden, the weight of caring for so many people for so long—it's, it's . . . well, it's something I would never want to do again without a long rest to recover. If you do go forward with this and start asking your managers to lead projects the way I've done, you'd better be prepared to give them at least a year of recovery time between projects."

Lamar paused one more time and said in a weary voice, "I just thought it was important to point that out before leaving."

The meeting ended. Roy and I said our thanks and good-byes to Lamar and headed to our homes.

That weekend, Roy called me.

"Cort, sit down. I have some terrible news," he said.

"What is it?" I asked.

"It's Lamar. He's died," he said. The line was quiet for a long while. "He had a heart attack today while duck hunting."

"My God," was all I could say. I thanked Roy for telling me and hung up.

As I set down the phone, I drew my hands to my face in devastation. How could God take a man who'd given so much to others? How could he rob Lamar and his wife of the retirement they had spent their entire lives building?

And then, I wondered, Had we asked too much of Lamar? Had we encouraged him to take on more than he could emotionally carry?

I took some solace in later learning that Lamar was hunting with a mutual friend I greatly respected, when he died. Our friend told me Lamar died peacefully and had passed on doing what he loved to do, duck hunting. He also said Lamar had a long history of serious heart problems, and there was no reason to feel that our work in any way contributed to his passing.

I wasn't able to attend the funeral. I had committed to a speaking engagement in Tennessee and decided that Lamar would rather I continue "spreading the word" than attend his services. I attempted to call his home several times over the next few days, but the line was always busy. I called the florist in his hometown to order flowers, but they said that for the first time in their history, they'd run out. I arranged for a florist in another town to deliver my arrangement.

Lamar's project finished with the best performance in the company's history. It came in 22 percent under budget, three months ahead of schedule, and the most serious injury was a hairline fracture to the tip of a mechanic's index finger. The project also had the best quality performance of any project then and since. This performance, according to Lamar's accountant, equated to tens of millions of dollars saved and earned in contract bonuses. The cost of the amenities, so resisted by company executives, was a microscopic fraction of the savings they had helped create.

Unfortunately for Roy and me and many others, the company was purchased by a much larger corporation about six months later. The new management had zero interest in continuing the legacy Lamar and his team had created. Roy still has good friends in that company, and they tell him the company has never repeated Lamar's performance, and no project of similar size has since been completed without a serious injury or fatality.

After my speaking engagement in Tennessee, I returned directly home. Like Lamar, I needed a long rest to recover from the physical and emotional investment I had made in Lamar and his project, and I needed to come to terms with his passing.

Also, I was eager to get back to defining my brand of coaching. I wanted very much to have that task behind me before I took on my next coaching engagement.

After coaching such great people as Hank and Lamar, I wanted to do nothing else. I knew that leaders like them—with extraordinary untapped potential, who are ready to shed their old paradigms and are courageous enough to pioneer a new model of leadership—would be few and far between. It would be some time until I finally crossed paths with another leader of such quality.

Chapter 20:
Navel-Gazing

"The older you get, the more you realize that the authorities are a bunch of troubled youngsters."

—Joseph Campbell

"Ivory Tower Feng Shui—obsessively rearranging one's 'mental furniture.'"

—Simon Hayes

"The symptomatic solution reduces the symptom, but also creates a side effect that has a negative impact on the fundamental problem. Symptomatic solutions only have a temporary benefit before things get worse."

—Tom Hopper

As is so with many coaches, work tends to come to me in bunches with extended periods of free time in between. I like to use these open spaces to be with family and friends, do research, read books, and attend seminars to improve my coaching toolbox.

During one of these periods, I was contacted by a coach I'd never met, Luke, who was interested in hiring me as a subject matter expert.

"I have a three-day session with a large petrochemical company next month," Luke said. "They've had a number of small explosions and some very serious near misses in several of their plants. Their CEO is convening their management to figure out what needs to change, and he's asked me to facilitate."

"What role do you see me playing?" I asked.

"I heard you speak at a conference last summer, and I'd like you to be there to coach me. This is a tough group, and I'm concerned I need someone there with your credentials to reinforce what I say to them. You would be working for me, and I would pay your rate. Can you help me out with this?"

"I can, but I have to tell you, I've dealt with this company before, and I don't have a lot of respect for them. They tend to be so sure of themselves; it's impossible to teach them anything."

"I understand that. Will you come anyway?"

A month later, Luke and I were in a large meeting room with about fifty top managers. I was seated at one of the tables of eight with my back to the wall. This vantage point gave me a clear view of the entire group.

On day one, I was surprised to learn a few of the company's explosions had been fatal. I listened the entire day to presentation after presentation explaining why the incidents had occurred and what each plant was doing to implement corrective actions. After lunch, I pulled Luke aside to offer my thoughts.

"What they're discussing won't make any difference," I told him. "They're treating these incidents as separate, unique events instead of symptoms of a systemic problem. If we continue with this approach, they'll come out of here with symptomatic solutions and without ever recognizing their disease."

Luke thanked me for my coaching, but in the afternoon and for the lion's share of the next morning, he employed the same process. I attempted to help Luke understand that we were talking about everything but what needed to be talked about, but it became obvious the concepts I was sharing were beyond his comprehension. Finally, I suggested to Luke that I should leave.

"I'm not sure I'm of much value to you," I said. "I think it best that I excuse myself and save you a day's fee."

"No," he responded. "Please stay, at least through lunch, and let's meet then and decide if there's value in you remaining." I agreed to stay.

About thirty minutes before lunchtime, some of the participants started to question if they were getting any value out of the session. As one put it, "We're just rehashing our incidents. We already know what happened. We all read the reports. We need to talk about what's in common with all these events."

It was obvious Luke was unprepared for the pushback. He stammered for a while and then turned his eyes my way.

"I'd like to ask Cort to share his thoughts at this time," Luke said. "He's been observing us for almost a day and a half. Cort, do you have anything to offer?"

I thought to myself, Luke's now going to get what he's paying me for. I wonder if he's going to regret asking for it.

I stood and said, "I agree with the folks who are questioning the value of the conversations you've been having. I say this because, in my opinion, you're avoiding the heart of the matter. You keep talking about what's happened out there in your facilities, but in truth the source of your performance is in here, sitting in your chairs."

I peeked at Luke. He was white as a sheet; his eyes wide open in terror. I was impressed by his courage to let me continue.

"Say more about what you mean, Cort," he said. "I think you're on to something."

The room was quiet as I continued. "Well, to be totally frank, what we've been doing for a day and a half is what I call 'navel-gazing.'" At this, the silence broke and I heard murmurs around the room.

"What do you mean by that?" the CEO exclaimed, sitting up in his chair. At least I knew I had his attention.

"I mean a mental exercise that serves no useful purpose. I mean that the conversations we've been having will make absolutely no difference."

Wisely, before the CEO could speak again, Luke asked, "What do you think would make a difference, Cort?"

"Talking about the leaders in this room and how each person is contributing to all we've heard this morning and yesterday," I replied.

"And what did we hear?" the CEO asked as he leaned back in his seat.

"That leadership is out of integrity with who you say you are. That this company doesn't do what it says it does," I replied. "That it doesn't follow its own policies, procedures, and practices. And its leadership allows that to happen."

I paused to let what I had asserted sink in. No one said a word.

"Ladies and gentlemen, if you want to get some value out of your time together," I continued, "I suggest you talk about yourselves—where you're falling short as leaders of this company and what you're going to change about your leadership to change this company."

"I disagree," called out the CEO, once again sitting up. "The problem is, we've been too focused on personal safety, and we need to shift our focus to process safety. We need to improve the training of our supervisors and operators so they know better how to safely operate our plants, and—"

"With all due respect, sir, you're wrong," I interrupted. "I'm willing to say that because I have empathy for your situation, and if I can't help you see that you're wrong, you're going to continue blowing up plants and people."

"How am I wrong?" the CEO asked, his jaw tight.

"You just said the solution is to train your people to operate safely. That's just not the case. Your people already know how to operate your plants safely. People knew how to do that before I ever set foot in a plant twenty years ago. What's missing is not the knowledge how but the will to. Your company, sir, is full of leaders who lack the will to do what you already know how to do."

The room remained silent. I paused to allow the tension in the room to diminish somewhat before continuing.

After a few moments, I said in a soft voice, "I know you don't know me, and you're probably thinking I have no right to say what I've just said. But I know you. I've been you. I've sat in meetings just like the one we've been having, and I don't want you to make the same mistakes I made. Don't wait until you've killed a lot more people to have the conversation that's begging to be had. Spend the rest of this session talking about you and how you're going to change yourselves to empower your people to do what they already know how to do: operate your plants safely, the way they wish they could operate them."

Luke intervened at this moment and broke the group for lunch. Several of the plant managers in the group made a point to find me during lunch and thank me for what I'd said. My reply to all of them was, "I've opened the door. It's up to you guys to walk through it and have the courage to drag some of your top leaders with you."

Near the end of lunch, Luke informed me that his client was not interested in me continuing the session. He thanked me for my contribution, and I gave him a few thoughts on how to keep the conversation I'd started alive, but I had little confidence he could.

Luke later told me he was unable to get them to face their fundamental problem, and they once again left implementing the same old fixes. As I ended my call with Luke, I encouraged him, "Don't ever let your client get away with taking an aspirin when they have a brain tumor. Even if you have to walk away, walk. If you don't, you become an enabler allowing them to continue their addiction to symptomatic patches, and even worse, you can become one of those patches yourself."

Unfortunately, years later, that company had two of the worst industrial accidents in history: one in a refinery and the other offshore. I was not surprised. The aspirin hadn't worked, and sadly, many lives were lost due to the leadership's unwillingness to face up to and address the tumor.

Chapter 21:
Slaying Dragons

"Life is like arriving late for a movie, having to figure out what was going on without bothering everybody with a lot of questions, and then being unexpectedly called away before you find out how it ends."

—Joseph Campbell

"The last of human freedoms—to choose one's attitude in any given set of circumstances, to choose one's own way."

—Victor Frankl

Years after working with Luke, I boarded a plane headed to Houston on my way to meet a potential client. I was seated next to a young woman who was studying her smartphone but looked up to say hello. After settling in, I noticed she was wearing a University of Texas T-shirt, and I asked about her studies.

Monica was a senior majoring in engineering. She seemed to be a typical UT female student, unconcerned with fashion or outward appearances. She wore little makeup, her wavy long brown hair was unkempt, and she dressed in worn blue jeans, her university T-shirt, and sandals. She shared that she was currently interning with a computer chip manufacturer in the Southwest, and the experience was causing her to question whether she was on the right career path. I thought back to my experience at the fab, and the "Imperial March" from *Star Wars* immediately played in my head, just as it had the day I visited the soulless facility years before. I suppressed a smile and instead asked what she'd learned so far during her internship. As our conversation progressed, she shared a recent experience she said was nagging at her.

"One weekend, management called everyone into the fab to work on a production problem," she told me. "When the fab manager was briefing all of us, he made a point to recognize a supervisor for her work ethic. The manager told us she had left her three-year-old son's birthday party to come into the fab and help with the problem." She paused, waiting for a reaction from me. I raised my eyebrows but said nothing.

"And all those people, they stood there and clapped for her," she continued. "I couldn't believe it. I felt horrible for her, but everyone else seemed happy. She actually stood there smiling and thanked them and even thanked the manager. It made me question whether I want to work in that industry. I'm not sure I want to live that type of life."

"What was so upsetting about the meeting?" I asked.

"That woman left her own son's birthday party for a problem at work! That's appalling to me, but the company rewards that type of stuff. I mean, the people there are very ambitious, but how could someone put their job before their kids? How could anyone think that making computer chips is more important than a mom attending her little boy's party?"

"Monica, in my work, I've met a lot of people in a lot of companies. What you've described isn't unique to computer chip manufacturers. I hear stories like this all the time. But I think you're making some assumptions that may be incorrect."

"What do you mean?"

"I'm not sure those people felt they had much choice. For most of them, sacrificing family for work is a way of life," I responded. "If you want to work and advance in those companies, you're going to have to give up a lot. Many of the people in those organizations are high performing, driven by social success. They convince themselves that they have no choice but to sacrifice much of themselves just to work there and advance. The myth is that you can't survive as a company without employees who are willing to sacrifice."

Monica's brow furrowed in thought. She looked sad as she said, "But how can they be so shallow and emotionless? I wanted to cry for that woman, and they clapped for her."

"I can tell you there's a lot of suffering going on in those companies. I know because I've had people cry when alone with me. I've had women cry because they're pregnant and believe they must get an abortion to keep their careers. I've seen men cry because they see no way to have quality time for their families. I remember one man who told me that the previous weekend his six-year-old son would not sit next to him in a restaurant because he didn't know his own father."

I stopped for a moment as Monica processed what I'd just said. I could tell from her expression that she was starting to connect to what I was saying.

"I'd bet that many of those people you saw clapping were thinking and feeling the same things you were, only they clapped anyway," I continued. "By the way, did you clap for her?"

"I'm ashamed to say it, but yes, I did," Monica replied. "I guess I didn't feel like I had a choice. Everyone else was clapping, and I didn't want to stand out."

"Have you considered that some of the others who clapped did so for similar reasons?"

"At the time, I didn't even consider it. But now that I've spoken with you, I'm sure some probably did."

We were interrupted by the pilot's announcement: the flight attendants would be doing the safety demonstration. As the attendants showed the safety manual and then grabbed a seat belt to demonstrate proper buckling, Monica stared ahead in thought. She waited until the demonstration ended before speaking.

"I know you say this isn't abnormal, but I don't want to work for a place like that," she said. "How do I find a good company?"

"Before I speak to that, I want to make something clear," I responded. "Those are not bad companies. Sure, I've met people who are unhappy working in them. But I've met just as many who absolutely love their jobs. Those companies make it very clear what's expected, and they reward people well for the efforts and sacrifices they make. If I'm coaching someone in one of those companies who is suffering, I'm going to help her see that she, not her employer, is the problem."

"How is she the problem?"

"She's making choices and living a life she really doesn't want to live. That's why she suffers. You know the guy I mentioned whose son was too scared to sit next to him at the restaurant? You know what my suggestion to him was?"

"Quit?" she asked with a grin.

"No," I said, returning her smile. "He had mentioned his son was just beginning to learn how to skateboard, so I suggested he might head home and take his son to the local skate park."

"What did he say?" she asked.

"He said he'd like to, but it wasn't possible. He began listing all the meetings he had to attend that day and how it was so important for him to go to each of them. He also described all the horrible things that could happen if he didn't attend them. And how his son's school would not approve of him taking his son out for something as dubious as skateboarding."

"That's how they talk where I intern. They've got lots of reasons for why things can't change," Monica said. "What did you say to him?"

"I asked him, if he was truly free to choose between attending his meetings or spending the day with his son, which would he choose?"

I went on to explain to Monica how this man had said he had no choice—that he must make those meetings or he'd become even further behind than he already was. And if that happened, he said he would have even less time to be with his son. I reminded him he'd just been crying because he had no relationship with his boy. I told him that from where I sat, he was choosing those meetings over his son—and that he would make such a choice was the source of his suffering.

"He started crying again," I continued. "But this time he was really sobbing. He slumped down in his chair with his head between his knees and wept. He just sat there sobbing for several minutes while I patted him on the back."

"How awful," Monica said. "What finally happened to him?"

"Something miraculous."

"Miraculous?"

"He got his life back. And that happened because he chose to."

"What do you mean, 'he chose to'?"

"Let me tell you the rest of the story, and you see if you can figure that out," I said. Monica nodded.

"After he stopped crying and composed himself, he asked me if I would walk him to the building lobby. When I asked why, he said, 'I'm going to walk out of this place and go be with my son. I want you to walk with me in case I lose my nerve.' So we packed up and headed to the lobby.

"As we were approaching the lobby, we heard a woman's voice yell out his name. We turned around, and he said, 'Oh, shit! It's my manager.' She approached us, handed him two three-inch binders, and instructed him to review them in detail for a 7:00 'emergency' meeting the next morning."

"Oh, no," Monica said, her eyes wide. "What happened next?"

"He turned to me and said, 'This will take all night. Now what do I do?' I told him he had a couple of choices. One choice was to abandon his plans to spend the day with his son, return to his cubicle cell, and spend the afternoon preparing for tomorrow's meeting. The other choice was he could hand me those binders and ask me to place them on his desk while he went home to be with his son."

Monica let out a breath. "You could have gotten him in a lot of trouble," she said.

"The guy had lost his life! He'd lost his son. He was miserable. What's worse is he felt he had no choice in the matter, when in reality, the entire situation was of his choosing. He was already in big trouble. Having his boss angry with him was chicken shit compared to the trouble he was already in."

"What did he say?"

"He said nothing. He just handed me the binders and walked out of the building."

I explained to Monica that for the first time in a long time, this man saw he did have a choice, and he'd finally chosen what he really wanted.

Monica listened as I told the rest of the story. I didn't see the man for a couple of days. I stopped by his cubicle a few times and left him some voice mails, but I didn't hear back. Then, one afternoon, I turned a corner and there he was. He came over to me and asked me to step into the conference room for a minute.

He said he went home that day and took his son and his son's friend to the skate park. He described in great detail everything that happened, and he was glowing with pride. He then thanked me for helping him see choice was possible. The last thing he said, which choked us both up, was how his son, when they arrived home, had given him a big hug and thanked him for taking him skating. And the meeting his supervisor had said was so important? It was canceled. His supervisor discovered another problem she felt was more urgent, and she postponed the meeting until the following week.

When I said this, Monica looked stunned, then relieved.

"Boy, he was lucky," she said.

"Luck had nothing to do with it," I replied. "That change in circumstances was generated out of the man's choice."

"So . . . you mean, if he hadn't gone home with his son, the meeting wouldn't have been postponed?"

"I'm not sure what would have happened. What I do know is time after time, I've seen people choose the life of their initiative, and all of a sudden their circumstances alter in a way that supports the choice. It's as if the universe hears their choice and lines up to support it. When that man said, 'I'm going home,' the world changed. He was different, so the world was different."

"You really believe all that?"

"I more than believe it; I know it. I've experienced it too many times with others and in my own life to not know it is so. The American Indians have a saying, 'Take one step toward the gods, and the gods will take ten steps toward you.' This man took a big step that afternoon toward his son and his life, and the gods, so to speak, changed the circumstances of his life to support that decision."

At this point, a flight attendant greeted us, passed us snacks, and asked what we'd like to drink. While the attendant poured soda into a plastic cup, Monica was lost in thought. As the attendant pushed the drink tray down the aisle, I waited for the next question.

"So, when people make good choices, their circumstances change," Monica began. "What happens when people don't choose the life they really want, when they compromise?"

"Last month, I was sitting in a crowded hotel lounge when a man asked if he could share my table," I responded. "After some chitchat, he shared with me how he was unhappy with his job. He was a senior project manager with a software company. By all traditional measures, he was very successful, but he said he was unfulfilled and never got the time at home he longed for. We talked for a long while, discussing what you and I have been discussing, namely choosing the life one wants. At one point, I asked the man, 'If you could choose what you really want to do, what might that be?' Without batting an eye, he said, 'I'd want to own a business that supports parents who do homeschooling.' He then went on to share with great passion how public schools are failing our children, how he and his wife were homeschooling their kids, and how much joy he got out of that work."

"Do you have this conversation with everyone you meet?"

"Only when there is someone already in this inquiry and suffering to the point that they'll share their thoughts and feelings with a stranger. Like you did at the beginning of our conversation."

"I did do that, didn't I?"

"Yes, you did. Just like the two men I told you about, you seem to be really questioning the path you're on. But don't think you're odd. That seems to be the norm nowadays."

"It seems so," she said. "What happened with the guy and his dream of a homeschooling business?

I shrugged. "When our conversation ended, he was still wrapped up in all the reasons why he couldn't leave his current company. Things like 'I've got twenty-five years vested in my career,' 'I don't have the cash to start up the business,' and many other reasons."

"Those sound like pretty good reasons for him to stay where he's at and just do his time until he retires."

"Do his time? You make it sound like he was in prison! And you know, a man who lives the life he thinks he should live, and not the one he wants to live, has condemned himself to a life sentence of unhappiness," I said. "As he stood to leave, I asked him, 'Have you considered that it's never too late to throw off the life you should do and take on the life you truly yearn to do? Or that just maybe if you do follow your dream, people and circumstances might come your way to support you?' He just stared at me, and his face got very red. Then he walked away."

"Sounds like you may have really hurt him."

"Oh, I agree he was probably hurting, but I don't think my questions were the source of his pain," I responded. "He was hurting because he was choosing not to live the life of his desire. I have known too many people who have spent their years climbing the ladder of success only to reach the top and learn they'd placed it against the wrong wall. I only hope our conversation helped him realize he was doing the same."

"I hope so too," Monica said.

At this point, Monica rose to visit the restroom. When she returned, she sat there staring out the window in deep thought. I concluded that our conversation was over, but a few minutes later, she turned to me.

"Can I share something with you?" she asked.

"Of course."

"I don't know why I'm majoring in engineering. I don't even like engineering. I really worry that when I graduate, I'll get a job in one of those companies and end up like those people, the ones who make good money and are the envy of other people with less things. Living in a big, nice home and driving expensive cars. Having two kids in private schools. Having all that stuff and being totally miserable. That's what scares me."

"What makes you think making good money, driving nice cars, living in a nice home, and giving your kids a good education will make you miserable? Sounds pretty good to me."

"But I know so many people living like that who are miserable. And you said you meet a lot of people who feel the same way."

"I don't think they're unhappy because they have nice things or the freedom to give their kids a good education," I replied. "In fact, there are plenty of people who have those things and are living very happy, fulfilling lives. On the other hand, there are people who don't have any nice things and can't afford to give their children the best education, and they're also living great lives. I think what all happy people have in common is that they're living the lives they choose to live. Discovering one's path and staying on it is the primary concern of every human being's life, because doing so permits them to experience being alive."

"Are you saying I have a path I should be on?"

"We all have one. It's your own, unique path, and it's been there for you all along. You'll know when you're on it and when you're not."

Monica looked confused, so I continued.

"The path is a metaphor for the life of your initiative, the life you're called to live. The American Indians have a concept they call the 'pollen path.' They say that when you're on it, there is 'beauty before me, beauty behind me, beauty to the left of me, and beauty to the right of me.' You must be aware of your thoughts and feelings and learn to notice what you're experiencing moment to moment. What is it that gets you in your gut, that when you're doing it, you experience the rapture of being alive? I know you've had this experience. Think back and remember a time when it happened. What were you doing, and what did you experience?

"Do you mean something like sky diving or bungee jumping?" she asked.

"No, you can experience the rapture of being alive in any task or activity, so long as you are on your path," I replied. "My grandfather loved being a dairy farmer. I observed him finding joy in things like herding and milking cows. You don't have to be a cliff climber to feel alive. In fact, I suspect some people take on extreme sports because their real life is so lacking."

"I know the answer for me is not doing engineering in one of those companies. I've never felt alive doing that. It's work. I do engineering so I can get a good job and make a good living."

"OK, then let me ask you this. Just imagine for a moment that you don't have to make a living. You're somehow free of the need to make money. Consider that you're completely unrestricted from doing whatever makes you happy. If this was the case, what would you choose to do? Think about that for a few minutes. When you're ready, answer as honestly as you can."

I took this opportunity to make a trip to the restroom and give Monica space to contemplate what I had asked her. When I returned and before I could get my seat belt fastened, she looked up at me, her face full of resolve.

"I'd teach math to kids," she said.

"You would?" I responded.

"I've done a lot of tutoring, and I love it. I get a charge when I can tell the kids really get it."

"Say more about this charge you get. What's it like?"

"It feels great. It feels like fun, not work. At that moment, I feel like I'm making a contribution to something worthwhile, and that I'm good at what I do. It feels like I belong, like I'm meant to be there with that student, and I'm doing what I'm meant to do. I feel, I feel . . ."

"Alive?"

"Yes. Much more alive than when I'm doing engineering stuff."

"You keep referring to engineering in a negative way. Let me ask you this: what if all along, you have been on the path to teach kids math, and the engineering studies and interning have been part of a plan to prepare you for that role?"

"I guess I'd look at it differently. But wouldn't it be a waste of time to put in all that work to get an engineering degree and not use it? My parents are both engineers and have invested a lot of money in my degree. They're looking forward to me getting a good job. How will they feel when I tell them I've decided to chuck it all and teach math?"

"I earned an engineering degree, and I can tell you that in all my years of working, I spent probably a few hours doing engineering," I replied. "But that degree got me in the door with a company where I could create a great life for my children and fund my family's future. I learned discipline, independence, and a lot about myself and what I was capable of while earning that degree. So my answer to your question is no, it wouldn't be a waste of time. You are confusing one's degree with one's path."

"Are you saying my path is to teach math?" Monica asked.

"No! Never, ever let anyone tell you what your path is. I don't have a clue what it is. I can only give you hints and tips that can help you find it and stay on it. Whether or not your path is teaching math, there's only one way to find out."

"By teaching math, right?"

"If you choose to teach math, you might find it is your path. If you find it's not, at least you've eliminated one thing you thought might be it, and you probably made a difference in a few kids' lives as well. You see, a vocation is not a life. Your life is your life. Sometimes I think the cruelest thing we teach our kids is the concept of a career. Most of the parents I interact with are more interested in their kids having a career than living a fulfilling life. The trick is to experience being alive as you participate in your vocation, regardless of what that might be at the moment. It sounds like when you're teaching kids, you experience that. All I can say to you is follow that feeling, and you'll never regret it."

"Well, my mom and dad—" she began.

"Even if they're initially disappointed," I interjected, "when they see you so content, they'll understand you made the right choice for you. All any parent really wants is for their kids to be healthy and happy."

Monica sighed. "But teachers don't make much money."

"No, they don't. And as far as I'm concerned, that's a crime. But I'll tell you something: if you sacrifice who you really are and what you really want to do for money, you might as well sell yourself into slavery. You'll have sold out, chasing money instead of happiness. Why, look at yourself. You already feel chained by money in the sense that you might not make enough of it if you teach."

"But how can a job that pays well, a job that others would die to have, have no meaning?"

"Again, I don't think jobs or neighborhoods or schools are the problem. The real problem is what people are doing with their lives—the lives they're living are not what they really want, or at least not what their spirits want to do."

Monica's brow went up in surprise. I chuckled—I could tell the spirit reference had caught her attention.

"When I use the word 'spirit,' I use it metaphorically," I continued. "I could as easily say your heart or your soul. You see, the spirit and mind don't always want the same thing. The mind is primarily interested in comfort, material things, and security. The mind looks for what is agreeable, what's fashionable, what's non-threatening. The mind is very much influenced by wanting to be accepted, to fit in. The spirit, on the other hand, has no aspiration to satisfy rationality or material desires or to minimize risk. It only knows what it wants, and that's to experience the rapture of being alive. In the case of all these people we've been discussing who've drifted off their paths, somehow their minds have gotten control of their lives and taken them on a journey that is not where their spirits want to go."

"But shouldn't our minds be in control of our lives?" Monica asked. "Wouldn't our lives be a mess if we just followed our guts?" At this, I laughed. Monica looked back at me, not sure how to respond.

"I'm sorry for laughing, but your questions are so logical . . . very reasonable. A few minutes ago, your heart was saying it wants to teach kids math. Your mind is using reason to get back the control your heart had a few minutes ago. I suggest that you listen to your heart and tell your mind to get with the program. You have to do what's unreasonable."

"Unreasonable?"

"There are two types of people in the world. First, there are those who have their reasons for not living their dreams, as you have many logical reasons for not becoming a math teacher. These people live ordinary lives, and today that means lots of conformance, comfort, and convenience—and very little experience of being alive."

"What about the other type of people?"

"Well, the other people live out of their impulses, the lives their hearts call them to live. They have no reasons, no explanations, and no justifications for the way they live. They may be poor, middle class, or high income, but regardless of their income level, they know that being rich and having wealth are not synonymous. Their lives are a wonderful adventure where every minute they endeavor to throw off the life they've planned in order to experience the life that is waiting to be theirs."

"How do you throw off your life?" she asked.

"Hmm," I responded. "There is a way of looking at life that may help answer your question. I first became aware of this perspective when I came across Nietzsche's 'Tale of the Dragon.'"

I continued explaining the tale to Monica. "The story goes that when we are children, we are spontaneous and uninhibited. We do and say whatever we want. But as we start to enter society, say around five or six, the uninhibited child must be transformed into a camel. Like camels, children squat down, and their parents and society load all the knowledge and rules required to be a productive citizen. This is appropriate since everyone benefits if people learn to be who they are and live the lives they are called to live in a way that contributes to the greater good.

"Later, as we grow into young adulthood, we leave our homes and go out into the world. By doing so, the camel that we are is transformed into a lion. The heavier the burden we carried as a camel, the stronger the lion we become.

"The function of the lion is to kill a dragon whose name is 'Thou Shalt.' On each of the dragon's scales is written a 'thou shalt,' 'because,' or 'should be.' The dragon's scales are made up of all the things that a person's community, society, parents, religion, and peers all say are, should be, or must be a certain way. All the things ego says someone can be, can do, should be, should do, can't be, and can't do cloak the dragon. Some of the scales are from several thousand years ago, some are from this month's fashion magazine, some are from yesterday's Internet headlines . . . even from today's corporate memo. These scales comprise the limiting belief system that every underdeveloped human carries throughout life and must throw off if she is to ever live a life of bliss.

"You must kill your dragon," I added.

"Kill my dragon?" she said.

"By killing your dragon, you throw off your life as a have-to-be, a supposed-to-be, or an ought-to-be. You see, when the lion kills the dragon, the lion is transformed back into a child."

"A child? Like a little kid?"

"No, the second child you become is metaphorical for a human being who has rediscovered the childlike freedom of a spontaneous life, a person who does not fear living her impulses. When you kill your dragon, life becomes an open possibility, an adventure waiting to be lived."

"And that's what these unhappy people that we've been talking about haven't done. They haven't killed their dragons."

"Exactly. These people are living the lives their dragons say they ought to, not the lives their spirits want. The scales on most people's dragons today are things like 'you can't be what you really want to be because it doesn't pay enough,' or 'if you're a woman, you mustn't give into any impulses to mother your children and instead must work in a meaningless job,' or 'if you're a minority, you have no chance of competing because the world is conspiring to discriminate against you,' and finally, 'you shouldn't throw your career away and chase your dreams because that would be selfish and irresponsible.'"

Monica's face showed that she was working through all she'd heard. She squinted her eyes in thought. I watched her for a moment, waiting for her next question.

"How will I know when I've killed my dragon?" she finally asked.

"Based on what you've shared with me, you'll probably know when your first math student looks up at you and really 'gets it.' At that moment, you'll experience the rapture of being alive."

"So, you're saying I should be a math teacher."

"No! No! No!" I responded, nearly shouting—not in anger but in emphasis. "There is no 'should' or what other people think. You see how quickly that dragon resurrects? You do what your gut tells you it wants to do, and don't let anyone tell you otherwise.

"But let's say, for the sake of discussion only, you do find that you really want to teach math, and you make the choice to become a math teacher. When you do, there will be other dragons waiting to take your life away from you. Your mind has an unlimited supply of dragons you must continually slay if you are to stay on your path. There is always the next one around the corner, so you must be vigilant. You kill that one, then another, and another, and another. You see, it's dragons all the way down."

"What do you mean by 'other dragons'?"

"Oh, the dragon that says you should teach junior high because it pays better even though you love teaching third graders. Or there's the dragon that tells you to move into administration because climbing the ladder to principal is where it's really at."

Monica looked at me for a long time. I imagined her seeing dragons dancing across her vision. I thought, This must be a lot to take in for a college student. But she's lucky to hear it now.

"But what if I become a math teacher and find out I don't like it as well as I'd hoped?" Monica said. "Or, if over the years, I get tired of it?"

"You know, every dragon I've ever met has that scale right smack in the middle of his forehead," I replied.

"What scale?"

"The one that says, 'You shouldn't try, you could be wrong, or worse fail, and that would make you feel bad.' You could find out that you don't like teaching math. But you might also find you love it and, in doing so, find your life. You've told me several times you love teaching math to kids, at least your heart did. Now your mind's summoning up all its dragons to generate all the reasons why you shouldn't. Can you see that this is what our conversation has been about for the last several minutes? Can you hear your heart and mind speaking in the conversation?"

Monica's eyes focused off in the distance for a moment. It was as though she was trying to hear herself. "Yes, I guess I can," she said.

"Wonderful. I suggest that you listen generously to both of them and then do what your heart calls you to do," I responded. "If you do this regularly, your mind will realize it's no longer running the show and will begin working for your true wishes instead of pushing its own agenda. As a young person, unless you're hit by a bus or become terminally ill, you'll probably live to be about one hundred. Given that, isn't it reasonable to assume that during your life, you might have lots of jobs? We're so fortunate today. Unlike our grandparents, who were lucky to live to sixty and basically had their work life and then retirement, we get to have many chapters in our lives. The big question is, will you be the author of those chapters, or will your circumstances and mind dictate them to you?"

I stopped talking as the captain's voice boomed through the plane's speakers, announcing that we were starting our descent. We listened to him talk through the weather and local time. When he finished, Monica leaned toward me with a hopeful expression on her face.

"You really think I can find bliss and live whatever life I want?" she said.

"Yes," I responded without hesitation, "you can, and you will if you follow where your heart's spirit calls you to go. Get on and stay on that path and put your mind to work for you and not against you, and you'll always have bliss."

"But that's not so if I fail. I could follow my heart and still fail, and then I wouldn't be happy."

"Don't confuse bliss with happiness. Up to now, we've been speaking of the two as if they're synonymous, but they aren't. Bliss is the experience of being alive, and being alive means sometimes you're happy and sometimes you're not. You're right; even when on your path, you will sometimes experience failure and pain.

But at least you won't be numb as so many people seem to be today. When happiness occurs, you'll know it's the result of your choosing, and that's also true of your pain. But since you'll know that you chose and caused them both, both will occur to you as bliss, as being alive."

"Pain is being alive?"

"You bet. Life can't exist without pain. There is the pain of birth, growth pains, the pain of losing loved ones and friends. These are all part of living. It may sound odd to you, but many people tell me that the two times when they felt most alive were at the birth of their children and the death of their parents. I know this is so for me. These are obviously on opposite ends of the scale of happiness, but somehow these people describe both as beautiful and sublime. For me, this suggests that you can experience bliss in all of life, even in failure, and not just during the good times."

She looked at me skeptically for a moment, then her expression softened. I waited for the question I knew was coming next.

"When will I know when I have reached my bliss?" she asked.

"You never will," I said.

"What? I never will? So why waste my time?"

"Bliss is not something you attain or some destination you reach. It's something you experience. You see, living a life of bliss is like climbing a mountain with no peak . . . or if there is a peak, we all die before we reach it. So, why not enjoy the climb? Why not choose to climb a mountain where every step is blissful, instead of choosing a mountain where we accumulate only material riches? Why not choose one where the richness of the quest is what accumulates?"

"But what do I have then when my life is done? After a lifetime of following my path, what will I have?"

"You'll have what you have, which could be nothing, or everything, or anything in between the two. At the end of our lives,

I don't think any of us will care, do you? I mean, both of us will be dead. Do you really think that when you're on your deathbed, you'll be looking around at all you have or don't have?

"I don't know. I'd probably want something to pass on to my kids."

"How about the example of a parent who lived the life she really wanted? A mother who killed her dragons and lived a free, spontaneous life, driven out of her own initiative? A parent who died a peaceful death, content in the knowledge she lived her life her way? Or how about passing on to your children the ability to follow and experience their own, unique path as they live their lives? I can't think of a more precious gift to leave one's kids."

Monica smiled. "Me either."

At this point, our conversation was interrupted by an announcement that we were about to land. The plane touched down, and after we withdrew our carry-ons from the overhead bin, Monica and I thanked each other for the discussion, said good-bye, and went our separate ways.

A few months later, I received an email from Monica, thanking me for giving her "a lot to think about." I replied, wishing her a blissful life. I can only hope the paths she chooses in her life are the ones her heart intends.

Chapter 22:
A Coonass in the Rough

"For the past 33 years, I have looked in the mirror every morning and asked myself: If today were the last day of my life, would I want to do what I am about to do today? And whenever the answer has been 'No' for too many days in a row, I know I need to change something."

—Steve Jobs

"Example is not the main thing in influencing others. It is the only thing."

—Albert Schweitzer

The potential client I was traveling to meet as I conversed with Monica was the senior-most manager of an offshore drilling organization working in the Gulf of Mexico. Michael had realized the old way of doing business was not going to be successful for much longer, and he was looking for someone to help him transform him and his organization.

Michael introduced himself by saying, "I'm just a simple coonass who grew up in the oil patch, took nearly twenty years to get my engineering degree, and finds himself in charge of a several-billion-dollar drilling operation. But I'm smart enough to know we have to change. I don't know what that new organization might look like, but I know it doesn't look like the one I lead today. And even if I did know, I'm not sure how I would drive such a change. That's where you come in."

I knew at that moment he had the potential to be an All-In Leader.

Michael was the sort of executive who was as likely to be seen in jeans as he was dress slacks. He was small in stature but enormous in heart. Tanned from years in the oil field and silvering at the temples of his crew cut, Michael only wore a suit when he was making a presentation to "the executives" or as a sign of respect when hosting business partners. Michael once told me, "I may be sitting in the executive's office, but I'll always be a driller."

Michael arranged for our first meeting to take place in a conference room midway up a forty-floor tower. Two of his lieutenants were waiting for Michael and me when we entered. Both men were new to the organization and their positions, and Michael was intent that they benefit from my coaching as well. When we spoke on the phone prior to the meeting, Michael told me, "I have two of the brightest and most talented managers in the business, and I want you to help them form a strong partnership and get off on the right foot."

At this first meeting, I agreed to engage with Michael and his lieutenants. The primary objective was to help the three of them form strong working relationships and work together as one aligned team. I convinced Michael to allow me to spend several weeks observing him and his people so I could "get the lay of the land." During those initial weeks, I discovered that Michael was mentoring some of the new supervisors in his organization. When I asked why, he responded, "I know what it's like to be a new supervisor, and I want to be sure these young folks succeed. Also, my lieutenants are new in their roles and too busy learning their way to have time to mentor their new supervisors." Michael's first concern was always the well-being and success of his people.

As a child of the oil patch, Michael knew everything there was to know about "keeping the (drilling) bit turning to the right." I overheard one of his lieutenants once describe him to a business partner by saying, "He may be wearing a suit, but if you cut him, he'd bleed crude." Michael's ability to easily morph between manager and driller was one of his strengths and afforded him great respect within all levels of his organization.

During those weeks, I attended a meeting with his senior staff. His people were especially down due to some recent bad press regarding their company, and Michael encouraged the group.

With a puffed chest and chin up, he declared, "Never forget the contribution we make to our country and our way of life," he told them. "We may not get the respect we deserve, but we know our mission is every bit as important as the U.S. military. And without us, our country and our freedoms would be in serious risk."

I quickly learned Michael was as beloved by his people as any manager I had ever come across. The most common phrase I heard from Michael's people was, "I'd walk on hot coals for that man." However, this phrase was sometimes followed by "but Michael is sometimes his own worst enemy."

As my observations progressed, I started to recognize there were aspects of Michael's approach that were affecting his organization's performance and his effectiveness as their leader. During a discussion with him one day, I focused on pinpointing those issues.

I'd caught Michael after a morning meeting with one of his mentees. He greeted me at his office door and directed me to a small table with two chairs next to a window with a twentieth-floor, panoramic city view. Michael's office looked more like an engineer's dorm room than an executive's office. Hanging above the windows were his favorite NFL and college team banners. On every horizontal surface sat a photo, plaque, or some memento commemorating his long and distinguished career. We sat and chatted for several minutes. Finally, I jumped in with a question I'd been wanting to ask.

"Who, more than anyone, do you think has the most impact on this organization's performance?" I said.

"That's easy," said Michael. "The frontline supervisor. That's management 101."

"It may be management 101, but I would disagree," I replied.

"You would?" Michael asked, somewhat surprised.

"I agree that supervisors have a significant impact on performance, but I wouldn't say they have the most."

"Then who does?"

"You do."

"Me? But I'm rarely on our rigs, let alone the drill floor, and that's where performance happens."

"It is. But I didn't ask where performance happens. I asked who in your organization has the most impact on performance."

"And you think that's me?" Michael asked again, pinching his slightly gray and closely cropped goatee.

"Yes, and here's why. I subscribe to the 'big wheel theory,' which says that the person at the top is the biggest wheel and everyone below him is a sequentially smaller wheel. Image six wheels stacked on top of each other, with the one below always a bit smaller in diameter. Can you see what I'm describing?"

"Yes, I understand what you're sayin.'"

"Now imagine that I turn the wheel at the bottom, the smallest wheel, about one quarter clockwise. How much does the big wheel at the top turn?"

"Hardly at all."

"Agreed. But now imagine that I turn the wheel at the top, the biggest wheel, a quarter clockwise. How much does the small wheel at the bottom turn?"

"Quite a lot," Michael said. "Maybe a few revolutions. Give me the dimensions of the wheels, and let me go get my calculator, and I can tell you exactly." Michael began to rise and turned toward his desk.

"That won't be necessary," I said. "This is a leadership problem, not an engineering problem. The point is, when you move one way or the other direction, you have an enormous impact on the direction of your organization. Can you see that now?"

"Not exactly. Say more."

"Well, you've asked me to help you transform your organization. What I'm suggesting is that you really don't need to transform your organization. All you really need to do is transform Michael. Change the way you manage and lead, and the organization will transform around you."

"How?"

"Because you're the big wheel."

"Give me an example," Michael replied, rubbing his index finger across his chin in thought.

"I'll do better than that. I'll let you give me the example. Imagine that you go to sleep tonight, and while you're asleep, this organization magically transforms into one that delivers every oil well on your schedule at or under budget, on or ahead of schedule. Have you ever been able to produce performance like that?"

"No," Michael replied. "Not even close."

"Well, in this imaginary exercise, it has happened," I said. "But you were asleep when it happened, so when you wake up the next morning, you're oblivious to the change. You head to work thinking that you're still in that old organization.

"Now, I want you to imagine that you observe yourself throughout a day in that transformed organization, the one that can perform like you've never been able to. As you watch and listen to yourself, what would be different about the way you would manage and lead in that new organization?"

Michael thought for a moment. "I guess I would spend a lot less time on operations issues because we wouldn't have many."

"So where would you spend your time?"

"Probably looking forward at what was coming rather than looking back on where we'd screwed up."

"Good," I said. "That's something you would do different. How would you be different?"

"I guess I'd be more confident, less worried, less likely to go off the handle if and when something goes wrong," Michael replied. "I'd be more composed."

"How would you lead differently than you do today?"

"I'd be much less controlling. I'd feel comfortable not knowing everything, and I'd trust my people to do the right thing."

"Is that transformed organization—one that reliably delivers wells on budget and on schedule—the kind of performance you think of when you tell me you want my help to transform your organization?"

"Not until just now. Until now, I hadn't even seen that level of performance as possible."

"Now that you do, do you want that level of performance to be part of the vision you imagine when you speak about transforming your organization?"

"Yes."

"Then we're agreed," I said. "Delivering wells at or under budget and at or ahead of schedule will be part of your intention going forward. I just have one last question to ask."

"Shoot," Michael said, leaning back with his hands clasped behind his head and grinning with possibility.

"When you see yourself in that transformed organization, you see yourself managing, being, and leading very differently. If that's the case, why don't you manage, be, and lead that way in this organization?"

Michael paused, unclasped his hands and leaned forward, his brow furrowed thoughtfully. "That's a good question."

"It is the question. Do you know why?"

"Because I'm the big wheel?"

"Exactly. When you transform, the organization will transform around you."

"Makes sense," Michael replied. "But transforming me will be a big job. I'm just an ignorant coonass who's been very fortunate along the way and finds himself in a situation for which I'm proud and grateful. I owe a lot to this company and what it has done for me. But—"

"Then give a lot back," I interrupted. "Give them the leader who transforms this organization into the one we've been describing here."

"You think I can do that?"

"I wouldn't be having this discussion with you if I wasn't convinced you can."

Michael sat pensively for several moments staring out at the city and looking down at the notes he'd been taking. He'd written the words "Big Wheel" and circled them several times. Then he looked up at me.

"What's the first step in the process?" he asked.

"The first step is for us to develop a list of people you want me to interview about you," I said.

"What will you ask them?"

Things that'll help reveal to you who you need to be and what you need to do to lead the transformation of this organization."

"You can get me that?"

"Yes."

"Then let's get started."

Michael requested that I interview about two dozen people from within his organization, including his managers and some of his business partners. I spent several days conducting the interviews. Afterwards, I developed a brief report summarizing that data to share with Michael.

Michael and I met late in the afternoon in his office. I had the report in front of me on the table. But before sharing the information with Michael, I walked to his whiteboard and wrote three words: justifying, defending, and investigating.

"What're those for?" Michael asked.

"These are things I will not allow you to do as we discuss this report," I replied. "You can't justify anything you read, you can't defend anything the feedback says, and you certainly can't seek to investigate who said anything in this report. Do you accept these terms?"

"I do. But is it that bad?"

"That will depend on you. I've gotten you what you've asked for, information that will help you see what you need to do and be to begin the transformation of this organization. If you accept it as the gift it is and in the spirit it is offered to you by the interviewees, it will show up to you as good. If you do any of these things"—I pointed to the three words on the whiteboard—"it will be bad."

Like most of the people I've coached who rarely receive truthful and specific feedback, Michael was very much disturbed by the responses, even though in an objective observer's eyes, they were overwhelmingly positive. People who aren't used to hearing the conversation that goes on when they're not around can be staggered when they experience it for the first time, and Michael was no exception.

He sat there as if stunned, listening to every word I said. When I was finished, he said to me, "This is devastating."

"Michael, let's get real here," I replied. "Devastating is when you are told your child has an incurable disease. This hurts a little. But as they say, no pain, no gain."

I instructed Michael to spend a week with his feedback report. I asked him not to share it or his thoughts about it with anyone, and not to attempt to do anything about it until I returned for my next visit. I explained that I wanted him to just "be with the feedback and do nothing about it until the pain stops." Only then would he be able to drill down into the responses and discover the gold that was there to be mined.

Michael did as I asked. The next time we met, he shared with me three specific changes he wished to make as he began his personal transformation.

"This has been invaluable," Michael said. "I'm sorry I reacted so negatively when I first read the report."

"Most do," I said. "Don't give it a second thought. What do you want to change?"

"I want to get much better at creating expectations. And along with that, I want to become much better at holding people accountable for those expectations. It is obvious from this feedback my people need that from me."

"So, first, create clear expectations and hold people accountable."

"Right. Second, I want to give more control to my managers and supervisors. I'm way too much in their business, and according to this feedback, they want me to push decision-making and accountability down to them so they can do the same with their people. Everyone wants to be accountable for more, but they can't be accountable until I pass on to them the power to make decisions, manage the budgets, and lead their teams."

"Second, then," I responded, "you want to give control to your people, which you defined as decision-making and spending authority, which you believe will cause them to be more accountable. Accountable for what, though?"

"Accountability for performance," Michael replied. "Right now, since I'm holding onto control and decision-making, I'm the only one accountable. I see from the feedback report that to get accountability down in the ranks, I have to give up control and push decision-making down."

"Excellent. What's the third change you want to make?"

"I want to be a more composed leader. I was surprised by the amount of feedback I received that said I am too emotional, too critical of management decisions I don't agree with, and too easily controlled by my emotions. And what surprised me most was the feedback that helped me see how much my emotions and lack of composure affect how my people feel and the composure of the entire organization."

"Big wheel theory again. Did you notice in the feedback how many people shared that the first question often asked early in the morning is, 'What kind of mood is Michael in?'"

"Yeah. I was disappointed to read that, but at the same time, I learned just how much my emotional state affects my people. I want to get control of my emotions and show up as composed, regardless of the situation."

"Perfect," I said. "The third change, then, is to become a composed leader, regardless of the circumstances. I think you've chosen three personal changes that are very much in line with the feedback you've received and will go a long way toward preparing you to transform this organization. How do you plan to make these changes?"

"I thought you'd tell me that," Michael replied. "You're my coach. I expect you to help me solve problems like this."

"I could tell you," I said, "but I'd serve you better by helping you learn the answer yourself. Transforming yourself or your organization is not a technical problem to be solved based on knowledge and experience. It's a challenge that is overcome by learning and adapting your way to a solution. There's no problem to be solved here, so the linear problem-solving that you and your people are so good at will not help you get to a solution."

"I'm not sure what you're saying."

"When you wanted to transform yourself from a single man into a husband, what did you do?"

"I got married."

"And how did you get married?"

"My wife and I stood in front of our friends and God and said our vows."

"And at what exact moment in the ceremony did you stop being single and start being a married man?"

"I suppose the moment the reverend said, 'I now pronounce you husband and wife.'"

"Exactly. So, then, at what exact moment will you stop being the leader you are today, the one who gives unclear expectations, holds onto control, and is often flustered, and become the leader you just told me you plan to be?"

"When someone pronounces that I am?" Michael asked, his voice anxious.

"And who should make the declaration?" I said.

"I will."

"Agreed. Now all you need to decide is when, how, and to whom you will make that declaration. I'll leave you to noodle on that. Please let me know what you decide."

For the next several months, I guided and advised Michael and his two lieutenants as they formed a strong partnership and as Michael worked on his three development areas. At an off-site communications session with his entire organization in attendance, Michael declared the three changes he was committed to making in himself and asked for patience and support as he made the transition. He also allowed me to help him explore what was driving his perceptions and behaviors that led to microman- agement and emotional outbursts. Through our work, Michael became extremely effective managing the three behaviors he'd committed to improve.

These changes were a good first step in Michael's personal transformation, but all the while, I was keeping an eye out for the event or circumstance that we could leverage to complete his transformation and begin the transformation of his people. That moment came in April of 2010. While drilling the Macondo well, the Deepwater Horizon oil rig exploded in the Gulf of Mexico, killing eleven men, severely injuring seventeen others, and changing the drilling industry forever.

Michael and his lieutenants attended the funeral services for the eleven perished men. He told me on his return that after the service, he had committed to doing everything in his power to make certain nothing like that ever happened again. I knew then that my coaching pursuit was to help Michael keep that commitment and, in doing so, help drive the transformation for which he had engaged me.

Chapter 23:
The Drift

"Basing one's future plans on what exists now simply generates plans for more of the same. The difficulty in planning forward from the present is that it invisibly locks in the very constraints that produced today's frustrations."

—Alan Scharf

"I don't know if we each have a destiny, or if we're all just floating around accidental-like on a breeze, but I, I think maybe it's both."

—Forrest Gump, played by Tom Hanks in *Forrest Gump*

Although I had worked with industries of all types and cultures, I'd never run into one quite like Michael's. Companies in his industry spent hundreds of millions of dollars like other industries spent thousands. At the end of the company's financial calendar, I made a presentation to Michael's leadership team estimating the cost of my coaching for the following year, which was six figures. Afterward, one of Michael's managers pulled me aside and said, "Cort, you don't need to waste our time discussing small expenditures like a few hundred thousand for coaching. We have much bigger fish to fry."

This attitude was partly because, at that time, the industry was enjoying record high oil prices. But it was much more than that. In this industry, especially when it came to the big players, not only did cost seem unimportant but performance as well.

There were times when Michael's people would make mistakes that cost hundreds of millions of dollars, with no one being held accountable, or at least not in the way most would define accountability. And because of the extreme complexity of the work his people did, it often took two or three attempts to correct a mistake, incurring tens or hundreds of millions more of unnecessary costs.

Although there was no accountability for what I considered massive and avoidable waste, after the problem was finally corrected, Michael would issue a congratulatory email to the rig team. I once told Michael during one of our coaching sessions, "You're the only leader I've ever run into who sends his team congratulations for getting it right the third time."

But as I say, Michael and his team were thinking and operating the way people in that industry did. There was a global energy boom going on, and many of them had forgotten what it was like when funds were limited. I knew the Macondo disaster was going to change all this, and that Michael had better get his people in front of that wave or they would be overwhelmed by it.

Although the full impact of the Macondo disaster wasn't yet clear, it was obvious to me that it was going to have a profound effect on how Michael's industry would operate in the future. I attempted to warn him and his leadership team.

"They're going to shut you down and come in here and tell you how to go about your business," I told them. "There is an old axiom in business that applies here: if you don't manage your business, someone else will manage it for you. Well, your industry just had a historic slip up, and you'd better get ready for all the help that's coming your way."

Although many of his team were skeptical, Michael was open to listening to what I had to say. I wasn't sure he accepted my prediction, but I could tell he was worried about the future of his people and his industry.

My prognostications became more believable a few weeks later, when I stood with Michael and dozens of his people one morning, watching the president deliver a televised national address regarding the Macondo incident. The president declared that he was ordering offshore drilling in the U.S. to be shut down immediately, abolishing the regulatory agency that oversaw U.S. drilling, and referred to the oil industry as "criminals." Michael was both shocked and very much hurt by that announcement.

I also took offense to the president using such rhetoric to slander an entire industry. I had witnessed just how hard Michael and his people worked every day to provide their fellow citizens with the energy they needed and the high standard of living they enjoyed. I understood their mission was every bit as vital to our national security as that of the armed services and felt they deserved the same adoration and respect. As I looked around at his people that morning, I saw in their expressions that they too were severely offended and hurt by the ignorant and insensitive remarks.

Once the upset generated by the president's speech subsided, Michael and I made our way to a nearby conference room to talk through what had just happened. As we sat down, I jumped right in.

"Given what has happened," I asked, "what can you predict for the future of your industry?"

"The gravy train is over," Michael replied, looking down, his hands flat on the table, still obviously devastated from the president's speech. "From this point forward and for the remainder of my career, our industry will be highly regulated by the outside and overseen from within." I could hear the regret in his tone, but at the same time, I was pleased he was facing reality.

"That's very perceptive. And how might that change affect you and your people?"

"It means that, in the very near future, performance is going to matter. And I don't mean just safety. Of course, safety, especially process safety, is going to get a total reemphasis. But things like productivity, cost, and quality will also matter like they never have."

"I concur completely," I said. "During the 1980s, when I was a young manager in the chemical industry, we had our equivalent to Macondo. Do you remember the disaster at Bhopal?"

"No," Michael replied, to my surprise.

"Like the Horizon rig, a chemical plant lost containment of some very hazardous materials, but in this case, nearly four thousand employees and members of the surrounding community were killed. Years later the death toll was estimated at twenty-five thousand. It was by far the worst industrial disaster in history."

"Twenty-five thousand! How terrible. I'm surprised I've never heard of it."

"Well, I can tell you it totally changed my industry. At that time, the company I worked for employed over eighty thousand people. When I left several years later, we had about twenty thousand. That incident destroyed my industry, just like Macondo is going to destroy yours if someone doesn't stand up and lead your industry into a different future."

"I think you're exaggerating a bit," responded Michael.

"Really?" I replied. "When is the last time you heard of a community welcoming the start-up of a new chemical plant?"

"It's been a while."

"About thirty years. And frankly, I don't blame them. My industry failed to change after Bhopal, at least in any meaningful way, and our lack of vision and leadership cost us our industry."

"But that's really not the same as our situation, is it?" Michael asked. "I mean, what happened to those men on the Horizon was tragic, but we didn't kill thousands. Surely we won't suffer the same fate as the chemical industry."

I looked Michael squarely in the eyes. "You heard the president. Do you have any doubts he would hesitate to put an end to your industry if he felt it was politically expedient or that there are millions of people out there who would support him doing so? I live in Austin, and I can tell you those people are out there. In the president's and their eyes, you guys are criminals. If someone doesn't stand up and convince them your industry is not what they think it is, and help them understand the critical role you play in their lives, it will happen. It's not a question of if but when. And I can tell you from experience that 'when' can come a lot sooner than you might ever imagine."

"But what can we do other than wait to see what happens and respond as best we can?" Michael stood and walked to the window, staring at the skyscrapers and highways.

"A better question for the leader of this outfit to ask would be something like, 'What can I do?'"

"Fair enough. What can I do?" he said, turning toward me.

"You could wait and see how this all shakes out and react as best you can, as you suggested. But I wouldn't call that leading. I'd call that drifting."

"Drifting?" Michael asked.

I explained to Michael that drifting is what people do when they allow themselves to be at the mercy of events and circumstances. Like a leaf drifts in the wind, people who drift turn over their future to circumstances. And like the leaf, they let the wind take them where it may. Leaders are instead intentional; they know who they are and what they stand for. Leaders are never willing to drift—the moment they do, they stop leading. Leaders are on a mission.

"Have you ever seen the movie *Forrest Gump*?" I added.

"It's one of my favorites," Michael replied as he leaned back in his chair.

"If you really want to learn the difference between drifting and being intentional, watch that movie. It shows how one intentional person—in this case, Forrest—can make an extraordinary difference in the lives of people he comes in contact with, even those who at the time are drifting through their lives."

"I'm not getting your point."

"My point is, Michael, you are that intentional person. I see that in you, and I think you see it in yourself, but your humility sometimes blinds you to it."

Michael looked out the window, considering how to respond. I waited quietly.

"I don't like giving myself credit, but I do agree I'm very intentional," he said.

I nodded. "Over the next weeks and months, you'll need to ask yourself some very important questions," I said. "Questions like, am I willing to be the one who stands up for our industry and leads our people into a different future, not the future that is predictable, given the current circumstances, but a much brighter future that wouldn't exist if it weren't for my leadership?"

"I don't know. I don't see myself as some great leader or anything like that."

"You don't? That's a shame because your people need a great leader at this moment, probably more than ever. It's also a shame you're unaware of the potential you have as a leader."

I rose and stood directly across from him. "You'll always get only the truth from my perspective, and from my perspective, you have the greatest leadership potential of anyone in this business unit. The problem is you're not aware of it, and even if you were, you don't know how to tap into that potential."

"And that's where you come in?" Michael said, looking at me, his brow wrinkled in doubt as he tried to gauge whether I was really being straight with him.

"If you decide you want me to continue coaching you, that would be my primary purpose—to help you realize your potential as a leader in a way that leads this industry into the future, while at the same time causing your organization to produce performance like it has never seen."

"You can do that?"

"We can, if you're willing."

I ended the conversation by suggesting that Michael think over the possibility I had put before him. I suggested that we meet again in a couple of weeks to continue exploring our relationship. If he was still interested in acquiring my coaching, I would explain what the relationship would look like, the time commitment required, and the other particulars that would go into our coaching agreement. He agreed to consider what we'd discussed and meet again in a few weeks.

I knew that if Michael did decide to engage me, I would need to guide him to develop himself in several areas. First, when Michael spoke, it was usually about drilling wells and rarely in terms of leadership. He seemed to be unmindful that leading people was as much a part of his role as managing drilling.

On the other hand, he openly expressed his concerns that his organization was no different than those associated with the Macondo disaster and not immune to such catastrophic failures. Michael regularly asserted to his people and management that they must change the way they operated. In fact, he had prepared a dramatic presentation to that end, which he presented to his entire organization and management during their annual communications meetings.

He had clarity about what was wrong with the present but was missing a clear and compelling vision of what a right future might look and feel like. He had strong opinions and was willing to express them, but this merely made him a critic of the status quo. He was declaring the problem, but he lacked a vision to offer his associates, and he had not declared himself as the one who would lead others to the solution. In other words, he was not yet "all in."

Moreover, although Michael was actively searching for new ways of doing things, he was relying on his experience and applying old, well-worn solutions. He was attempting to problem solve his way into the future based on experience. Instead, he needed to learn and adapt his way into the future. He had not yet discovered the difference between solving a technical problem and learning one's way to an adaptive solution.

In short, Michael had no practical experience dealing with such a leadership challenge. He was a brilliant, caring, and skilled drilling manager, but his reality called for an entirely different skill set and knowledge base, of which he was lacking.

In "hero journey" terms, Michael had been tossed by external events over the threshold and into the forest. His adventure had begun, but he was unaware of it. He was lost in the forest and couldn't successfully complete the journey unless a guide accompanied him. Without my coaching, I worried, he was going to be eaten by the dragon. He would go down after putting up a gallant fight, but he would go down.

Chapter 24:
Baton Rouge—Part 2

"If one does not understand a person, one tends to regard him as a fool."

—C. G. Jung

"Until one is committed, there is hesitancy, the chance to draw back, always ineffectiveness. Concerning all acts of initiative (and creation), there is one elementary truth that ignorance of which kills countless ideas and splendid plans: that the moment one definitely commits oneself, then Providence moves too. All sorts of things occur to help one that would never otherwise have occurred. A whole stream of events issues from the decision, raising in one's favor all manner of unforeseen incidents and meetings and material assistance, which no man could have dreamed would have come his way."

—William Hutchison Murray

"Love is the only force capable of transforming an enemy into friend."

—Dr. Martin Luther King

Max, the coach I'd worked with in Baton Rouge, met with Oscar, the plant manager of the chemical plant, in the aftermath of his employee's death. A couple of days afterwards, Max called me to see if I was interested in partnering with him. By this time, Max was out on his own as well, and he was convinced the plant manager, now several years wiser, was ready and willing to change. I was not so sure.

In my experience, fatal incidents have a short-term effect on leaders. For most of them, it's similar to passing a fatal accident on the highway—for a few miles, you drive the speed limit, but before long, you're flying down the road at eighty miles per hour.

I agreed to join Max on his initial revisit to the plant but held off making a long-term commitment. As we'd done years earlier, Max and I interviewed a representative sample of the plant's population to gain their perceptions. But this time, the issue of race dominated their comments, regardless of the interviewee's skin color. Our three primary findings were (1) the people in this plant saw everything through the lens of race; (2) there was a widespread perception that plant management and supervision were unfair and unjust when it came to dealing with black employees; and (3) the company could expect the poor performance to continue, and even worsen, if this perception stayed unchanged. Our recommendation was that management secure a consultant experienced in dealing with race relations to coach them on how to address these issues.

During our meeting with the plant staff, the humbled but still highly confident plant manager, Oscar, sat quiet and still as he read his employees' descriptions of what it was like to work in his plant. The room was dead silent as each staff member contemplated the report. Then, just as we began to discuss the team's reactions, Oscar rose from his seat and darted out of the room, which drew a collective gasp from his staff.

Max and I paused and waited, thinking Oscar had left to grab a notepad or something and would soon return, but when he didn't, we continued the discussion. Oscar's team had a similar reaction to the report as they had during our meeting years prior. They made the same arguments and accusations; Max and I did our best to remind them that the report did not reflect our interpretations but rather what was actually said in the interviews.

Then suddenly, the conference room door opened. The staff turned to see who was at the door and let out a second collective gasp. There stood Oscar, his long, thin face pale and covered with sweat. His black hair gleamed, and the top of his shirt was drenched in perspiration. His eyes were red and sad. My first thought was that Oscar had just received some terrible news.

A staff member nearest the door stood and said, "Oscar, are you alright?"

Oscar did not respond and slowly walked to his chair at the end of the table and sat down. For what seemed an eternity, he sat silently, rolling up the report tightly in his hands and then releasing it. I thought to myself, I bet Oscar wishes that report was Max's or my neck.

He pressed the paper flat on the conference table. Finally, he looked up at the man who had spoken to him and said, "No, Louis, I'm not alright."

"Where did you go? Where've you been?" asked another man.

"I've been in the bathroom, throwing up."

Oscar's response drew a third gasp from the group.

"I've been in the bathroom cleaning myself up and thinking about this report. My first reaction was to come back here and throw Max and Cort out the door. But as I stood at the faucet, I looked into the mirror and there I was: the so-called leader of this plant. And I have to say, gentlemen, I did not like who I saw."

There was a long, awkward pause as the team waited for Oscar to continue.

"I had no idea things were this bad," Oscar said, waving the report in the air with his right hand. "I just assumed the plant was a reflection of the community, and we all know we have a ways to go when it comes to relations between whites and blacks. But as I looked in the mirror, I realized this report is not a reflection of our community. It's a reflection of me and my leadership."

Oscar paused and collected himself. As he did, I noticed each member of his staff was sitting low in their chairs with bowed heads.

"I don't have any idea how to fix what's in this report," Oscar went on. "I have no clue what to do after reading something as ugly as this. But I do know this. This will not be my legacy. I will not go down as the guy who sat by and allowed what this report reveals to continue."

At that point, Max recommended we take a break so Oscar could get a clean change of clothes and we could all consider what he said. When the group reconvened, Max repeated the recommendation that the team secure a consultant experienced with race relations.

"We are outstanding at helping teams and organizations improve their business performance," Max said, "but the issues you face are something we have no experience with."

"I want you," Oscar said. "Not someone else."

"Why us?"

"Because our people have connected with the two of you. They trust you. It's obvious from this report that you have their confidence. Hire a race expert to coach you if you need one, but I want you guys."

After a lengthy discussion, Max recommended the team empower us to hold a two-day session where volunteer employees could meet to read the report, discuss it, and make recommendations to the leadership team. Max asserted, "This way, we get you some useful data on which you can begin acting, and we can get a better idea if there is a meaningful coaching role for us to play."

The team accepted Max's recommendation, and a month later, he and I were welcoming approximately seventy employee volunteers into the session room at a hotel a few blocks from the plant. Three of them were Jeff, the young laborer who'd given me a tour of his unit, and his father and grandfather.

As the volunteers took their seats at the eight-person round tables and Max led the introductions, five things became obvious. First, about two-thirds of the group were black. Second, all levels and departments of the organization were represented by at least a few attendees. Third, as expected, all the white attendees were foreperson level or above. Fourth, at no table did blacks and whites sit together. And fifth, the table at the front left, where ten middle-aged white men sat—some of whom introduced themselves by declaring their membership in the Ku Klux Klan— was going to be trouble.

During the first break, Max pulled me into a nearby storage room and said, "Cort, those eyes, they're back."

"What eyes?" I replied.

"The ones that wouldn't hesitate to slit my throat. They're here in the room. What are we going to do?"

"Who are you speaking of?"

"The KKK table. They're the same group that cornered me in the maintenance shop. I didn't recognize them out of their work uniforms, but they're here."

Max was genuinely terrified. I paused and gave great thought to his question. Thoughts like "we're over our heads" and "we should get plant management to the hotel just to keep this session from getting out of hand" leapt into my mind. But then I thought of my dad and all he'd taught me about fear.

"Max, I can see you're afraid," I said. "And I understand I don't know what it's like to be in your shoes. But we can't let our fear stop us. Remember Dr. King. What did he do when things seemed their most frightening? He kept walking and treating people with love and respect."

"Love those guys?"

"Yes, we're going to do what we always do. We're going to fall in love with everyone who's volunteered to be here and treat them with respect and dignity, even the KKK table. We're going to make sure everyone has a chance to speak and experience being heard by everyone else, regardless of their point of view."

"That won't be easy looking into those eyes."

"Then don't look into those eyes. See those men as they were when they were innocent little boys, before someone poisoned their minds. When you look at them and interact with them, see who they can be, not who they are."

"I'll do my best."

"Of course you will. Whatever happens over these next two days will happen. And what happens is all that could happen. We can't try to force this group to go anywhere other than where they're capable of going. They will get where they can get at this time."

"But what, then, is our objective for this session? What are we really working on?" Max asked.

"Our objective is to help these people speak authentically with each other about their reality and then listen generously to each other. If we accomplish no more than that, I'll consider this session a success. Are we aligned on this objective?"

"We are."

Max and I returned to the session and led the group through a series of conversations intended to have the volunteers capture their current reality. To say the conversations were challenging would be a gross understatement. There were arguments, accusations, justifications, and profanity-laced rants all morning. At lunch, the whites and blacks continued to sit separately, although the break and meal seemed to reduce the tension within the group.

After lunch, Max announced that he was going to show a brief video that demonstrated how the values, beliefs, and relationships within a team or organization profoundly impact performance. As Max began to darken the room, to everyone's astonishment, the men from the KKK table stood in unison, grabbed their chairs, and proceeded to line their seats directly in front of the projection screen. The men sat facing the group and staring in defiance as the video played, with the backs of their chairs against the screen. I knew this was the moment to which the session had been building. I signaled to Max to do nothing and allow the video to continue.

The KKK group sat leering back at their associates for the entire video, blocking the bottom third of the screen. No one said or did anything. The contrast between the KKK's obvious position and the video's message was stark and ironic.

While the video was playing, I left the room and called the plant's human resources manager, Dale, a youthful but competent professional. I told him of the situation and asked, "Can you and the local union representative please come to the session as soon as possible?" I was surprised when he agreed and said they would get there as soon as possible.

After the film finished fifteen minutes later, Max told the group we'd be taking a twenty-minute break. I walked to the hotel parking lot to meet Dale and the union officer, a white man about forty-five, dressed in pressed jeans and a flannel shirt. I approached them, introduced myself to the officer, and explained the KKK table's behavior. As I spoke, the officer's face became red with anger, and his lips pursed as he shook his head back and forth.

"Can you do something to stop this?" I said to the officer. "All we're asking is for people to speak openly and listen with respect."

The officer said without hesitation, "This bullshit will stop and now." He started to dart toward the hotel entrance when I grabbed his arm.

"Can I offer a suggestion?"

"I'm all ears."

"Instead of barging in there and laying down the law, how about you just sit with your members at their table and model the proper way to behave in a session like this. Give them an example to follow, and if they start getting out of line, gently guide them back."

"I can do that. You bet."

I was impressed with the officer's willingness to support Max and me and his members.

"Your people are fortunate to have such a strong leader as their officer," I said. The union officer gave me a tight smile and then immediately made his way to the session room.

The officer could not have been more effective. He remained the rest of the session, and the KKK table behaved appropriately the entire time. Max and I led the group through the two days, culminating with five specific recommendations the volunteers agreed to jointly present to the plant staff the afternoon of the second day.

After the lunch of the second day, Max led an exercise in which he put the white volunteers on one side of the room and the black volunteers on the opposite side. He then asked each group to list on flip charts everything they had "thought, felt, heard, or said about the other group."

The two lists were full of extremely malicious statements about the opposite group. One of the items the black group had on their list was that whites love white bread and Miracle Whip. When I expressed surprised at this, Max asked me, "Do you like white bread and Miracle Whip?"

"Yes, I love them," I replied, "but that has nothing to do with—" I was interrupted by the roaring laughter of the volunteers, both black and white.

Then Max asked one of the most important questions of the day, "What are the lessons we can take away from this exercise?"

Several people offered lessons they had learned. At one point in the debrief, a white woman stood and said, "These conversations are very uncomfortable. I don't like talking about this."

Max simply replied, "You're not supposed to be comfortable talking about this. That's the point, to get out on the table something unmentionable that's negatively affecting your performance."

One of the KKK team members named Delbert spoke up. "For me, the exercise shows we all have a lot of preconceived notions about the other group," he said, "some of which might be true of a few people but none of which are true of all."

Jeff then stood and nervously said, "I think both groups are missing the larger lesson from this exercise."

"What's that?" asked Delbert.

Jeff turned to Delbert, picked up his LSU cap from the table, and put it on with the bill facing forward. "What do you see when you look at me?"

"I see an upstanding young man."

One of the older black women said, "Someone I wish my granddaughter was dating." Everyone in the room laughed.

Then Jeff turned the bill of his LSU cap to one side and down a bit.

"Now what do you see?" he asked.

"A moron," said Delbert. Jeff turned to the woman and raised his eyebrows, indicating that he wanted her to respond as well.

"I got to admit, you do look pretty stupid. I'm not sure now I want you dating my granddaughter." Another round of laughter.

Jeff then turned his cap with the bill facing backward.

"A gang member," Delbert responded. The woman agreed.

Jeff then looked around the room for a moment, removed his cap, and softly said, "For me, what can be learned from the exercise is that we rarely see or experience the person we are with."

He then turned his attention back to Delbert and the woman. "When answering my three questions, neither of you ever saw me. Instead, you saw my cap. The person under the cap was the same in all three situations, but you never experienced him. That's our problem in this plant. We don't know each other; we only know our stories about each other, our preconceptions of each other, but not the person standing behind them. So we go about our day interacting story to story, not person to person. And from what I've learned from Cort and Max, it is our relationships that are the foundation of the performance we create together."

Jeff then put his cap back on with the bill facing backward and stepped toward the KKK table. "I don't know you gentlemen. But I've gotten to know you a little bit better than I did. I'm starting to see that you're not evil. You don't hate and fear me; you hate the story you have about people like me—a story others have given you, just like the story others try to give me about you. I hope we can get to know each other as part of this effort and, just maybe, we'll make up our own minds about each other."

I looked at Jeff Sr. as his grandson spoke. He was bursting with pride and nodding with every sentence his grandson uttered. At that moment, Max and I knew the session was going to meet its objectives.

Max and I led the group through the remainder of the day, culminating with five specific recommendations the volunteers agreed to jointly present to the plant staff later that afternoon.

Max helped the group develop their presentation while I called Dale and informed him it was time for him and the rest of the staff to make their way to the hotel. As the group practiced their presentation and made their last adjustments, Max and I sat on a bench in front of the hotel waiting for the staff to arrive. As we sat there, we congratulated ourselves for what we both felt was some of our best work. But our contentment would soon end.

A car pulled up to the hotel containing only Oscar and Dale. It stopped abruptly at the curve right in front of the bench where Max and I sat, and both of them quickly exited. Max and I stood expecting to receive congratulations. We were ready to coach the two men on how to receive their people's presentation, but to my shock, Oscar walked directly to Max and said, "I'm putting an end to this," and dashed through the hotel door. Max followed.

I stepped in front of the HR manager, blocking his path, and said, "Dale, what the hell is going on?"

Dale stopped. He could tell there was no way I was going to let him pass without an explanation. He took a deep breath, exhaled a long sigh, and proceeded to sit down on the bench. I sat next to him and waited for him to speak.

"Oscar's gotten cold feet," he said. "Some folks from the plant have been visiting him in his office the last couple of days, and they've convinced him this process is heading down a road where he doesn't want to go."

"When the lights go out, the cockroaches get to work," I said, looking down at the cement and laughing as I shook my head and clicked my tongue.

"He's had probably ten people visit him, just today."

"People who've been at this session have visited him?"

"No, no one who's at the session. Just people back at the plant. They've persuaded him that this session is a mistake. I tried my best to stop him, but the rest of the staff piled onto his fears and now he's pulling the plug on the entire thing."

"Son of a bitch, I forgot to warn him of the drift. The drift's got him by the short hairs, and it's my fault."

"The drift?"

"Never mind. I'll explain later," I said. I slapped Dale's thigh with the back of my hand, stood, and turned to the hotel entrance. "Let's get in there before he does something we'll all regret."

We proceeded to the session room. As we entered, Oscar was standing in front of the room speaking defiantly. The volunteers were mostly standing as well, having been abruptly summoned from their break by Oscar.

"I've asked Max and Cort to come help us improve our performance," Oscar said. "As you know, we've been the poorest performing plant in the company for some time, and last year a man died. But for some reason, they keep making this all about race, and I'm concerned we're just stirring up bad feelings and emotions that will do us no good."

There was a long pause as the volunteers stood in shock, many with their mouths wide open, and shook their heads as if to plead, "No! Don't do this!"

"So I've decided to end this session and pull the plug on this before it gets out of hand—"

"Baby, I don't know what session you're talking about," interrupted an older black woman who had played a pivotal role in the conversations of the past two days. "The session we've just gone through was not about race; it was about performance."

Many of the other volunteers nodded their heads up and down, their eyes focused on Oscar, as if to say, "What she said."

Oscar stood there stunned by her response, like a possum in headlights.

"I just think it's best—" he began.

"Who's been talking to you? Who changed your mind?" This time it was one of the white men who interrupted Oscar, a supervisor from the KKK table.

Oscar turned to the man, again in shock, especially since the person who spoke was the last person he'd expect to challenge him. Oscar was now the one with his mouth hanging open. It was obvious he was not prepared for this reaction.

I stepped forward. "Oscar, can we take a short break and allow the group to complete the presentation they hope to make to you and your staff?" I said. "I want to better understand your concerns and see if there's a way we can address them and still support these volunteers."

Oscar said nothing. He just nodded and proceeded to walk toward me. We left the room together. Max instructed the group to get back to work on their presentation, and he and Dale joined Oscar and me back outside. By the time they arrived, Oscar was seated on the bench, and I was sitting next to him.

"I made a fool of myself in front of my best people," he said. "This stuff, it's beyond my capability. I'm just a plant manager."

Oscar and I sat there silently for several moments while Max and Dale stood and observed.

"Oscar, none of us has ever dealt with something like this before," I replied. "It may be beyond all our capabilities. We're all scared."

"But—"

"Please hear me out before you respond." I paused to see if Oscar had accepted my request. He said nothing as he dropped his head and stared down at his well-polished shoes.

"Max and I are just as frightened as you are," I went on. "And so are your people."

"The people I just spoke to don't seem frightened," Oscar said. "Some of them are better suited to lead this place than me."

"That group is afraid as well. But they've spent two days working through their fears, and they've made a choice to move forward despite them. Today, their commitment to changing and turning around their performance is stronger than their fears."

I paused to see if Oscar needed to speak. He sat back against the bench while letting out a heavy sigh, but he said nothing. At least he was listening.

"But they won't remain that way without a leader," I said, "someone they know they can count on to stay the course, to not allow his doubts and fears to overcome him."

"I don't know if I can be that guy," Oscar replied. "There are so many back at the plant who don't want me to take us in this direction." His chin jutted out slightly, and his eyes were closed tight.

"Of course there are. But in that room you just left, there are about seventy people who are willing to help you make the changes necessary to get better performance—but only if someone leads them. They expect that person to be you. They stand ready to follow you, if you stand with them. But you have to be steady."

"I really let them down, didn't I?"

"For a moment, but you can go back in there and change all that."

"What could I say to make up for what I just said? There's no way they'll follow me. They're probably in there right now talking about what a coward I am." Oscar was once again slumped over looking at his shoes.

"Actually, they're in there working on the presentation they hope to make to you and your staff," Max said. "And they're hopeful Cort and I can help talk you off the ledge and back to being their leader."

As Oscar looked up at Max, he appeared every bit as ill and uneasy as he did after throwing up upon reading our report. He paused and turned to me.

"How do I earn back their respect?" he asked.

"First, you have to forgive yourself for not being the leader you hope and need to be," I said. "Let's face it. You fell well short of that this afternoon. All leaders fall from time to time. The trick is not to avoid falling; it's to stand right back up, brush yourself off, and march forward with renewed commitment."

Dale stepped toward Oscar. "There are a lot of folks who are going to resist you if you lead this, even some of your staff," he said. "But I'm with you, and I won't abandon you. And there are a lot more like me than you realize."

Oscar looked at him and smiled. He turned back to me and sat up, as if he'd made a decision.

"Any more advice for me before I go back in there and apologize to my people?" he asked.

I paused in appreciation of Oscar's courage. I wanted him to bask in the shower of his fears as it gave him the energy he would need upon returning to the room.

"Try to do more than apologize; tell them the truth," I responded. "Tell them this scares the shit out of you. Tell them how much you appreciate their courage and support. And if you can, tell them you will never again waver, that they can count on you no matter what comes. And then tell them what you plan to do about this session and their presentation."

"I'm not sure I'm ready to say all that."

"Say whatever you can authentically say, and you'll do fine."

We returned to the room. The volunteers became immediately silent, watching Oscar intently as he slowly walked to the center of the room. He stood there for several moments. Every eye was on him, each person waiting in anticipation. He took a deep breath while looking at the ceiling, then leveled his head, looked at his people, and spoke.

"I want to apologize to each of you for not being the leader you deserve," he began. "I've let you down today. I got scared and let some people who are even more frightened than I am convince me that I needed to end this thing."

Oscar paused and took another deep breath. He glanced at Max and me. We smiled and nodded our encouragement to continue.

"I've been outside thinking, mostly about you folks and the courage you're showing in facing up to our performance problems. And let's face it: race is a big problem we'll have to face if we're to ever get better."

I looked around the room. The collective feeling of relief was palpable. His volunteers were resting back into their seats, smiling as they nodded their heads and glanced at each other as if to say, "Thank God, he's back."

"But I have to be honest with you. I'm not sure if I can be the leader you guys need. I want to be, but I'm not sure it's in me."

"So, here's what I propose as a path forward. Please hold onto your presentation, complete your session, and head home with my appreciation of the efforts you've made. I'm going to go home as well and decide whether I can lead this plant going forward."

The group was obviously taken aback by Oscar's honesty and once again sat stunned.

"If I decide I can, I'll ask you to meet with my staff back here at this hotel for lunch tomorrow. Don't worry; we'll make the necessary arrangements to get you all back here, even if we have to shut down the plant."

Oscar then paused for a long period, taking several deep breaths and working up the nerve to say what he wanted to say.

"If I decide I can't, I'll inform my boss that it's time for me to move to a new assignment and do my best to help him find the leader you deserve. That's the least I can do for you good people."

This last statement by Oscar obviously moved the volunteers. Many eyes were glistening, including his. Several people told me later they had never seen their manager be so transparent and vulnerable. It was noticeably endearing to them.

Oscar thanked the group for their attention and departed with Dale. Max stayed behind to complete the session with the volunteers. I followed Oscar.

As I walked them to their car, I made clear Max's and my stance on the matter. Since Oscar was being more responsible for his emotional state, I felt I could be more direct with him than earlier. And he needed to know where we stood before he made his decision.

After acknowledging him for what he'd shared with the volunteers, I looked him directly in the eyes. "Oscar, I want you to be clear on where Max and I stand," I said. "If you decide tonight that you cannot lead this, then there is no need for Max or me to continue coaching you or your people."

I paused to ensure Oscar was hearing what I was saying. The dead serious look in his eyes confirmed that he was.

"If you don't call me and tell me you're up to leading this by 10:00 tonight, I'm going to call the airline, and Max and I will take the first available flight home tomorrow. Do you understand what I'm saying?'

"Yes, but what if I call and say I am?" he asked.

"Then we'll be at the plant at 6:00 tomorrow morning to meet with you. At that meeting, you'll have to convince both of us that you're truly committed to this and will not bail on us and your people ever again. If you convince us, we'll remain and coach you in preparation for the lunch with your volunteers and staff. If you don't convince us, we'll head to the airport. Am I communicating clearly?"

"I hear you loud and clear."

"Good. We're simply not willing to partner with someone who's not all in. We're destined to fail if we're partnering with anyone less than an All-In Leader."

"I get that. I'll decide tonight and let you know."

At 9:50 that night, Max knocked on my hotel room door.

"Has he called?"

"Not yet."

"I checked, and the first flight we can get tomorrow is at 2:00 in the afternoon."

"He's still got a few minutes. If we go, we go. Anyway, we've earned a good sleep-in after the last couple of days."

The phone in my room rang. It was Oscar.

"OK, I'm in. I'll see you tomorrow morning at 6:00. You and Max have a good night."

"Thanks for letting us know. See you at 6:00."

Max and I arrived at Oscar's office promptly at 6:00. His administrator escorted us into his office, where Oscar was leaning back in his chair, staring out the window at the plant. He stood and walked around his desk, shook both our hands, and invited us to sit at a table in the corner. Dale soon joined us. Oscar closed the door and turned to us.

"I left the hotel yesterday convinced I wasn't the right person to lead this plant. I was just getting ready to call and inform you of that when, at around 8:30, my doorbell rang. I went to the door and there stood Jeff Sr.

"He asked if he could speak with me. I invited him in. My wife and I sat and had coffee with him for an hour. As we chatted, it dawned on me that Jeff Sr. was the first employee to ever visit me at my home."

Max leaned forward. "What did he want to talk about?" he asked.

"His message to me was very simple. He said, 'Mr. Oscar, I've worked in your plant for over fifty years. I started when I was thirteen. My son has over twenty-five years, and my grandson is in his second year. Together, we've had the good fortune of spending over seventy-five years in your plant. But the last two days, the days with my son, grandson, and the other volunteers, those two days have been my family's best days in this plant. Please, sir, please do not take that away from us. We've waited seventy-five years for this day."

Max and I sat silently, dealing with what Oscar had just shared. Max was obviously moved by what Jeff Sr. had said. He struggled to keep his emotions intact, holding his closed fist against his nose and mouth. Once composed, Max turned to Oscar.

"How did you respond?" Max asked.

"I didn't for a while," Oscar replied. "My wife and I just looked at each other for an eternity. She and I had discussed the situation earlier and had agreed it was time for me to move on. But as we looked at each other, I could tell Jeff Sr.'s plea had a profound effect on her. She teared up, made some excuse, and went into the kitchen. I thanked Jeff Sr. and told him how much I appreciated his visit and that he was welcome in our home anytime, and he left."

No one said anything for several moments. Max and I made eye contact and signaled to each other to remain silent. Finally, Oscar walked to the window and looked out at the plant.

"I can't take that away from that man and his family. I can't abandon these people now, after years of serving me and this company, just because it's getting hard and just when they need me most."

I decided it was time to chime in. "What happened after Jeff Sr. left?" I asked.

"My wife and I sat in the kitchen and agreed to stay. In fact, she wants to have dinner with all of us tonight. She wants to be part of this thing too. It's like it's become our mission as husband and wife. We agree that together, we can help make this happen."

At that moment, I knew Max had his All-In Leader—in fact, from the sound of things, two of them. Oscar stayed true to his word. He and his staff had lunch with the volunteers that afternoon; as a team, they developed a performance improvement plan.

The following year, the plant's performance was above average in the company. The turnaround was so dramatic, Oscar and his people were presented the company's performance award for most improved. Many years later, I ran into Oscar. He told me, "I've worked a lot of years for this company, but those few years with you guys in Baton Rouge, I did the best work of my career."

Chapter 25:
The Pinnacle of Leadership

"Many are called. Few are chosen . . . and it's only because the few put themselves to it."

—Joseph Campbell

My next meeting with Michael occurred in his private conference room directly across from his office, a room in which he and I would spend countless hours over the next few years. The room was well equipped with a large wooden table and eight comfortable leather chairs. Michael's seat was at the head of the table nearest the door. Behind his chair was a projector screen with a marble counter below it for serving meals during meetings and guest visits. To the right were mounted two large LCD television monitors and a video conferencing camera. To the left, and curving all the way around the opposite end of the table, the wall was covered in whiteboard.

Michael said, "Only my staff and administrator, Lisa, have access to this room. I've asked her to give you security access as well." He sat in his customary seat and indicated for me to take a seat directly to his left, which I did, unaware it would be my seat for many future meetings.

It was obvious Michael had spent the weeks I was away considering whether to take the next step with me as his coach, and welcoming me into his private conference room was an indication of his decision. But prior to sharing his decision, I wanted him to recognize a few things about himself. Before he could speak, I spoke first.

"How would you describe a leader who has reached the pinnacle of leadership?" I asked him.

"That's not an easy question to answer," Michael responded. He sat there pondering my query for a minute, and then finally said, "I guess I'd say our CEO. He's certainly at the top of leadership."

"He is. But I want you to think beyond just a person's level in a company. What is it your CEO has that's helped him reach the top, something other leaders have in common? What describes a leader who's reached the pinnacle of leadership?"

Michael again thought for a long while. "I can't answer that. What's your answer?"

"I believe you've reached the summit of leadership when you can create extraordinary results while caring for people.

"That's it?"

"That's it."

"So, you're suggesting I'll have reached the top of leadership when my group has great business performance and my people are well taken care of?"

"That's not what I suggested; in fact, I didn't suggest anything. I declared to you that I believe you've reached the summit of leadership when you can create extraordinary results while caring for people."

"I don't understand."

"Are you a leader if you can't create extraordinary results?"

"Not likely."

"Not likely at all. The top leaders get the best results. They lead their fields, whatever those might be. This is true in sports, business, politics, and everyday life. Leaders are leaders when they get results. No results, no leader. Would you agree?"

"I would," Michael replied.

"So, we're aligned that until you can create extraordinary results, you haven't reached the summit of leadership," I said. "That's one-half of what makes a leader. Let me ask the second half in a negative way. Is it OK for a leader to create extraordinary results and harm people in the process?"

"Absolutely not," Michael asserted, his voice passionate.

"Even if the people who are harmed don't work for you?"

"It's unacceptable to create results if you have to harm anyone in the process."

"Is it acceptable for a leader to create extraordinary results and harm the planet in the process?" I asked.

"No, it's not," Michael said, the same passion in his voice.

"Is it acceptable for a leader to create extraordinary results and harm the team, the franchise, the school, the business, your neighbors, your state, your fellow citizens, or anyone else in the process?" As I listened for his response, my thoughts wandered back to my presentation years earlier where I was called a witch for uttering such foolishness.

"It's unacceptable to produce results at the expense of any of those. You just can't do it."

"Says who?"

"Well . . . says me."

"So, you're saying a person is a top leader when they can create extraordinary results while caring for all those things. Is that right?"

"Right."

"Well, then, we're completely in agreement. For you and me, it's as simple as this: when you can create extraordinary results while caring for people, you're a leader. If you can't, then you're not."

Michael nodded as I spoke. I could see I was starting to get through to him.

"Furthermore, you must be able to deliver on both halves," I continued. "It's not good enough, as you say, to create extraordinary results if it's at the expense of others, and it's equally inadequate to care for people but fall short on the results side. Leaders can do both."

"Yes, they can," he replied.

"You know," I said with a chuckle, "my Texan father used to say, 'Boy, you're half-assed no matter what cheek you're missing.'"

"That's a good one," he replied, laughing.

"It is, and I'd say it applies to your industry's predicament. Has your industry been delivering both halves of this equation? Or have you been operating half-assed, and it's finally caught up with you?"

"I'm not sure what you mean." Michael drew back in resentment to my question.

"Has your company and industry been creating extraordinary results?"

"You bet. We're in the middle of another financial boom," he said, leaning forward with pride.

"Now, while creating that boom, have you taken care of people—of all that stuff you listed a moment ago?"

"It's hard to say yes after what's just happened in the Gulf of Mexico."

"How about before the Macondo incident in the Gulf? Were you taking care of people before then?"

"Not as good as we might have. Certainly not as well as our stakeholders expected."

"In other words, you're creating extraordinary results but not caring for people. Is that a true statement?"

Michael's eyes dropped. After a moment, he looked up at me and said, "I'd be lying if I said it wasn't true."

"Fair enough," I said. "Then, given our description of a leader, you, your company, and your industry have been half-assed. You're delivering great results but at the expense of people, the planet, and your company's and industry's reputation. In other words, you aren't leading."

"You're right. It's just hard to swallow when you put it that way." Michael stood, walked to the serving counter, and retrieved two bottles of mineral water and snacks from the basket Lisa kept stocked for him.

"The good news is a leader can change all this," I said, watching him make his way back. "Someone who can create results and care for people can turn this around much quicker than you might think. And from my perspective, you're a person with the potential to be that leader."

"Because I'm the boss, right?" he said, returning to his chair and setting a bottle of water and pack of raisins in front of me.

"No, being the boss says nothing about your potential as a leader. I say you have the potential to lead a turnaround in this industry based on my observations of you. You approached me initially because you were dissatisfied with the status quo and wanted to lead a change."

"Of my organization. I didn't say I wanted to lead a change of my industry."

"No, you didn't. However, circumstances have changed, and now merely transforming your organization might not be enough.

Your first step is obviously to save your organization and, in doing so, help save your company, but someone had better change the industry as well."

"What do you see in me that tells you I'm that person?"

"Being a leader requires certain faculties, awareness, and skills," I said. "You have some of these already and, from what I can see, you're capable of acquiring the others, if you are so inclined."

"What faculties?" Michael responded. "What do I have that makes you think I can turn this around?" Michael stuck his hands out in a quandary.

"For one, you're aware. You're not drifting with the circumstances. You realize a tectonic shift has occurred, the future will be very different, and something must change if you're to succeed in that new reality."

"I do seem to be one of the few who recognizes the magnitude of what's happening."

"You are. In fact, you're the only person I've run into who is fully awake and capable to lead it out of this predicament. Not that the others are not good, talented engineers, supervisors, and managers. They're actually among the best. However, none but you, in my opinion, is ready or able to take on the type of leadership needed. Like it or not, you're the guy. The question is, are you up to being that leader?"

I looked at Michael carefully, letting the moment settle in. Michael tilted his head back in thought.

"How can I, alone, lead this industry?" he asked. "I'm just one person." Michael rose and tossed his snack package into the trash can next to the door. I could tell that a part of him wanted to exit that door and be done with this conversation.

"You won't be alone, Michael," I replied. "Some will follow you if you lead, and that's all you need. You don't need everyone in the boat with you—just enough to tip the scale in your favor. The only one who needs to change is you. You think differently, and others will think differently. You change and they'll change. Not all of them, but the right ones, the ones who are ready to follow you and grow into leaders in their own right."

"But what about the ones who don't follow?" Michael turned back to face me and leaned on the serving counter.

"They'll leave because they no longer fit in, or they'll stay and fake it so they can get along until they retire or exit. Either way, you'll do what's necessary to keep them out of the way of those who are following. It's them, the ones who have opted in and are changing, that you'll want to focus your attention on."

"So, let's say I sign up for this role and decide I'm the one to lead the industry. How would it work? What would the process look like?"

"Before we go there, I first need a decision from you. We agreed to meet today so you could tell me whether you've decided to continue engaging my coaching. Have you made your decision?"

"I'm not sure. What would you be coaching me about?" Michael returned to his seat.

"About what we've been talking about!" I shouted. "About you leading the turnaround of your organization and transformation of your industry."

"Why does it have to be that at this stage?" Michael asked in a loud, frustrated voice. He stood, walked behind his chair, and placed both hands on the chair back. "Why can't you just teach me about being a better leader . . . teach me about leadership? Why do I have to agree to change the world before you can coach me?" By now Michael's hands were waving in the air as he spoke. It was obvious I was asking him to do something of which he was not sure he was capable.

I said in a soft tone, "Michael, sit down. And please try to stay seated."

Michael dropped into his chair and let out a long sigh. I lowered my voice and spoke gently.

"Again, you won't be changing the world. You won't even be changing your industry or your people. All you will be changing is you. That's what leaders do. They get better, and everyone around them gets better. You want me to teach you about leadership? Well, that's lesson one."

I slowly began returning my voice to a more normal tone. "And by the way, leadership is not about learning about leadership; it's about learning about yourself. That can't happen in a classroom. It pains me to see companies waste their resources on leadership courses. They send their managers, without any meaningful assessment of their leadership potential, to courses designed by academics who themselves possess virtually no leadership faculties or skills. And then they're disappointed when the managers return unchanged.

"You don't become a leader by attending a leadership class," I continued. "Anyone can do that. You become a leader by doing something few others are even willing to take on, like leading the turnaround of a business unit or industry."

Michael was watching me carefully, listening to every word, but I could see objections rising to the surface.

"I get it. I really do," he said. "But why save my industry? Why not just improve my organization? Why do we have to aim so high?"

"Because that's what leaders do," I said. "You want lesson two about leadership? Here it is: leaders play a big game. And they do so for three reasons. First, who wants to waste a good leader on a small game? I could agree to coach you about some small game, but that'd be a colossal waste of the rare commodity you are. Leaders like you are literally one in thousands. It would be a crime to waste that, especially when your industry is crying out for a leader.

"Second, leaders know that to enlist any meaningful followers—ones who can and will lead on their own—they must invite them into a big game. Who's going to follow a leader into a small game? As a colleague of mine used to say, 'We don't remember Dr. King because he said he had a strategic plan.'"

I paused a moment and let the King quote sink in. Michael offered a shy grin.

"And third, it has to be a big game because I don't coach people who play anything less. Like all leaders, I won't play a small game. Where's the fun in that? I coach leaders who are all in and willing to put themselves in service of a big game. And I can't think of a more meaningful or larger game than helping you first transform your organization and then, having created that foundation, lead this industry into a new future."

There was a long pause. Michael and I sat in silence as he contemplated the weight of what I'd said. This is the moment I come to with every potential All-In Leader—the moment when he realizes the magnitude of what he's considering and asks himself whether he's up to my invitation. He must decide whether he trusts himself and me enough to accept the call.

I left Michael alone with his thoughts and excused myself to take a short break. When I returned, Michael was sitting completely still, reflecting on my invitation. I sat down close to him and said, "Michael, it is perfectly OK to say no to what I've proposed."

Michael looked up at me with surprise and started to speak, but before he could, I continued, "You can join the others around you and drift into the future like they are. Believe me; they'll accept you with open arms. You can complete your last few years of tenure here and enjoy a nice retirement. No one will blame you if you choose not to lead. In fact, you and I will be the only ones who'll ever know that you even considered doing so."

He watched me thoughtfully as I went on. "I've purposely placed a fork in the road in front of you. One branch leads to a life of drifting. You'll be like Lieutenant Dan in the movie *Forrest Gump*, drifting along, doing his duty, following orders, and destined to die on the field of battle. That path is well lit, and you'll have lots of company along the way. But let me warn you, that path can rob you of your destiny. You won't actually die on the battlefield, but your spirit will.

"The other branch leads to a life of leading, and when you first take it, you won't find anyone there but me. I'll be waiting to support you if you choose to take that path. And for a long part of the journey, especially at the beginning, you and I will be alone. But if you invite others to join you, as I have you, they'll follow. Not all, but enough."

I was quiet for a long while, letting Michael think. He somehow knew I didn't expect him to respond.

"The choice is yours, Michael," I said. "You contact me once you've decided, and if you choose to commit to leading, I'll make two promises. I'll hear your commitment and hold you to it, and I'll guide you to being the leader necessary to transform this organization and turn this industry around—the leader you already are but have not yet fully realized. When you make your choice, let me know. I'll accept either. Thanks for considering my invitation."

I left Michael in his conference room. Although I've had this conversation with many people, to this day, I never know what they might choose. There is so much that goes into such a momentous decision. I was, as I had told Michael, perfectly OK with either choice, and something told me Michael would make his decision quickly. I was right. The next day, Michael called me into his office.

"I'm all in," he said before I even sat down. "What's the first step?"

"The first step is we negotiate a simple coaching contract where you and I get clear on roles and expectations," I said.

"Great. Let's get to it," Michael replied.

We immediately sat at his office table.

Michael's demeanor was very different than the day before. There was no reservation or hesitation in him at all. He was all in, alright, and ready to get going. He'd made his choice quickly—in fact, quicker than do most of my clients.

"The contract works like this," I said. "We'll partner in developing a strategy and plan for first turning your organization around, and once we've accomplished that, we'll turn our attention to transforming the industry. I estimate it will take you eighteen to thirty-six months to do the first.

"Then, with the turnaround behind you, you'll turn to transforming your industry. All the while, I'll be in the wings as any guide should be. You'll be the face of the change, and I'll essentially be invisible. You and your followers will take all the credit, and I'll enjoy watching you receive the accolades you've earned."

Michael said nothing but sat quietly, listening to all I had to say.

"I'll be the one person in your life who tells you the truth," I went on. "I'll let you know exactly how you're perceived by your followers and critics, what you're doing that's working, what you need to adapt or adjust, and what you need to stop that isn't working.

"When I offer you coaching, you'll either accept it, decline it, or propose an alternative. If you and I agree on something that you're to do, you'll follow through, or I'll be very upset with you. On the other hand, if I commit something to you and don't follow through, you'll be upset with me.

"And when there are breakdowns, we won't keep our upsets to ourselves or share them with others. We'll take them directly to each other, get them on the table, deal with them, and move on. Do you understand and agree to my terms?"

"Yes," Michael replied. "Let's get on with it."

"Wait a minute," I said. "We are getting on with it. We're negotiating the terms under which our partnership will operate. We have to get this right or we'll pay a heavy price later on. This negotiation is important, and by the way, you'll be having this same type of conversation soon with your potential followers. This is what leading looks and sounds like. So, again, do you understand and accept my terms?"

"Sorry, I'm just eager to get going. Yes, yes, I do understand and accept your terms."

"Fine. And do you have any terms of your own?"

"Only this: Just don't ever bullshit me. Don't hesitate to give it to me straight when I need it."

"I'll be straight with you always, even when you don't need it. And if I'm ever not, you should fire me."

"Agreed."

"So, now for the first step," I said. "I want you to imagine that you have a grand invitation you want to share with your people. A possibility that you want them to consider and either accept or decline. In your case, it's the possibility that the future of your organization and industry can be very positive, even in the face of the Macondo tragedy and all its aftermath. How might you go about putting that invitation and possibility in front of your people?"

"I'm not sure," Michael said.

"Would you send them an email?"

Michael scoffed. "Of course not. I can do better than that."

"What's the best you can do? What's the most creative and impactful way you can imagine of putting that possibility and invitation in front of your people?"

Michael thought long and hard, the idea forming slowly and carefully. Finally, he looked at me with the appearance of one with a great story to share.

"We could call a large meeting and invite my managers and supervisors most essential to the change," he said.

"Tell me more."

"I'll share my vision of the future and invite them to join me in making it happen. That'll give them the opportunity to make a choice to opt in and follow me or opt out. But how will I know what they choose?"

"You might not know for sure, and it's not important at that stage that you do. What's most important at this meeting is the future you offer them. We have to get that right. Everything else hangs on it. It must be extremely compelling—something they want to be a part of making happen. In fact, it needs to be so captivating that a critical mass of them say to themselves, 'I want to be a part of that future so much I'm willing to change to make it happen.' They must go through an experience in which they change their relationship to you and their future and choose to embrace both."

"Keep talking. I'm liking what I'm hearing. Sounds like you've done something like this before."

"I have, many times. Arranging for the meeting, which you might call a summit, is easy. All we need to do is schedule the venue and work the logistics. Anyone can do that. In fact, most organizations do that annually—they get their people together and inform them of last year's performance and next year's goals. It's what I've seen you do at your communications sessions."

"I love those sessions. Are you saying doing those was wrong?"

"They're fine if you want to inform people and have next year be some version of this year, maybe a little improved . . . in other words, for an organization that's OK with drifting into the future. But if you want to transform your organization and create a totally different future, to lead people into the future, those sessions are grossly insufficient."

"Then what would be sufficient?"

"A summit like the one we're exploring where you place your managers in a container."

"A container?" Michael asked.

"The container I speak of is a psychological container. You'll start creating the container with how you invite the participants, and you'll end it with your closing comments on the last day. This means your people will be in this container for weeks."

"Weeks?"

"That's right. Think of it as an old-fashioned popcorn popper. Remember the ones where you placed the oil and kernels inside the popper, attached the lid, and turned up the heat?"

"Sure. We had a round one when I was a kid with a transparent domed lid."

"Exactly. That's what you're going to create with your summit. The summit process is the popper itself, the people are the kernels, your vision is the oil, and you're the source of the heat. The trick will be to orchestrate this entire event in a way where as many of the kernels pop as possible. If the container doesn't get hot enough, no kernels will pop, and if it gets too hot, the kernels will burn. You'll also have to understand going in that even if you get the temperature perfect, there will always be some kernels that don't pop—but as I've said from the beginning, you don't need them all, just enough to tip the scale in your favor at that stage."

"This sounds complicated."

"Oh, it is. Extremely. It'll require meticulous planning and preparation by a team of people, and you'll spend hours, with my guidance, developing your vision and preparing yourself to lead the summit. A summit like this is something very few people know how to do and even fewer can pull off. But I know how to do it, and I'm convinced you're a leader who can pull it off."

"You sure about this? A summit is the right way to go?" Michael asked. "I only offered it as one possibility."

"It is," I replied. "It's the first step in any movement. That's what you're leading—a movement to change your organization and your industry. And the first thing any leader of a movement needs is what?"

"Followers. I get it now. But how many followers will I need?"

"My answer may shock you. You only need a few."

"A few? I have over five hundred people! How can a few be enough?"

"How many matches does it take to start a forest fire? How many leaders and followers were needed to create Apple? It took one leader and one follower. You're forgetting the principle I offered you: the only person who needs to change is you. That principle applies to everyone associated with the change. Believe me, you and a few others can transform this organization. You'll lead your few followers, and they'll lead and grow other followers, and so on."

"OK, I trust your experience."

"Why not trust your own experience?"

"What do you mean? I've never experienced anything like this."

"Of course you have. I've led you through this entire process over the last few weeks."

"You have?"

"Yes. Through the series of conversations we've had, I intentionally placed you in a container and turned up the heat. I kept the heat on while you simmered and ultimately chose to pop when you said to me, 'I'm all in.' At that moment, I knew you had popped and were ready to get going. Looking back, can you see that's what happened?"

"I guess I do. Yeah, I see that now."

"Good. But I want to be crystal clear that I didn't make you pop. I only created the container where you could pop if you chose to. The same will be so with your summit. Your job will not be to make people pop—if you try to do that, you'll burn the kernels. Your job will be to create and maintain the container long enough so people have time to consider your invitation and choose whether to pop. And by that, I mean to accept it and choose to follow you."

"I get it now. I'm excited about the summit," Michael said. He rubbed his hands together. "What's next?"

"We've got to get moving on two fronts: the team you and I will work with to design and plan the summit itself and the vision you'll offer the participants."

Michael and I completed this coaching session by deciding who he would invite to lead and populate the planning team and how they would be recruited. We also aligned on the process we would use to develop his vision for the future.

I left the meeting more confident than ever that I had chosen to partner with the right person. I was looking forward to the three months of work leading to the day Michael would stand before his people at his summit.

Chapter 26:
The Vision

"Frank O'Connor, the Irish writer, tells in one of his books how, as a boy, he and his friends would make their way across the countryside, and when they came to an orchard wall that seemed too high and too doubtful to try and too difficult to permit their voyage to continue, they took off their hats and tossed them over the wall—and then they had no choice but to follow them. This Nation has tossed its cap over the wall of space, and we have no choice but to follow it."

—John F. Kennedy, remarks at the dedication of the
Aerospace Medical Health Center, San Antonio, Texas,
November 21, 1963

"Intentions compressed into words enfold magical power."

—Deepak Chopra

Michael and I formed the summit planning team, and the group began meeting. Their first assignment was to develop the invitation Michael would send to the invitees. Michael identified his invitee list by telling the planning team, "I want to invite those

I feel must be in the boat with me from the beginning." He landed on eighty people.

Coaching the planning team relative to the invitations was equally as simple. First, I instructed them to come up with an invitation that sent an unmistakable message that this event was special and different; second, capture the invitees' attention and cause a "buzz" within the invitee community; and third, make sure they knew this was a personal invitation from Michael.

The team came up with the idea of using a 3-D picture slide viewer as the main mechanism for the invitations. They placed viewers in a black box branded with graphics the team developed for the summit and sat the invites on each of the eighty people's desks while they were away. When the invitees returned to their offices, they found the box, opened it, put the viewer to their eyes, and were surprised to see pictures of Michael with a message inviting them to the summit.

The approach could not have been more effective. Not only did it create the intended buzz, but it generated much anticipation for the summit itself. Several of the invitees visited Michael in his office and shared with him how honored they were that he viewed them as a leader and how much they were looking forward to his summit.

Once the invitations were out, it was time for us to turn our attention to Michael and the vision he would offer to the summit attendees. We met in his conference room one afternoon.

"A few weeks ago," I began, "I said of all the preparations you'll do for your summit, your vision is the most important."

"Yeah, you said something like, 'We gotta get it right,'" Michael recalled.

"Precisely. And because it's so critical, I propose we spend several weeks meeting off and on until I help you get it just right. Are you up for that?"

"That's more than I expected. But OK, I'm up to whatever it takes."

"Great. Let's start by me explaining the process I suggest we use."

I went on to detail for Michael how I'd interview him for about an hour or so each week and ask questions intended to help him see the vision for himself. Once he'd given me enough of a picture of what his vision was, we'd shift gears, and I would help him write it down so it could be shared with the attendees. I would then assist him in preparing to present his vision to the invitees of the summit. So, three steps: interviewing, writing, and preparing to deliver the message. Michael agreed to the process.

"Then let's begin," I said. "Let's spend the next hour exploring the future you'll be leading from and inviting the participants to join you in creating that future."

"Leading from?" Michael asked. "I'm not sure what you mean by that."

"Good question. Up to now, I've been speaking in the way most people think of leading— leading forward, into the future. But actually, the best leaders don't lead into the future, they lead from it."

"I'm still not following. I don't see the difference between the two."

"Let me see if I can distinguish the two for you. Leading into the future is not really leading; it's just good management. It involves developing a strategy and plan to get from the present to the future and then executing that plan. In this way, the future is predictable; it's known and doable. All that's required to bring a predictable future into being is to follow the plan from A to B. This type of so-called leading is done every day in business and elsewhere. Am I making sense so far?"

Michael nodded.

"Good," I said. "Don't hesitate to stop me if I lose you because this next part can be more difficult to grasp. Now, what I call leading is very different than good management. It's not better, just different. We need good management as much as good leadership.

"When leading, there's no strategy or plan, at least not until well along in the process. The future is not predictable—in fact, that's the very essence of leadership. Leaders lead to where no one has gone before, into a future that doesn't exist and would never exist if not for the leader's vision and leadership."

"I'm with you so far," Michael said. "But why leading from the future?"

"Because that's the place from which leaders lead. They stand in that future and look back to others and say, 'Hey, join me over here. Follow me, and together we'll create a new and better future.'

"I'm proposing that's what you do at your summit," I added. "You alone will be standing in the future, the future you'll spend the next few weeks articulating, and you'll look back at the invitees and say, 'Join me over here in this future, and we'll create it together.' And then they'll spend much of the summit considering your invitation."

"I like it," Michael said.

"Great. Now, let me ask you a few questions about your vision."

"This is where it's going to get tough. I mean, I've never done anything like this before." Michael rose and began erasing some marker dust from the whiteboard. I waited as he confronted his fear. He turned back to me and placed the eraser on the table, staring at his reflection in the LCD monitors on the other side.

"But now that the invitations are out, there's no turning back," he said. "I have to succeed, or I'll let my people down."

I rose and placed the eraser back in its holder on the whiteboard. I turned and stood next to Michael, speaking to his image in the TV screen.

"You're right," I said. "You've never done this. But I have, and I've helped a lot of leaders with their visions. And no, it won't be easy to envision the future, and the summit won't be easy either. But on the last day of that summit, when everyone else is gone, you're going to look at me and say, 'I did it,' and you're going to tell me something like, 'This is the most fun I've ever had at work and the most meaningful work I've ever done.'"

I pointed Michael toward his chair. As he sat, he picked up a marker from the table and began twirling it in his right hand while biting his lower lip and looking at the tabletop. I waited until his eyes rose to mine.

"If we're going to be successful, Michael, I need you to place your doubts aside. Trust that you signed up with the right guy, and believe you already have everything you need to pull this off. I want you to have faith in the process that we'll cocreate. Can you do that?"

Michael paused, staring at me with wide eyes. He placed the marker back on the table, looked up at the ceiling, took a long, deep breath, and exhaled. Then he looked back at me.

"I trust us, Cort, and I'll trust the process," Michael answered.

"Thank you, Michael," I replied. "Let's take a break and get some coffee."

We left for a fifteen-minute break. I arrived back just a few seconds before Michael. As we took our seats, I continued our earlier conversation.

"Before I ask you about your vision," I said, "I want to point out that the circumstance you described before we broke—having no choice but to go forward, not being able to turn back—well, that's what's known as commitment."

"Please don't use that word," Michael replied. "I'm so tired of that word."

"Me too. It's way overused and often misused. I just want you to understand what's happening to you, and I don't have a better label to give it than commitment. Can you forget everything you know and feel about that word and let me redefine it for us?"

"I'll try." Michael's face gave away his skepticism.

"I define commitment as 'an intentional choice to eliminate all choices but the choice to move forward,'" I said.

"That sounds like a load of consultant-speak. Try using English this time." Michael leaned back in his chair and turned away from me and toward the door. I could see that I was at risk of overstaying my welcome, but I wanted Michael to get my point about commitment.

"Michael," I replied in a calm tone, "I did use simple English. Try and listen to what I'm saying without hearing consultant-speak."

Michael said nothing, so I continued. "Commitment is an intentional choice to eliminate all choices but the choice to move forward. It's what you've done with the summit invitations. You sent them out knowing that the moment you did, you were obliged. You had to go forward. Did you not realize that?"

"I did. That's why it was so hard to do." Michael turned back in my direction.

"Yes, but you did it anyway. Why?"

"Because this was too important for me not to."

"And you made an intentional choice to eliminate, for yourself, any other option but to now go forward. When you made that choice, I knew you'd committed. But I'm making a point here that I'm not sure is landing with you."

"What's that?" Michael leaned in to get my point.

"That leaders do what you did intentionally. They orchestrate the circumstances and events so that they have no choice but to go forward."

"Give me an example."

"Burning the ships so there's no way to return home," I replied. "Blowing up the bridge behind you so there's no possibility of retreat. Signing the Declaration of Independence. Kennedy declaring we were going to the moon. And while we're on the subject of declaration, declaring in front of friends and family that you'll love and honor another person until death do you part. All of these meet my definition of commitment."

"The best we do around here is to all sign a poster," Michael said, chuckling.

"There's nothing wrong with that approach if it eliminates any choice but the choice to move forward. If it doesn't, however, I'm not sure there's much value in it. In that case, it certainly wouldn't be what I define as commitment."

I then stood, picked up the marker Michael had been playing with, walked over to the whiteboard, and drew a symbol, which consisted of a two-foot-long straight line with a large, rounded "W" resting on the top of the line.

I pointed to the symbol and said, "The upshot is, if this doesn't happen, we're wasting our time."

"What the hell is that?" Michael asked.

"That is the international symbol of commitment," I said, and then paused for a few seconds while Michael attempted to solve my riddle. Michael's head tilted back and forth several times. I finally pointed to the symbol and said, "Butt on the line?"

Michael groaned and laughed, closing his eyes and shaking his head. "I like that one. But I do see a theme with you, Cort. I mean, butt on the line . . . half-assed?"

"That's the last one," I said, laughing. "I promise." Michael raised his eyebrows and smiled as though he didn't believe me.

"The point here," I continued, "is that the first step to creating an unpredictable future is for someone to commit to it. In this case, that someone had to be you for reasons we've discussed many times.

"But if you'd somehow been unable to make that choice, this future of yours would never have had a chance. However, you did make that choice, and that's a huge accomplishment for someone who's just beginning their journey as a leader. And I wanted you to be fully aware that it's you who made that choice, of your own free will, and that's, as I have said, exactly what leaders do."

"Thanks for helping me realize that. I did do what you're describing, and it does help to understand that I did," Michael replied.

"You're very welcome," I said.

"But going forward, can we try to avoid the word commitment? If I get up in front of my people and start using that word, they'll literally puke. I'll lose them in an instant."

"No problem. The only person who has to commit to your vision is you, the person leading from it. There are other ways to speak about commitment that are much simpler to discuss and understand. My favorite is to simply talk about being 'all in.' When you're all in, there's no option other than to move ahead—there's no retreating or returning back to the status quo. At the summit, you'll not be asking or attempting to get anyone to commit to your vision. But through the summit process we'll design, some people will willingly choose to be all in and follow you."

"And I only need a few, right?"

"Right," I said. I looked at my watch. "We only have a few minutes left, and I want to be sure we begin working on your vision. Can we spend our last few minutes together doing that?"

"Of course," he replied. "But I've got another meeting in ten minutes."

"That's plenty of time. I just need to give you an assignment to complete before the next time we meet. I want you working on this assignment everywhere you go for several days. It's a mental exercise and will take only mental energy and virtually no time out of your calendar."

"OK, shoot."

"I want you to imagine that you go to sleep, and while you're asleep, you're magically transported to another universe exactly like this one—"

"We've done this exercise," Michael interrupted.

"We've done a version of this exercise, but this one is a little different. I want you to imagine that you go to sleep, and while you're asleep, you're magically transported to another universe exactly like this one . . . down to the last detail, the last molecule. And in that universe exists you, me, your people, your company, your industry, and everything else you know in your world.

"There's one thing that's different about the universe you've woken up in. In that universe, Michael and his people have already accomplished the turnaround that you hope to lead."

"Lucky sons of bitches," Michael chuckled.

"Your assignment is to spend a few moments throughout your days, when you have time to daydream, and imagine yourself in that universe, in that industry and company, and with those people. I want you to use all your senses and see, listen, and feel what would be different about that world, one where your vision already exists.

"What would you notice that's different about the people, their beliefs, their values, their myths and legends?" I continued. "What would be different about their processes and systems, their metrics and measures? How would people feel about their industry, their company, their leaders, about you? What would the work environment look and sound like? What would be on the walls? What would the working conditions be like? How would people work together?

"And then, finally," I added, "what would you notice about that Michael? How would he speak? What would he believe about himself, his people, and his industry? What would he say? What would he do differently than you? What would he not do that you do? What would he do that you don't do? What would he know and be able to do that you can't?"

Michael looked at me thoughtfully as I continued. "The assignment is to ask yourself these questions, over and over, for the next few weeks and just see what comes up for you. Don't try to force it. This is not problem-solving; it's a very different type of inquiry, and it's something leaders do often. This exercise is intended to help you start developing your ability to imagine the future, not to predict—that's a management skill. To imagine, to dream—that's a leadership skill."

"I'll do my best," Michael said. "Would you send me a list of those questions?"

"I will if you'll promise to read them at the beginning of each day," I replied.

"Deal."

Michael left for his next appointment. I emailed him a summary of our meeting with an outline of the "parallel universe" assignment. It would be three weeks before we met again.

I interviewed Michael in his conference room approximately six times over the next couple of months, asking him about what he envisioned for his organization, his industry, and his people. Gradually, a vision for the future began to emerge. Ultimately, Michael was able to craft a two-page letter to his people that shared his concerns about where they and their industry were headed and articulated his vision for the future.

I asked the summit planning team to review and edit Michael's "vision letter," as it came to be called, and brand it with special summit graphics they had developed. It was to be printed on one piece of paper, front and back, and distributed at the summit. Then I turned my attention back to Michael. It was time to enroll him in honing his delivery skills.

At our next meeting, I said to Michael, "You've made a lot of progress. You've formed a planning team that's excited about the summit and working hard on the preparations. You've identified your key leaders and sent them an attention-getting invitation. You're close to having a vision you'll offer the attendees. The next item on our summit checklist is you."

"Me?" Michael asked.

"Yes, you. We need to get you ready to offer that vision in a powerful manner."

"I assumed we'd just hand out the vision document."

"We will," I said, "but not until after you've offered your vision to your people. Never forget, Michael, it's your vision—you authored it, and you'll use it to author a new future for your people and your industry."

"Author the future? What does that mean?"

"Many, if not most, people relate to the future as if it is preordained. But leaders know the future is a blank page waiting for them to author and their followers to build. Dr. King authored the future when he shared his dream. His followers then went to work making it a reality."

"But I'm no Dr. King."

"No, you're not. There's only one Dr. King. But never forget: there's only one Michael."

I paused for a moment to let Michael absorb what I had said before continuing. "As human beings, we determine our future through thoughts, words, and deeds. It's as simple as that. Change what you and your people think, and the future changes. Change what you and your people say and do, and the future changes."

"So, at the summit, I'm going to change how people think, what they say and do?" Michael asked.

"No," I replied. "Again, the only person who needs to change is you. At your summit, you're going to show your people a changed Michael, one who thinks, talks, and acts differently. One whose thoughts, words, and deeds are an embodiment of the vision you'll be offering them. It's critical that at the summit, you're completely in tune with your vision.

"Think of it this way," I continued. "Your vision is the sheet of music, and you're the instrument on which it'll be played. If you're out of tune, the music won't resonate as well as if you are."

"And you're saying I need to be tuned," Michael said.

"You're very much out of tune with your vision, but that's to be expected. This new way of thinking and being is as new to you as to them. Leaders are often just a few steps ahead of their followers. But with a little effort and practice, you can be primed to deliver your vision at the summit. And when you do, it'll be music to some of your people's ears—the ones who will become your followers."

"What do I need to do?"

"In short, you need to learn how to look and sound like a leader."

"I figured I'd just make up some slides and give a presentation."

"That's not what I suggest at all. Leaders don't give presentations with slides. They don't read from teleprompters, either. Managers make presentations. Politicians read from teleprompters. Leaders hold conversations with their people, and that's what you must do at your summit."

"How can I have a conversation with eighty people?"

"You will learn, that's how," I replied. "The main idea is that you'll have a one-on-one conversation with every one of those eighty people. I suggest we erect a large backdrop behind you with an image that captures the spirit of your summit—'leading from the future.' Then you'll stand in front of your people, alone, in front of that backdrop, and share your vision. But when you do, you won't think of it as making a presentation to a group of eighty people. You'll think of it as an intimate conversation with each one of them. There is a powerful message you must send."

"Which is?" Michael asked.

"I am Michael," I answered. "I'm standing for a different future. I say it can be different. I say it can be better. I'm declaring to each of you that future. And I'm inviting you to join me in making it happen."

"I have a dream," Michael said.

"Exactly. You'll stand in front of your people and author the future for them. They'll then engage with that future and ultimately choose whether they accept or decline your invitation. Those who pop and decide to join you will choose to eliminate all choices but the choice to move forward. They'll be standing with you."

"It's all coming together for me. I can see it now. This will work."

"Of course it will, but there's a lot to be done to get you ready. I see two areas where you need to focus your attention."

"What areas?"

"First, if you want to be seen as a leader, you have to sound like one," I said. "A leader can have a wonderfully written vision, which by the way, you do have. But if the delivery doesn't equal the might of the vision, the context and content of what you say will be lost. I want you to work with an associate of mine who will help you hone your delivery so that it's of the same quality as your vision. Are you willing to invest a few days' time with him?"

"Yes, but what will he do with me?" Michael replied.

"He'll make sure you sound and look like a leader. He'll help make sure your instrument is in tune. He'll teach you how to use your voice, your inflections, your eyes, your expressions, your hands, and your body to communicate effectively. He'll also teach you how to deliver your vision in a way where you create STAR moments. That's the second thing you'll need to work on."

I went on to tell Michael that STAR moments are "something they'll always remember" moments. I explained that my associate would help identify those moments in his vision and deliver them in a way his people would never forget.

"Trust me, it'll be fun," I said. "And we'll find a place where you two can work in private so you'll be comfortable trying out what he teaches you."

"I'll reserve the auditorium downstairs for our practice sessions," Michael replied. "What's the second thing I need to work on?"

"Before I answer that, I want to ask you, when you look at your vision, what are the STAR moments—the elements of your vision that have the most effect on you emotionally, the ones you'll always remember?"

Michael thought for a moment. "For me, there are a few that are really big."

"Read them, please," I said, handing Michael his vision draft.

Michael looked over the document and then began reading,

"We hold great responsibility in our hands. Not a day goes by in which I don't feel humbled by this. For me, there is a strong sense of pride in the contribution our people make, both to our nation's security and the luxuries of daily life. But it scares the hell out of me when I think about what could happen to our planet and its people if we were to fail in that responsibility.

"The conversations we'll have over the next few days carry an enormous weight. Lives will be saved or lost based on our discussions and the resulting actions. If we succeed at the immense task ahead, a bright and promising future awaits our world and its people; if we fail, that future is equally dark."

Michael stopped reading and looked up at me through glistening eyes. I could see his words touched him, which is always the case with a leader. Leaders cannot touch others if they are not touched by their own words.

"Well put, Michael," I said. "Is there another STAR moment for you?"

Michael browsed the document for a moment and then read, "In the future, the world will see us differently. Never again will a president call us 'criminals.' Instead, our people will be honored just like other men and women of service who work to assure the safety and well-being of their fellow citizens. The global community will celebrate us alongside firefighters, police, and the military for our contribution to their nations and the world. World leaders will give national addresses from our drill ships, thanking us for our sacrifice. Our people will think of themselves as elite professionals who contribute to the freedom and security of the world."

"In the sixties, we looked up to aerospace engineers and astronauts. Future generations will hear stories and listen to history lessons about the incredible trials we overcame to give them a bright future. Kids will grow up wanting to become 'heroes' like us."

Michael paused and looked at me. "That's where I've attempted to paint a picture of what the future could be for our industry," he said.

"And your people," I added. "It's very well done, and I agree that'll be a STAR moment for the people in the room. Is there another STAR moment for you personally that you see in your vision?"

Michael glanced through the document one more time. "There's this part where I speak about me."

"Read it," I said.

Michael read, "I now want to discuss me, because when I think of that future, I see a changed Michael. I see a transformed individual leading in a new way.

"Today, I see myself as a senior drilling manager who constantly needs to know what is happening and what everyone is doing. But in the future, I won't think about my work that way. I'll recognize that I'm not there to drill wells but instead to foster a compelling vision. I'll know I'm responsible for instilling pride and commitment to that vision. My job, and the jobs of many in this room, will not be to fight today's fires but rather to impart knowledge, build competency, and mentor those we lead.

"I won't be troubled by daily issues as I often am today. Those will be challenges for the people I'm leading to solve—people I will have every confidence in to handle those problems without my intervention. My energy will instead be used creating work environments that build a sense of value, purpose, pride, confidence, and positivity. I will leave the important job of planning, drilling, and completing wells to capable people; my job will be to establish an environment in which they can do their best work to protect and support the world around them.

"This is where I start to bring them into the conversation," Michael said, "where I get them to start seeing me differently and hopefully themselves too."

"I agree," I replied, "and it's just the right balance. At this point, as the person leading, most of your speaking needs to be about you . . . the future you're declaring and how, in that future, you'll be different."

"Good point."

"I'll put you in touch with my associate so you and he can begin honing your delivery. I encourage you to read your vision often, aloud, so that your mind and body get used to saying those words. For you to be most effective, you must get your vision in your bones. It needs to transition from something you wrote to who you are. You need to have said your vision so many times that it's not something you've memorized but something you'll always remember."

At this, I stood, said good-bye, and walked out. Behind me, Michael sat staring at his vision letter, as if attempting to absorb every sentence, every word, down to the last period.

Chapter 27:
The Corporate Audit

"I know one senior manager who keeps up his visibility by sending occasional e-mails to important people in the organization, and every quarter coming up with a really good idea. The rest of his time, he spends playing tennis."

—"Dear Lucy" blog post from *The Financial Times*

While Michael and his summit project team were busy preparing, I received a call from a past client, Ed, who had changed companies a couple of years prior. I hadn't conversed with Ed for several years, other than the occasional season's greetings note, and was pleased to hear his voice. He cut right to it.

"I've somehow allowed myself to be the victim of a corporate compliance audit comparing us to our company's new operational standards," he said.

"You have my sympathy," I replied.

Ed snickered and continued. "The auditors will be sitting down with me to share their findings. They want to get my reaction before they finalize their report. I'd like you to be here to help me prepare my response to their findings and coach me during that meeting. I should only need you three or four days."

"Tell me more about how you became the victim of this audit."

"Well, a few of the other business units have gone through this audit. My manager floated the idea in a meeting a few months ago, and in a moment of weakness, I said yes."

"Like a fish on a hook."

"Yeah, that pretty much describes it."

"What's your assessment of the auditors?"

"Actually, I've been very impressed with them. They both have significant industry experience, but I get the idea they're new to auditing and can use some help there."

"I'll support you in whatever way you feel appropriate and them as much as they'll let me. So when's this meeting?"

"Next Tuesday."

"Next Tuesday?"

"Yes, I'm sorry for the short notice, but I've been distracted while they've been doing their audit and forgot to call you until now. Can you make it?"

"I can, but it'll cost you my last-minute add-on fee."

"What's that?"

"Thursday night, you'll host me at the Red Sox game. I see they're in town playing the Rangers."

"You've got it."

We met with the auditors Tuesday morning. Ed was right—they did know their stuff and had identified some significant shortfalls in Ed's organization. And as he suspected, they were unskilled in communicating their findings and writing an effective report. Their draft report, which was over seventy-five pages and seemed to be one run-on sentence, was as painful to read as their presentation was to sit through.

During a break, I suggested to Ed that he offer them my coaching and support. He did so when we reconvened, and they were surprisingly open to any support I might give. The auditors asked to meet a second time Thursday afternoon, after they had time to work with me on their report. Ed agreed.

The auditors and I spent all day Wednesday condensing the report down to a one-page executive summary with nineteen pages of backup data and information. I also coached the auditors on how to present the findings so Ed could understand them and take action.

Late Thursday morning, I met with Ed to share a concern I had with his leadership. As I sat across from Ed, I noticed he was just as thin and tall as I remembered him. His short hair, starched shirt, and pressed pants were remnants from his days as a Marine officer. Ed had always possessed great technical skill and knowledge but despite his military training, was often lacking "situational awareness."

"I want to chat with you about the findings the auditors are going to report," I began.

"We're meeting on that this afternoon, aren't we?" Ed replied. He leaned back in his chair. Ed was only a few years from retirement, and it showed in his body language.

"You're meeting then with the auditors; I want to meet with you before. I'm concerned you're taking this audit too casually and don't see the threat it is to you and your team."

"Threat? There's no threat. I invited them in, for Christ's sake."

"Hear me out. Is it possible I might be able to see something from my vantage point that you cannot?"

"I guess. I forgot what a pain in the ass you can be sometimes."

"Better the pain of dealing with me than with your management after they see your audit report."

"What do you mean by that? The report's not so bad, and anyway, no one expects us to be perfect. Besides, my boss has my back."

"It's not your boss I'm concerned about. It's the bosses above him. What are you going to do when one of them gets her mitts on this report and calls you up to her office to explain the findings?"

"Oh, it will never make it that high." Ed looked sure of himself.

"I'm not going to argue with you whether it will or won't," I responded. "I'm asking, what if it does? Don't you want to be prepared for that contingency?"

"Really, Cort, I'm not going to invest time on the off chance they see it. I have better things to do."

"A boss I once worked for wished he'd done so. He was like you. He had a cavalier attitude to an audit like this. He went from 'I'll be retiring in five years' to saying his good-byes at his early retirement party."

"I think you're blowing this way out of proportion. Are you just fishing for some more billable days?"

"I'm dead serious. And I resent that question."

I paused to let Ed know just how serious I was. I scooted my chair closer to his and said almost in a whisper, "My God, Ed, yesterday those auditors showed us a report that said your organization has poorly written procedures, your people and management lack the discipline to follow those procedures, and employees are not held accountable for their actions and performance."

"It said all that?"

"Jesus, Ed, I realize the report was poorly constructed, but wake up. Yes, it said all that, and now that I've helped them develop a much better report, it will say it ever more clearly."

Ed's face became tense, and I could see the uncertainty beginning to creep in. I waited for him to respond.

"But again, that's compared to the new company standards," he said. "And I've only been in charge a couple of years. No one expects us to be in full compliance at this stage."

"Are you hearing yourself?" I replied. "No one expects you to have good procedures and follow them? No one expects you to hold people to account?"

Ed sat silently. He covered his mouth with his right hand for a moment and then lowered it to speak.

"I've got a problem, don't I?"

"No, you're going to create a problem, a big unnecessary one, if you continue to take such a lax attitude toward this audit. The auditors are thinking the same thing."

"What? Did they say something to you?"

"They didn't have to. I could see it in their eyes and body language yesterday. They were very concerned about how you might react to their findings, as any auditor would be, but when you behaved in such a ho-hum way, I could see the disbelief in their eyes."

Ed didn't say anything. He just sat there looking at the seventy-five-page draft report on his desk.

"How do you think these auditors will respond when your management asks them, 'Do we have the right person leading this business unit?'"

"They wouldn't ask that . . . would they?" he replied.

"They will," I said. "I guarantee it, and you know from our previous interactions I'm usually right about this stuff."

"But why would they ask that?"

"Wouldn't you? If you had a manager who'd been in a seat for two years and got a report like that, wouldn't you question if he's the right guy?" I pointed at the report on Ed's desk.

"But they wouldn't touch me. I mean, they know I only have a couple of years before I leave."

I was taken aback by Ed's statement and said nothing as I contemplated what I needed to say next. Ed silently flipped back and forth through the pages of the report. I knew it was time for me to say to Ed what I'd really been wanting to say ever since yesterday's meeting.

"You surprise me, Ed. I never thought you'd be an RIP."

"RIP? What's that?"

"Retired in place."

Ed just sat there looking at me. His face glowed in anger, and I could see his cheeks expanding and his lips tightening as he gritted his teeth. He took several breaths and then spoke in a low tone.

"You need to leave my office," he said.

I left immediately.

After I left Ed's office, I took a walk around the grounds. I needed to internally debrief the conversation I'd led him through. I asked the same questions I guess all coaches ask themselves: Did I push him too hard? Is he right? Am I overdramatizing his situation? These doubts all crept into my thoughts as they always do. But I quickly put them aside and asked the only question a coach needs to ask in any time of doubt: am I totally in service of my client, or am I pushing my own agenda?

I returned to Ed's office a few hours later. He was still sitting at his desk, tapping his fingers on the report. I cautiously peeked inside his door, and when he looked up, I said, "Are we still on for the ballgame tonight, or do I need to call the airline and get a flight home tomorrow morning?"

"Sit down, you son of a bitch," Ed replied. He picked the report up and slammed it on his desk. I sat down.

I waited silently as Ed rose and paced the room. He had something to say, but it was obvious he was finding it painful to vocalize. Finally, he turned to me.

"You really think I'm an RIP?"

"You know the deal when you partner with me. I'm not going to bullshit you. I'm going to tell you what I see."

"And that's what you see when you look at me?"

"It is."

"How can you say that to me?"

"You've caused me to say it by the way you've been leading the last day and a half. You're not the same leader I knew years ago."

"How so? Give me an example."

"I'm not going to give you an example so you can tell me why I'm wrong. I thought I cured you of that racket when I coached you before. All I'm telling you is you're not the same leader I knew, the leader I said good-bye to years ago. You've gotten too comfortable and lazy."

As I moved toward the door to leave, I saw Ed open his mouth to respond, but I continued talking. "That's my observation of you. You can do what you want to do with it. You can tell me to f---off and go home, or you can take my feedback to heart and use it to show up tomorrow as the Ed I know you still are and can be. It's your choice." As I reached the door, I turned back to Ed. "I'll take a rain check on the game tonight. I want to give you the space to noodle on what we've discussed. If you don't email or text me to say I'm no longer welcome, I'll see you at the meeting with the auditors tomorrow morning."

Ed and I never discussed RIP again. It wasn't necessary. The next morning, he was the old Ed, taking the report dead serious, working with the auditors to understand how he'd contributed to the findings. After the meeting, the auditors shared with me their amazement of the change in Ed. They also said they'd been asked to review their report with Ed's boss's boss a few weeks later. That did not worry me a bit. Ed would be ready for that meeting, and when it happened, he would blow his bosses away with his ownership of the findings and a plan to address them.

Chapter 28:
The Summit

"Today, anyone of the billions of people on the planet can start a movement that spreads like wildfire. . . . [T]hey can start out with just a small group of people who believe passionately in something and they can end up changing the culture."

—Scott Goodson

After my work with Ed, it was time for Michael's summit. The event was held over three consecutive days. I was impressed with how calm and confident he was the evening before the summit began. Over the months of preparation, Michael had seen the impact of his behavior changes and what a group, such as the summit planning committee, can accomplish when provided clear expectations and given control by a composed and intentional leader.

The room was arranged with ten round tables with eight persons at each. The attendees included senior staff managers, onshore team leaders and engineers, and offshore management and supervision. All were well aware they had been invited because Michael wanted them there. They entered the room early and quickly took their seats well before the scheduled starting time. Some were simply eager to get going, others were curious to see what Michael might have in store. For all, this was the first summit-type event to which they'd ever been called.

On the morning of the first day, Michael led the attendees through a version of the "parallel universe" conversation I'd had with him, only this time it was the summit participants who described that other universe. By the time the early morning was done, the attendees had covered the walls with large poster sheets describing what they saw, heard, and felt when visiting their counterparts in that other universe.

Then, after lunch, standing in front of a fifteen-foot-high, thirty-foot-wide banner, Michael stood resolute and declared his vision for the future. At the left edge of the banner, a lone figure stood on a rock in the Gulf of Mexico. In the distance behind the figure was one of the organization's drill ships and the company's world headquarters building. The figure was standing at attention with his left arm and hand pointing upward and outward to the right, toward the future.

Unlike most executive presentations, as Michael spoke, everyone listened intently. One reason was the environment the planning team had created. Starting with the invitations and ending with the venue and its setup, the team sent the unmistakable message that this session was different and significant, and anyone who was invited was important. But the main cause of their undivided attention was Michael.

The attendees had never seen one of their top managers facilitate an introspective conversation as Michael did that morning or stand alone and speak from the heart so passionately and eloquently. Seeing Michael dressed in his best attire, as the instrument, describing a vision that he'd written, was entirely new and unique for them, and it had two effects.

For the many members of Michael's organization—some with the most experience in drilling and in working with Michael—the day was somewhat disconcerting. At the social event that evening, many of them said things to me like, "that wasn't the Michael I know" and "that was too touchy-feely for me." I didn't share this feedback with Michael; it was expected and insignificant at that stage of the process. These were the people who would likely decline Michael's invitation, the kernels that weren't going to pop but which he had to be careful not to burn. He would later have to keep these individuals out of the way of those who did accept.

The morning's conversations and Michael's invitation had the opposite effect on many others, especially the junior managers within the group—the third layer of management who were a long way from retirement and dissatisfied with the current state of affairs. These managers shared with me comments like, "Michael was unbelievable; what an amazing leader," "I love what he said about our industry and how we could be different in the future," and "I'd follow that guy anywhere." These were the kernels that, if Michael kept the temperature hot enough, would pop the next day.

During the morning of the second day, Michael led the group through a series of conversations where they explored their relationship to his vision. He made sure the conversations were introspective by saying early in the day, "You're going to have a lot of conversations today about this vision, but the most important conversation is the one you'll have with yourself."

The first discussion Michael had with the participants was to explore all the reasons why it would be difficult to realize this vision. Michael said to them, "I want you to give me every reason you can think of for why we can't realize this future." They had no problem covering the walls with hundreds of ideas.

The second conversation Michael had with the group was to explore all the reasons why he and his people could realize the vision. Michael said, "I've heard your reasons why we can't; now I want to hear your reasons why we can." This conversation was much more challenging for the group. Unlike the "why we can't" conversation, it was difficult for them to conjure up reasons for the "why we can" conversation, despite spending most of the morning attempting to do so.

After a long break, as Michael began to reconvene the group for the third discussion, one of the members asked the group, "Why do you think the second question was so hard for us?"

None of the attendees gave an explanation that seemed to satisfy the person, so he turned to Michael and asked, "Do you understand why?"

Michael was a bit taken aback by this question. He looked at me as if to say "please help," so I stood up and said, "Michael, if it's OK with you, I'll take a shot at answering this question."

"Please do, Cort," Michael said. I stood, and he handed me the microphone.

I turned to the questioner. "First, I want to thank you for asking that question, because it's probably one a lot of people are asking."

Then I turned to the group and said, "The answer is really very obvious when you stop and think about it. It's hard to say why something can be done when you've never done it before, but it's easy to say why not. You have a lot of history and experience with things not being the way Michael has described in his vision, would you agree?" A lot of heads nodded.

"And because of that, it's very easy to go to that history and bring forth reasons for why it can't be," I continued. "In fact, you came up with hundreds of reasons because you have years of experience you could draw from. Am I making any sense?" Again, I saw lots of heads nodding.

"But you have no experience to go to when considering why Michael's vision can become a reality," I added, "and because of that, you can't retrieve answers to that question from your experience. Are you following me?" The heads continued to nod.

"Therefore, there is only one way to come up with a reason why Michael's vision can be, and that way is to what?" I asked. My question was met with a roomful of blank stares. "I'm asking you to answer that question. What is the only way to come up with a reason why you and Michael can realize his vision?"

I heard someone mumble something a few tables to my right. I turned to the table and asked, "Does someone have an answer?"

A young woman at the table, who I later learned was an engineer, said quietly, "We have to make it up."

"Yes!" I said. "What's your name?"

"Sharon," she said.

"Sharon," I said, handing her the microphone, "would you please say what you just said so the entire room can hear?"

Sharon took the mic, confidently placed it near her mouth, and said, "We have to make up our answers for the second conversation, because we've never created that future before. If we go there, we're going to have to invent it."

I retrieved the microphone from Sharon and said to the invitee who asked the original question, "Have you gotten the answer you were seeking?"

"I have," the invitee replied. I returned the microphone to Michael, who looked grateful. It was time for him to lead the third and final discussion.

"I have one more conversation before we end this morning," Michael told the group. "I want us to explore whether we'll make the vision a reality."

Michael instructed the groups to reach consensus at their table as to whether or not they would do what it took to create that future.

"I want one of two responses from each table," Michael said, "and I want your table to reach consensus before you give me your response. I'll accept a yes or no response. I won't accept a 'yes-but' or 'yes-if' response—there can be no qualifier. I'll also not accept a 'no-because' or a 'maybe' response. Do you understand what I'm asking of you?"

The room was completely quiet, but people's heads were nodding. Michael said, "Great, please get to work." The group remained silent and inactive for several moments, but gradually each table began effecting Michael's request.

Once the tables were engaged in their conversations, I approached Michael and said, "Well done, sir."

"That should turn up the heat on the kernels," Michael replied.

"Yes, it will. And they'll decide whether they pop."

"Who do you think might pop first? Do you think there'll be a lot of them?"

I turned Michael away from the group so as not to distract them and whispered, "There will be what there will be. Try not to get invested in who or how many, or you'll destroy the container you've worked so hard to create. Right now, and for the remainder of this conversation, do your best to be totally OK with none of them popping. Your focus for the remainder of the day needs to be on you and who you're being."

"Thanks for setting me straight," he said. "I'd forgotten that."

"You're doing outstanding. Trust the process we've created, and you'll get a great outcome."

Michael and I returned our attention to the group.

The tables worked on their responses to Michael's third conversation for nearly an hour. Finally, one of the team's spokespersons said, "I don't think we'll ever reach consensus."

Michael and I had discussed this possible scenario, and he responded exactly as I had coached him to. He paused the conversations and had each table report their status. About a quarter of the tables reported that they had reached a consensus of yes; about half had reach a consensus of no; and the remainder had either not reached a consensus or had a sole dissenter at the table.

The table Michael invited to speak first was one that had not reached a consensus. Within a few minutes, the conversation spread to the point where the entire room was engaged. At many times, the opt-outs, who were by far in the majority, would speak and give all the reasons why what Michael proposed was un-achievable. At other times, the opt-ins would stand and advocate for Michael's vision and declare their intention to do whatever it took to make it happen. All the while, Michael, the "undecideds," and I sat back and observed.

Michael allowed the conversation to sway back and forth for about ten minutes. At that point, he approached me and asked, "How do I end this in a positive way?"

I looked at the room, and the group was still totally engaged in their conversation and oblivious to Michael and me. I pulled Michael behind a temporary black curtain that hid equipment and supplies, so we could chat privately.

I reminded Michael of the coaching I'd given him a few weeks prior, when we had talked through how he would close the conversation down but in a way that maintained the container for the remainder of the afternoon.

"As we discussed, I suggest you let the group go on for about ten more minutes and then get their attention," I went on. "At that point, you must declare two things to them and make one request. First, we agreed you were going to tell them that you intend to create the vision you've shared—that for you, there's no going back."

"Put my butt on the line," Michael said, grinning.

"Yes. Second, tell them you invited them to this summit so they can choose whether to join you. And then you'll request they make their choice before leaving this summit."

"Remind me," Michael said, "how might I say it?"

"Once they've quieted down, look them in the eyes and say something like, 'I've shared with you my vision of the future I intend to create. I've made my choice and, for me, there's no turning back. I invited you to this summit to give you the opportunity to choose, as I have, whether to continue to drift into the future or take charge of it. This summit is your opportunity to decide whether you choose to join me and do your part in making the vision a reality.'

"And then pause," I said, "and make eye contact with every person in the room before ending by saying something like, 'So, my request of you is very simple: before you leave this summit tomorrow, make your choice.'"

"I've got this," Michael said with confidence. "Thanks for grounding me." He patted me on the shoulder and immediately returned to the front of the room.

After about ten minutes, Michael quieted the group, slowly looked around the room to make eye contact with every person, and said, in his own words, what we had agreed he would say. But because he, the author of the vision, said it to the room, and not me or some facilitator, it was a hundred times more powerful. At that moment, I knew Michael was going to get an outstanding outcome from his summit.

Afterward, Michael thanked the group for their participation that morning and announced lunch. As the group left the main room and proceeded to where lunch was being served, Michael and I stayed behind to debrief the morning.

Standing in front of the large banner gazing out at the empty chairs in the room, Michael asked, "What do I do with the people who don't choose? What do I say to them?"

"Let people choose at their own pace. Just like popcorn, some kernels pop early, some pop last, and some never pop. Tomorrow, when you end this summit, the container that you've created will be gone. You'll have given them a fair opportunity to choose. After that, it's up to them and their associates to keep this conversation going. They'll create their own container, so long as you do your part."

"And my part is what?"

"To remain all in, and make that fact unmistakable to your people; to take care that your thoughts, words, and actions are in integrity with your vision. Never forget, you are the leader of this movement; they are the followers. If you stay true, they will grow into leaders in their own right."

"I keep forgetting that I don't have to make it happen all by myself. My followers will take care of that for me."

"They've got the easy part. You've got a much tougher job. You have to do battle with the drift."

I moved and sat at one of the large round tables. Michael joined me.

"What do you mean?" Michael asked.

"You've just announced your vision to the world, and that's a serious threat to the drift. It now knows you exist and that you intend on leading its members into a different future."

"You speak about the drift as if it's alive." Michael was wide-eyed.

"It is, Michael. The drift is a living entity, and what is the main goal of any living entity?"

"To stay alive?"

"You've got it. Now that you've announced yourself and your intentions, it knows it's in a fight for its life."

"But how can the drift fight me?"

"The drift itself can't, but its members can. The drift will take hold of its members like a puppeteer takes hold of a puppet. It will, in a way, possess them and use them to do its bidding, to fend off its enemy—and that's you and your followers."

"This is getting spooky," Michael said, looking at me carefully. "Aren't you being a little melodramatic here?" Michael leaned back in the chair, shaking his head in skepticism.

I leaned over the table toward Michael. "Just wait, and you'll see what I mean," I said, and then leaned back into my chair. "Before this summit ends, you'll look straight into the eyes of the drift. And I warn you, it may take possession of the last person you might expect to do battle with you—even people you thought were your best friends or advocates. From this moment forward, you have one job: to stay all in, to stay on mission. Are you still up to that?"

"I am," Michael answered with defiance. His neck arched and head tilted upward.

"I know you are. I just wanted you to say it for yourself. If you ever doubt it, just remind yourself what's at stake in this movement you're leading."

"Our industry, our nation, and the lives and futures of thousands of people are at stake," Michael replied.

Michael and I ended the debrief, discussed plans for that afternoon's session, and headed to lunch. Little did we know the drift would be waiting for us when we returned.

Chapter 29:
Mr. Drift

"Our doubts are traitors, and make us lose the good we oft might win by fearing to attempt."

—William Shakespeare

"Blind belief in authority is the greatest enemy of truth."

—Albert Einstein

"When you can't understand the negativity, doubt, or lack of support directed at you just remember this. They are not looking at you . . . they are looking in the mirror. After that the true clarity of their self-doubt will emerge."

—Carl Henegan

During the lunch break, Michael was pleased to see the level of energy among the attendees as they dined. The conversation that had occurred in the morning session ran over into the restaurant, with the opt-ins and opt-outs still attempting to enroll each other in their points of view.

I walked over to Michael's table, leaned down, and whispered, "Can you see it? Your troops are doing battle with the drift."

Michael looked up at me, smiling, and said, "As they say, 'The battle is afoot.'"

After finishing our meals, Michael and I returned early to the session room to prep for the afternoon. Waiting there was one of Michael's senior-most managers, who said he wanted to talk to us about the summit. The manager had sat in during the morning and, to this point, had not offered any comment.

Michael and I sat at a table with the manager, a gentleman about ten years our senior whom Michael revered. We listened as he listed his concerns about the summit. What surprised Michael was that the manager was worried not about Michael's vision or the summit content but rather things like the cost of the audiovisual team and the need for the large banner that served as the session's backdrop. As Michael began to rationalize the expenditures to the manager, the manager's cell phone rang.

The manager looked at his phone and said to Michael and me, "Gentlemen, I have to take this call. Excuse me, please." He stood and walked to the other end of the room.

As soon as I was sure the manager was engaged in his call and couldn't hear us, I leaned over to Michael and said, "Say hello to Mr. Drift."

"Him?" Michael said. "Nah, he's a good guy. He's just concerned about the optics of some of what's going on here. We probably shouldn't have spent so much on the video stuff."

"Michael, you can't let your personal feelings for your managers blind you from what's going on here. We're sitting here talking about a few thousand dollars spent on video professionals when we should be discussing what we're going to do this afternoon to save a billion-dollar business unit. That's ludicrous. Can't you see that?" Michael blinked at me, unconvinced.

"He's a great person, and I know you think the world of him," I continued. "But right now, he's possessed by the drift. What, do you think the drift only uses assholes? It'll use anyone it can to get you off track."

"You're saying the drift chose him because it knew he would be someone who has influence over me and could take me off track?" Michael asked.

"Of course it did. And it worked. We've now spent five minutes of precious time talking about video stuff and the drift and not preparing for this afternoon. Right now the drift is winning."

"So, what should I do?"

"Remember that you're talking with two distinct entities: him and the drift. Love and respect him, but don't give in to the drift," I replied. "When he's done with his phone call and returns, stand for your vision and speak as the leader of a movement would to someone he loves and respects but who is drifting and drawing him off his mission. If you spoke to him in that manner, what you would say?"

Michael thought for several moments. "I would say something like, 'Dan, I have all the respect in the world for you and your input. But right now, I'm in the process of transforming a business unit that's facing a very uncertain future. I need to focus on that mission at the moment. I'd be happy to talk with you after the summit about the optics, but right now I need to prepare for this afternoon's session.'"

"Perfect. Just remember this: be vigilant for the drift. Never let your personal relationships or feelings blind you to it. And when you encounter it, love the messenger and send the drift a clear message that you won't be taken off mission. You do that, and you'll be fine."

Just then, Michael's manager completed his phone call and returned to speak with Michael. I excused myself and stepped away to let them talk privately.

After they were finished, Michael walked over to me. He explained that the manager had to return to the main office to deal with an issue. But before the manager had left, he had expressed that he was extremely pleased and impressed with the summit and Michael's leadership, and he was sorry for distracting Michael with trivialities like banners and video equipment.

"Of course he did," I said to Michael. "After lunch, sitting at the table with your manager, the drift observed a bowing, cowering subordinate. But when you spoke with your manager after his phone call, you were being a leader, an All-In Leader with a vision. The drift knows it doesn't have a chance battling such an enemy. The drift has no power other than what you give it." Michael was quiet as he thought about what I'd said.

"I'm starting to see it now," Michael replied. "If I stay all in, I can win this battle, but any time I weaken, the drift will be waiting there to pounce."

"I think you've got it. You have the ultimate power, and going back to one of the first lessons I offered you, that's why the only person who needs to change is you."

"But that sound exhausting. To be ever-vigilant, I mean."

"It can be at times. You'll need to get your rest and take care of yourself. But it's much less taxing if you counter the drift with love and respect and calmly stand for your vision. If you do that consistently, your battles will be briefer and fewer and more enjoyable."

"Enjoyable? Battling the drift can be fun?"

"Well, yes. That and leading. In fact, if you're doing it right, it's a blast. I mean, what's more fun than leading people into a bright future? What's more fun than saving lives and futures and dueling with one's detractors? It's all fun when you approach it with love, respect, and intention."

"You really do believe all this stuff," Michael said.

"I more than believe it," I replied. "I know it. And the reason I approached you and offered to coach you is, deep down, I know you know it too."

Michael and I then turned our attention to preparing for the afternoon session. This was to be the point in the summit where Michael handed the reins to his people and began to see the product of his hard work and leadership.

When the summit attendees returned from lunch, they entered a room that had been converted into one large circle of eighty chairs. All the tables had been removed, and the room had been arranged for the very special event that was to be a highlight of the summit.

In the center of the large circle was one small table with a flip chart sitting on top of it, one large black marker, and a microphone on a tall stand. The room was dimly lit with a spotlight on the table.

As the participants entered the room, they were surprised to see the dramatic change and were understandably curious about what Michael was planning for them next. Michael, sporting a welcoming smile, greeted the group and instructed them to take a seat of their choosing. Within a few minutes, everyone was seated and settled in. Michael then raised his hands, quieted the room, and stepped partway into the circle, visible to the entire room but not in the spotlight. He spoke softly but purposefully. You could have heard a pin drop.

"As of this moment, this summit is an open space; you will decide what we discuss and work on for the rest of today. I only have one expectation: that whatever you discuss and work on is directly related to realizing the vision we've been exploring for the last couple of days."

There were slight murmurs around the room, but they quickly died down as Michael continued. "I also have a process I want you to follow that will assure you get the most out of whatever you choose to discuss and work on. Here's how it'll work."

Michael then went on to point out the large meeting room schedule, about six feet tall and twelve feet wide, posted on the far wall. On the left side of the schedule, listed vertically, were the names of eight breakout rooms that the summit planning team had reserved. Across the top of the schedule, listed horizontally, were time blocks.

"We've provided these rooms so you have space to have whatever conversations you might wish to have," Michael said. "In each are all the equipment and supplies you might need. As you can see, we have time today for about twenty-four different conversations, if needed.

"Now, let me explain how a person can call a conversation. All you need to do is walk to that table"—Michael gestured toward the setup in the center of the circle—"write on that flip chart the name and objective of the conversation you intend to call, and then step to the microphone, introduce yourself, and announce your intentions. For example, someone might say, 'My name is Michael, and I'm going to call a conversation to discuss how we can improve our relations with our drilling contractors. My objective is to identify at least three concrete actions that can be taken to improve that relationship. I'll be holding my meeting in the Bluebonnet Room from 2:00 to 4:00 this afternoon.

"Then, after you've called your session, you'll walk over to the room schedule on the wall and post your flip-chart page in the box corresponding to your session room and time. Does everyone understand how this process works?"

Michael looked around the room and saw a large circle of extremely apprehensive people all nodding their heads.

He paused a moment and then said, "I'm dead serious about what I'm saying here. Anyone can call a conversation about anything they want. But if you do, you have to bring some deliverables back to the group." Michael paused again, and looking at each face in the circle, he smiled to help alleviate some of the uneasiness in the room.

"First, those who call a session will attend a short meeting this evening where the planning team will provide you a simple template for capturing the topic and outputs of your session," he continued. "Then, overnight, the planning team will convert your completed templates into posters. They have arranged for a large room tomorrow, and they'll place all the posters in the room along the walls. You'll be expected to stand in front of your poster and discuss your session with anyone who visits you." The group seemed somewhat more relaxed now that they better understood the process.

"For those not leading a session but visiting them, you can plant yourself at one session for the duration, or you can bounce from session to session. Have I made it clear that you can go wherever you feel best serves you and the vision?"

"Yes," the room said in loud unison.

"OK," Michael said. "I have one last piece of instruction to give you before I open the floor and let whoever wants to call the first session. As we go about creating this open space this afternoon, there will be some guiding principles that we'll embrace." Behind Michael, two principles appeared on a large video screen. "One, whoever shows up for a session is in the right group. And two, whatever happens in the session is all that could have happened. Do I have your assurance that you'll embrace these principles?"

"Yes," was the group's thunderous reply.

"Outstanding," Michael said with a large smile, laughing as the participants laughed with him. "Now, I'm turning the floor over to you. If and when any of you wish to approach the table and announce a session, you're free to do so."

The room was dead silent as Michael slowly turned and strolled to his seat in the circle. He sat and leaned back with his hands folded behind his head as if to say, "My work is done. It's now up to you guys."

You would need an atomic clock to calculate the "billisecond" between when Michael sat and about fifteen of the attendees rose and headed for the table and microphone. In less than thirty seconds, there were twenty-five in line waiting to call their sessions, and most were the third level of managers in attendance.

I looked at Michael, still seated with his hands clasped. He was beaming. I turned my gaze toward his senior leadership team, some of whom had been highly skeptical about using this open-space approach. Their jaws were on the floor.

There were too many sessions called that afternoon for the rooms reserved, so the session callers quickly convened at the large session schedule on the wall and worked to combine and rearrange sessions so all could be accommodated. It took them less than five minutes to ensure that all sessions had a time and room.

Soon, the large session room was empty except for Michael and me. All the others were attending sessions. I walked over to Michael, who was standing in front of the posted meeting room schedule, looking up at all the various sessions. He said, "It's a beautiful thing, isn't it, Cort?"

"What's that?" I asked, knowing exactly what he meant.

"When something you work so hard to plan and prepare for goes off better than you could've imagined," he replied, motioning toward the wall.

"It sure is. And it's all because of your leadership."

Michael turned to face me. "I had no idea so many of them would pop. And several of them are the young ones, the new ones to the unit. They couldn't wait to call a session, and they meant what they said when they called them. It was a thing of beauty."

"We've still got a ways to go, even with completing this summit. But now you have followers, several of them. And they're with you and committed to your vision. You're not all alone anymore."

"And they're expecting me to keep this going," Michael replied, staring at the other end of the long, empty room. "How will we avoid losing momentum? How will I live up to their expectations of me?"

"You'll cross that bridge when you get there," I said, stepping in front of him to get his attention. "Right now, enjoy this huge accomplishment and milestone. You've created dozens of passionate followers. Go sit in on some of the sessions and enjoy what you've created. I'll catch up with you afterward to debrief the day and prep for tomorrow morning."

The following morning, Michael, the other summit attendees, and I conducted what the planning team called a "gallery walk." The planning committee turned a large room into what resembled an art gallery, and on each wall, every few feet, was a poster summarizing the conversations and outputs of each of the open-space sessions. Standing in front of each poster was the person who had called the session and, in some cases, two persons who had combined their sessions and jointly facilitated. It was inspiring for Michael to see so many of his followers standing for his vision and doing their part to make it happen.

After the gallery walk and before lunch, the entire group was to meet back in the main room for the completion of the summit. As the attendees assigned action items from the open-space sessions and aligned on their path forward, Michael asked me for my thoughts on how he might best finish the event.

"You don't need to do more than send three simple messages," I replied. "First, thank them for coming and actively participating. Second, tell them that you'll assume everyone in the room is with you and on board until they give you a reason to believe otherwise. And third, tell them they can depend on you to embody the vision and do everything in your power to work with them to realize it.

"Make it short and sweet," I added. "These people have worked hard for three days and are ready to move forward." When the group gathered for this final conversation, Michael did a great job of closing the session and received a booming round of applause and cheers at the conclusion.

At lunch, Michael asked me if we could meet in a couple of weeks to talk through the summit. Something told me he was looking for more than just a debrief.

Chapter 30:
A Day in My Life of Bliss

"It seems the mind, working in pictures, knows no difference between a picture from the past and a picture from the future. If you create a vision as a memory in the future, it will have the same power as a memory of the past."

—Harvey Austin

"Students achieving Oneness will move on to Twoness."

—Woody Allen

Upon returning home from Michael's summit, I was approached by my daughter, Katy, and son-in-law, Trent, with a difficult request. They wanted me to coach them.

Katy and Trent had met soon after finishing high school. Trent played baseball on a college team on which a friend of Katy's also played. Within a year, they were engaged and they married soon after.

When I look at Katy, I see my mother. Like Mom, Katy is thin and pretty with long, thick, wavy brown hair, gorgeous blue eyes, and a slight overbite—the kind that, as my dad used to say when describing Mom in her youth, "drove the boys crazy." And like her mom, Julie, Katy was born to nurture. During adolescence, Katy was always the one to bake and take cupcakes to school to celebrate a friend's birthday because she was devoted to relationships.

Katy also showed artistic talent and resolve at a young age. While in seventh grade, she once got a low grade on a history report, even though the report's cover was a beautiful work of art. It was obvious that Katy had spent hours decorating the cover. However, the report itself was obviously copied from something she'd found on the Internet. When she questioned her grade, the teacher told her the school gives no credit for report covers.

But Katy was satisfied with the report, despite her poor grade. As she put it, "I can't expect a school that's eliminated art to appreciate what I bring to the world. I'll graduate with my C average and then I'll find people who will appreciate me."

Trent was an only child raised by his mom. Where Katy enjoyed the benefits of living in an upper-class home, Trent grew up watching his mom toil just to make ends meet. He once shared with me that when he played little league baseball, his mom could not afford the league fees, so they were paid out of the charity of some of the other parents. Trent's good grades and baseball skills earned him a four-year scholarship at a private college where he excelled on the field and in the classroom. While Trent is small in stature, beneath his compact frame lies a man of great passion, character, and heart.

Upon hearing Katy and Trent's request for my coaching, I recalled my dad explaining to me why he never attempted to teach me the game of golf. "The best way to destroy a close relationship is to try and teach the other person something difficult to learn," he'd said. "If I'd tried to teach you golf, you might have ended up hating the game and possibly me."

I shared this concern with my kids (as I still and will probably always refer to them), and after some lengthy discussion, I agreed to lead them through an exercise I often use to kick-start the hero journeys of emerging leaders. I call the exercise "a day in my life of bliss."

I explained to Trent and Katy, "The exercise works like this. You will write a movie script detailing a day, or week if you prefer, in your life of bliss. By that, I mean a day or week where you know and feel you're living the life you were meant to live; the life in which you're playing a big, meaningful game; the life in which you like and respect yourself, know you are appreciated by others, and are totally confident in your ability to produce the results you want from your life; the life in which you feel like you belong and are in the right place, at the right time, doing the right thing; and lastly, the life in which you feel you're making a worthwhile contribution to the world while constantly learning and growing as a human being."

"Write a movie script?" replied Katy. "We don't know how to do that."

"Neither did any script writer before she wrote her first script. It's easy to do, I promise. But it will consume hours of your time over the next several weeks."

"The exercise is to write a movie script in weeks?" asked Trent.

"Of one day in your life or a week if that makes more sense to you," I said. "The idea is to get crystal clear on the life that's always been there deep inside, calling you to live it. If you take on this exercise and really go for it, I promise you'll have something very few people possess: clarity on who you are and your intentions for your life. Most people are drifting through a life determined by others and circumstances. I'm offering you a way to live a life of your choosing—one that you author. Does that interest you?"

"It does," they both replied.

"OK, then let me further explain the exercise so you'll fully understand what you're signing up for," I said. "Your movie script will begin with the moment you first open your eyes on that day of bliss, or the first day of your week of bliss. From that moment forward, you'll write a detailed description of everywhere you go, who you're with, what you do and say, and what you think and feel—in other words, everything a movie director would need to produce a movie."

"Is this a day I document as I live it or one that I imagine?" Katy said.

"Imagine. The exercise is not about capturing a day in your current life but in the life of your dreams. I assume you're not living that life and that's why you're here asking for my coaching."

"Yes, that's why we're here," Trent replied as Katy nodded.

"So, is the exercise clear? Do you have any other questions?"

"How will this exercise help us?" Katy asked.

"I'm going to ask that you trust me on this, and have faith the exercise will help," I responded. "I can tell you this: about thirty years ago, a friend of mine, a doctor working in the Middle East named Patel, took me through his version of this exercise, and it helped me choose to create and live the life I do today."

"What did you describe in your day?" Trent said.

"The life you've seen me live. The one I chose a long time ago and have been creating every day since. I don't want to share much more than that."

"Why?" asked Katy.

"Your script is extremely personal. You'll be recording your innermost thoughts and feelings. If you feel it will be shared with others, you might hold back. So, I suggest you assume you'll not be sharing any of your script with anyone. Does that make sense?"

"I guess it does. So, Katy and I won't be sharing ours with one another?" Trent asked.

"And won't we have to share them with you since you're coaching us?" added Katy.

"Again, my advice is no, but that will be your decision to make. It's not necessary to share your script with anyone for this exercise to work. For now and until you're done writing your scripts, can we assume no one else will see them unless you decide to share?"

"I'm OK with not sharing if you are," Katy said to Trent, with a casual shrug.

"OK, I guess we won't," Trent added.

"Just consider it a possibility for now. You can decide later if both of you agree to share," I said. "Any other questions?"

Katy and Trent left my office and headed off to begin writing. Two weeks later, they emailed me their scripts. They had decided to share them with each other and me only. I met with them a couple of days later.

"These scripts are a good start, but they still need some work," I told them over coffee at my dining table. "As a movie director, I couldn't make a movie of what you've written. I might be able to shoot a few scenes, but several of your scenes don't have enough detail. For example, Katy, you say that you're out with your five children, but I don't know their names, what they look or sound like, or what their personalities are like. I don't know where you and the kids are going or what they're doing and saying. And most importantly, I don't know why you're there, what you think and feel about each child, and about whatever it is you're doing with them. In short, I don't know what it is about the experience that makes it blissful for you."

"You need that much detail?" Trent asked with surprise.

"No, you do—if you are to create the life of your bliss. Before Michelangelo sculpted David from a block of marble, don't you think he had a pretty good idea of what his final product would look like? Or do you think he just winged it?"

"He probably had a good idea," Trent replied.

"Of course he did. Without that clarity, sculpting a masterpiece like that would be impossible. Can you see it was that clarity of vision and the desire to realize it that drove him and kept him moving forward, despite whatever challenges he faced? And I'm sure he faced his fair share." I paused and let both Katy and Trent absorb what I was trying to help them realize.

"I guess I see what you're saying," Katy said. "Is that why we're doing this exercise?"

"That's some of it, and it's why I'm suggesting you take another go at your scripts and chip away at the ambiguity in them," I said. "Use this exercise to reveal the life of your bliss as a sculptor does her masterpiece. Go spend another few weeks writing, and bring me a script from which a director can make a movie of your blissful day. Do that, and we'll then discuss how you will use your script to start living that life."

Trent and Katy returned three weeks later with detailed scripts in hand. They entered my office, smiling and eager to discuss the days they had written about and explore how they might make those lives their reality. After they both finished reading their scripts aloud, I asked them the questions this exercise creates.

"So, these are the lives you would live if you followed your dreams?"

"Yes," they both replied, obviously pleased with what they'd created and proud of the effort they'd put forth.

"Katy, this is the life you feel you are meant to live that would have you wake each morning enthusiastic about the day ahead?"

"Yes," she said as she leaned toward me. "I wasn't sure about this exercise, but I'm very happy with the life I've written about."

"Trent, this is the life that would provide meaning and purpose, where you like and respect yourself, know that you are appreciated by others, and are totally confident in your ability to produce the results you want?

"It is," he said, moving closer to Katy and taking her hand. "Each time I read my script, I get jazzed about what our lives could be."

"If you choose to live the lives you've described here, you'd feel like you belong in that life and that you're in the right place, at the right time, doing the right thing?"

"Yes," both replied.

"And lastly, is the life you've written about a life in which you feel you're making a worthwhile contribution to the world while constantly learning and growing as a human being? Please think long and hard, and look to your heart before you answer."

After a long pause, Katy and Trent both agreed they would.

"So," I said, pausing several seconds for effect, "if the two of you were able to set your fears and doubts aside and live the life you are called to live, the one you feel in your gut you're intended to live and will make you the most blissful, it would be these lives?"

"Absolutely," said Trent.

"Yes, this is the life I wish I could live," said Katy pointing to her script.

"OK then, I only have one last question to ask: why are you not living these lives?"

As does just about everyone else I lead through this exercise, Katy and Trent were stunned by this question and sat there with their mouths half open for about thirty seconds. Then, as others often do, they began to list all the reasons why it was not possible to live the life they had just said was their dream.

"You can't make a living teaching young boys how to play baseball. That's something you might do in your spare time, but not as a full-time job," Trent exclaimed.

"We'll never be able to own a home if I don't work," Katy added.

I explained to the two of them that they were allowing their minds to speak for them.

"Your brain is doing its job," I said. "It's been programmed by millions of years of evolution to conjure up all kinds of scary possibilities whenever we're faced with something new or unpredict-able. That made sense a few thousand years ago when we were hunting for food in the jungle and being hunted. Back then, it was essential to our survival that we imagine all the things that could harm us when in a new environment.

"But sitting here in my office, neither of your lives is at stake. No one is going to die in this conversation. What's at stake is whether the life you live is one of your choosing or one created by your frightened brain."

"But this is scary, Dad," Katy replied. Memories of Katy overcoming childhood fears, such as her first dive, first recital, and first day at a new school, entered my thoughts. Despite being a young woman, I heard in her voice the sweet but frightened child her mom and I had the privilege of raising.

"To your mind it is, Katy," I replied, speaking to that frightened child. "So I suggest you give your mind a breather and start using your heart—which, by the way, has a totally different purpose than your brain."

"What's that?"

"Your bliss. Tell your brain to move aside and ask your heart these questions: Why can I live the life of my dreams? Why can my days resemble the ones I've described in my script?"

Katy and Trent were able to rest their minds and listen to their hearts. They each came up with compelling reasons why they could live the lives of their choosing. And once they chose to live those lives, I was able to help them develop strategies and plans to realize them.

When the two of them first approached me, Trent was a math teacher hoping to someday become a high school baseball coach—he saw that as the best he could ever hope for. Today, he and Katy own a thriving youth baseball development business, which uses baseball as the means to develop boys into men who excel at baseball and life. Trent's devotion to and love for the game and his players are some of the major reasons why so many parents have been attracted to his company and the principles from which it operates.

Katy was a job hopper seeking employment that would fulfill her desire for meaning while volunteering at the church day care because that's what gave her true purposefulness. Katy had told Trent and me, "I want to be a stay-at-home mom, like my mom and grandmother, and play an active role with the kids in our church, but I can't see how we can make that happen financially."

Today, Katy is a homemaker with two young, healthy, and rambunctious boys, living in the modest home Trent and she are buying. The two teach youth religion classes at their church, and they host the church's annual summer youth camps along with other church volunteers. In short, they are pretty much living the lives they had described in their movie scripts, and where gaps still remain, they are working on closing them.

Of course, they don't have the BMWs and large homes others of their generation so covet. They understand that true wealth comes from living the life of your bliss and not from costly possessions.

One day, Trent was sitting with me in my office, thanking me for all the support I'd given Katy and him over the years. I asked him, "What is it that I've given you that has been the most valuable?"

Without hesitation, he replied, "Cort, you see in me potential that I cannot. And then you help me see it and realize it."

I cannot think of a better description of a coach.

Chapter 31:
The 5 Conditions
of Performance

"Employee engagement is the emotional commitment the employee has to the organization and its goals. This emotional commitment means engaged employees actually care about their work and their company. . . . When employees care—when they are engaged—they use discretionary effort."

—Kevin Kruse

"Welcome to Taco Bell. My life is pointless. May I take your order, please?"

—Taco Bell drive-through employee in Austin, Texas

"We are all standing on a whale, fishing for minnows."

—Polynesian proverb

A few weeks after his summit, Michael and I sat in his office, reliving a few of our favorite moments and debriefing the event. At one point in the debrief, Michael brought up what he'd asked me at the summit.

"How am I going to live up to the expectation I set for these people?" he asked. "They're counting on me to lead them into a new future and industry." Once again, Michael was staring off into nothingness, a casualty of fear.

"Have you considered that you're already doing that?" I replied. "Moreover, that you're already not just meeting these folks' expectations but exceeding them?"

"I hadn't thought of it like that." Michael looked out the window, as though attempting to see the solution that might rid him of his worries.

"Don't lose sight of that or allow yourself to get too overwhelmed by the enormity of this thing. You're going to have bouts of fear and doubt. But my dad taught me that fear is just your body getting ready to face a challenge. When you feel fear, welcome that feeling and know your body is working with you to assure you're ready to meet whatever you might face."

Michael sat silent, still gazing outside. I tapped him on his forearm. He turned to me.

"Yeah, it's a big game you're playing," I said, "but you now have a whole group of great people on your team. All you have to do is stay on mission and embody the vision. Your people will do the heavy lifting for you if you just give them the space."

"Is there something specific I can give my followers to keep them motivated and making the change happen?"

"Now that's a great question, a question an All-In Leader asks. But it'll take longer than a few minutes for me to answer it."

"I've got all morning," Michael replied. He leaned back in his chair to get comfortable, anticipating another provocative conversation.

"OK, then," I replied. "Although everybody is unique, we all have brains and central nervous systems. As a result, we all share the same fundamental psychological or, if you prefer, emotional needs. Our behavior is simply an attempt to meet those needs. Are you following what I'm saying?"

"Yes, so far."

"This is good news for those who want to influence people's behavior to drive performance."

"How?" Michael looked skeptical.

"Because if you can determine what needs or conditions are most conducive to the highest performance and help people meet them, you will get the best from your people."

"And you know those conditions?"

"Yes. In fact, there are five conditions that, if you reliably create them within your followers, will keep people motivated and in action toward your vision, mission, priorities, and goals."

"Five. That seems like a lot."

"You know, Michael, there once was a very busy man. And every morning, he'd stop at the bakery on his walk to work to eat a blueberry muffin. He loved those muffins but always complained to the baker that he was a busy man and it took too long for him to be served.

"The baker became tired of the busy man's complaints," I continued. "One day, he gave the man his secret muffin recipe and said, 'Now you can bake yourself a muffin each morning and you won't have to stop by my bakery.' The busy man took the recipe home and his wife offered to make him the muffin each morning."

"Are you going somewhere with this story?" Michael asked. Michael tilted his head to the right and raised his left eyebrow.

"I'm taking you somewhere you need to go," I said. "Can I continue?"

"You can," Michael said.

"The next morning, the busy man entered the bakery," I continued. "The baker approached him and asked, 'What are you doing here? Didn't you try my muffin recipe?' The busy man said, 'My wife did and the muffins were terrible.' 'Oh,' the baker said, 'you wanted a good muffin? I thought you only cared that the muffin be fast, so I gave you a recipe with four of the five ingredients.'"

I paused to see if Michael understood the point of my story, but he just stared at me with both eyebrows raised and said nothing.

"Do you get the message I'm trying to send here?" I asked.

"I get it," Michael said. "But was that story really necessary?"

"I'll make a deal with you. You never ask me again for the easy solution, and I'll never pain you with another fable. Deal?"

"Deal."

"The five conditions are a big game to play, commitment to and confidence in victory, positive self-image, sense of belonging, and the last one is personal growth. If you create within your people those five conditions reliably, every day, and stay on mission and embody the vision, they'll stay motivated and do what's required to realize your vision."

"I would have expected physical conditions. But, as you say, these are more psychological," Michael said.

"These are psychological conditions that occur inside of people and which all great leaders are good at creating within their people."

"How can I give my people these conditions?"

"Over time you will learn how, but for the sake of this conversation, let's start with the first two. The first one is one we've discussed many times: a big game to play. A big game, as I define it, is a vision, mission, or goal your followers want to be a part of so much they're willing to evolve and adapt to make it happen. The bigger the game, the more of their potential and discretionary effort they'll give."

"Wow, the summit gave them that," Michael said.

"I agree; you gave them that at your summit. You can definitely check that box for the time being," I replied.

"The second condition is commitment to and confidence in victory. This condition exists when your followers believe they, their leaders, and their teammates will provide and do whatever it takes to win the game—that each of them is into and up to the game they've have chosen to play. And the only choice they have is to move forward."

"We've made progress on that one as well, I'd say. People know I'm committed," Michael replied.

"Yes, they undoubtedly do, but there's the second aspect of this condition—confidence in victory. This confidence is the culmination of three distinct elements. First is the belief the game is winnable—it's something your followers believe they are capable of pulling off. Second is their belief they have control over whether they'll win, and third is their expectation they will win. Do you think your followers believe they can realize your vision—that they have control over whether it'll happen and are optimistic that it'll happen?"

"Much more than before the summit, but we still have a long way to go on this one," Michael said.

"I agree with one caveat. It's not that your followers don't have self-confidence; they do. You saw that at this summit. The only reason this one could become a problem is if they lose confidence in you, and you have total control over that."

"That's a good point."

"So, can you see now that a key component of being an All-In Leader is positively affecting the psychological states of his people? And can you see that you're more than capable of doing that?"

"I can."

"Excellent. We can discuss the other three conditions at another time. Right now, I want to change gears for a moment."

"What do you want to discuss?"

"I know that the safety of your employees is very important to you and your company."

"Absolutely," Michael said. "It comes first with us, before anything else. It's my primary accountability. The ability to produce safety results is the first measure of a manager in our company. We've got one of the best safety programs in the industry."

"I can see that," I replied. "But can you see that your approach to safety, despite being world-class, is half-assed?"

"What?" Michael replied. He sat up straighter, his face angry. "What do you mean by that?"

"Hear me out. Performance can be created in four distinct fields: the systems field, the behavior field, the self field, and the social field. Your company's approach to assuring the safety of your people exists almost entirely in the systems and behavior fields but seems to be oblivious to the critical role of the self and social fields."

"Go on," Michael said, this time with less anger in his voice.

"You just called your approach to keeping people safe a 'program,'" I continued. "Programs exist in the systems field. And you guys are always clamoring about behavior-based safety. That's the behavior field. But it's the other two fields, the self and social, that keep people safe."

"I'm not following."

"All performance, including safety performance, begins with what goes on inside of people and between people, the self and social fields, not just with the systems they have or their behaviors. And when it comes to these fields, all leaders need to know and work on are the five conditions we've been discussing. Leaders who adopt these conditions and foster them within their people have gotten much better performance in all areas, not just safety, than your company gets with all its systems and programs."

"I can't see how that's possible," Michael said.

"I know you can't. That's why we're having this conversation," I responded. Michael looked at me thoughtfully but said nothing.

"I tell you, Michael, these conditions are a magic formula—only most managers are too blinded by their systems and behaviors paradigm to even see what I'm offering."

"I'm hearing you. But give me an example where one of these five would have such miraculous results."

"Let's take the fourth condition, belonging. Belonging is a sense of community or interconnectedness with others or the task or mission at hand. All forms of belonging involve some sense that I'm the right person, doing the right thing, in the right place, right now."

"Many of the people I saw leaving the summit definitely felt they belonged and were in the right place. But how can something like belonging lead to miraculous results?"

"The word 'belonging' is just the business-correct way of speaking of love. For some insane reason, we can't talk about loving each other at work. So, instead of talking about love, we use the word belonging."

"What does love have to do with performance and keeping people safe?"

"Everything, Michael. It has everything to do with it. Without love, no system, no program—even one as robust as your safety program—is worth the paper it's written on."

"You're losing me again," Michael said.

"Loving one another is built into our DNA," I continued. "We are designed and intended to love one another. Not romantically, the way we think of love in the West, but the love that all great leaders have spoken about for thousands of years. The love of your fellow man and woman. That form of love."

Michael leaned in and listened intently as I spoke. I knew he was getting what I was attempting to communicate.

"You and folks who see safety as a management system designed to regulate behavior have forgotten or never learned the role that love, or belonging, plays in performance. As human beings, we have evolved to where we reserve love for those we consider one of us, one of our group, those who belong to our tribe . . . our family, if you will. And we'll give our very lives to protect the safety and well-being of anyone who is family. Are you following me?"

"I'm with you now," Michael said.

"But the reverse is true," I said. "For those who aren't part of our group, who don't belong to our family, we won't protect them or intervene for their welfare. In fact, we'll sit back and allow them to hurt, suffer, or even die. But—and I can't overemphasize this point—it's not because we're selfish or hateful; it's how we're wired. It's built into our emotional operating system. We love our own and could care less for those who aren't one of us."

"Wiring. That's why people don't care? Give me an example," Michael said.

I told Michael a story of how I was shopping in a market in the Middle East about thirty years earlier. "The sidewalks and streets were jammed full of people, with very few foreigners. A young Asian man on a bicycle barely missed avoiding a truck in the middle of an intersection. He took a terrible tumble, and his bike was badly damaged.

"I stood there and watched hundreds of people walk and drive past the man, without any consideration at all for his safety or injuries as he lay there in the middle of the intersection, hurt and helpless. It reminded me of how cows will just stand there and watch one of their own drown without attempting to offer aid."

"Did you help him?"

"Yes, I helped him to the safety of the sidewalk, dodging cars and trucks along the way. The police arrived soon after and ordered me to move on.

"That's what a lack of belonging will do to human beings," I said. "It can turn us into cows if we aren't aware of it and don't act to counter it. What good is a safety program in the hands of a team of cows? I'll tell you, it's almost worthless. I would much rather have my loved ones working on a rig where people cared for each other and took care of each other than a rig that has all your systems and programs. Wouldn't you?"

"I guess I would," Michael said, his tone uncertain. "But I'm not sure how talking about love on a rig will go over."

"Unfortunately, it won't," I said. "I hope that someday as a society we grow up, but for now, we're dealing with an emotionally immature society. Consequently, I don't talk about love; I talk about and get people to work on building a strong sense of belonging."

"And that has the effect on performance you've described."

"Every time, without fail. In fact, if there's only one thing I could work on to improve performance, especially safety performance, it would be building a strong sense of belonging among people."

"Now that I'm beginning to understand these five conditions, they don't seem as hard as I first thought."

"I've worked years to hone this list down to the few that are most critical to performance. Later, you and your followers will build strategies and plans to create them in your people."

As our conversation came to a close, I thanked Michael, and we set up our next meeting. I was glad he seemed to enjoy these talks since we still had some important conversations ahead of us.

Chapter 32:
The Big Leadership Lesson

"Man is buffeted by circumstances so long as he believes himself to be the creature of outside conditions, but when he realizes that he is a creative power, and that he may command the hidden soil and seeds of his being out of which circumstances grow, he then becomes the rightful master of himself."

—James Allen

"Often the difference between a successful person and a failure is not one has better abilities or ideas, but the courage that one has to bet on one's ideas, to take a calculated risk—and to act."

—Maxwell Maltz

My work with Michael and his organization expanded significantly after his summit. It was time to help translate the energy and support he'd generated into concrete plans and actions that would have an immediate effect on performance. I enrolled Michael in expanding my coaching team to add the resources I needed so I could continue to focus on coaching him and his direct reports, while my associates worked with his other levels of managers and supervisors.

My skill set is the ability to recognize emerging leaders, as I did with Michael, and to develop them into All-In Leaders. These are very special leaders who, as I've explained, possess a unique set of faculties, realizations, and skills. That made me the right coach for Michael and his direct reports.

However, I needed a coaching partner who was equally as skilled at translating a vision into plans, priorities, metrics, and goals, in other words, someone who could help Michael's followers do the heavy lifting necessary to quickly turn his team's performance around. I turned to an extremely skilled coach named Stephanie, who I knew fit the bill.

Stephanie and I aligned on our roles as our first order of business. I was to help Michael fend off the drift, stay on course, lead through his direct reports, and keep his organization informed of the transformation's status and progress. Stephanie was to help Michael and his followers build the capability within his organization to reliably deliver the performance expected by its stakeholders.

A few weeks after her first meeting with Michael, Stephanie facilitated a three-day marathon session with Michael's senior leadership team where they hammered out the mission and plans for the upcoming year, including the process for enrolling all personnel. After several hours of exploring, the group decided its mission was to "deliver wells on budget, on time, the first time."

Stephanie then helped the team identify what she called the "mission essentials" for the coming year, which the team decided would be "operating with discipline and accountability" and "clear priorities and goals." She also prepared the team to facilitate a series of cascading conversations designed to enroll the rest of the organization in the mission and mission essentials.

Their efforts could not have been more effective. I sat in on the first enrollment session, where the leadership team enrolled the next level of management. After they were finished, one of the most respected and influential managers stood.

"I've worked in this business unit for over ten years," he said. "And for the first time, I know exactly why we're here, what we're expected to do this year, what I need to know to develop my plans, and what success looks like. Thank you for giving that to me."

I knew Stephanie and Michael's team were right on track, and even when they inevitably met resistance, they'd have the staying power to achieve the mission.

For my part, I continued to coach Michael in his three development areas: creating clear expectations and holding people to account for performance, giving control, and being a composed leader. With my coaching, he developed specific action plans for each area. I observed him in meetings, and afterwards we would debrief so I could reinforce where he performed well and offer what he might adjust to be even more effective.

I also continued to help Michael see that performance can be created within the four distinct fields: systems, behavior, self, and social. I had given him a brief introduction to the four fields concept previously, but I wanted Michael to realize that a key skill of an All-In Leader is the ability to create performance via all four fields. Only through the mastery of this skill can a leader realize the full potential of his people and grow a healthy performance culture.

Sitting at his office table one morning sharing a bagel, I said to Michael, "Stephanie is working with your managers to build systems and behaviors that help support the mission of delivering wells on budget, on time, the first time. I'm presently helping you work on your three behavior development areas. In other words, she and I are working to help you and your team get better in the systems and behavior fields of performance."

"That's right," Michael replied.

"But most of the work I've done with you, and most of the work you've done with yourself and your people, have occurred in two other fields," I said.

"Self and social, right?"

"Yes, and that's why you're seeing such immediate and extraordinary change and results. The systems and behavior fields are essential, but without the work you've done in the other two fields, this turnaround would not be occurring."

"What exactly have we done in those two fields?"

"Well, we did a lot of work on you in the self field. In fact, that has been my primary intention as your coach—to help you choose to change yourself." Michael looked inquisitive, so I continued. "Do you see the world the same way today as you did before we met? Has your vision of the future changed?"

"Definitely," Michael responded. "My perspective is completely different."

"What about you? Do you see yourself the same as you did prior to our working together?"

"Not at all."

"What's different about you?"

"I'd say I see myself as a leader now. Before our work together, I saw myself as a driller. Today, I'm still that driller and always will be, but I'm also an oil company executive who leads drillers."

"How else are you different?" I asked. "What about your self has changed?"

"Well . . . ," Michael replied, hesitating as he thought. "I'm very clear about who I am."

"And who are you?"

"I'm the person who's going to change our industry. I'm the person who's going to make my vision come true. I'm the person leading a movement and who has created dozens of followers who are helping me make that happen. I'm the guy leading this turnaround."

"That you are, Michael. Now, I want to ask you a question, and I want you to think long and hard before you give me your answer," I said. "Who caused this change in yourself?"

Michael thought for several moments and then looked up at me and said, "I did."

"Bingo! Give that man a cigar!" I shouted. I clapped Michael on the shoulder. "You know, many people don't get that."

"Get what?"

"That they can change their *self*. That they can intentionally work not just on their behaviors and systems, but their *self*. That's what you've done so well, and that's what makes you different and more effective than most.

"Anyone can work on their systems and behaviors," I continued. "That's basic management. But it's been my experience that there are very few who are willing to acknowledge the self field of performance, let alone work in it. It's a main reason why I've enjoyed coaching you. You not only get the self field, you're willing to till in it, knee deep, if necessary." At this, Michael's body seemed to straighten a bit, and his chin rose slightly.

"Virtually all the coaching I've provided you has been intended to give you opportunities to choose who you are, how you see yourself, and your personal mission in life," I said. "I've sought to help you choose how you see people and the future, what you stand for, and what you believe. Can you see that's what I've been working on with you since the day you signed up for my coaching?"

"Yes, I can," Michael said. His voice was even, but his eyes told me he'd just had a realization.

"And do you recognize that it was your choosing to change yourself—your willingness to explore who you are and your intentions as a person—it's that work and those changes that you made in yourself that are the true source of this turnaround? That you changed and so your people changed? That you got better and so your people improved as well? Can you see that?"

"Yes, but it's hard for me to say it because I don't want to take the credit. My people are the real ones to thank. They deserve most of the credit."

"Bullshit," I said.

"Bullshit?" Michael replied. "You think my people are bullshit?" Michael slid his chair back from the table. It was obvious that he was taken aback and even slightly insulted by my comment.

"No, your people are wonderful. I love your people and have great respect for them and what they've done to realize your vision. But saying you don't want the credit and that your people are the real ones to thank—that, I say, is bullshit."

Michael scooted back to the table, so I continued. "Why, Michael, do you find it so hard to say that you made this happen, that it starts and ends with you, that without your leadership, this turnaround would not have occurred? Why are you so hesitant to embrace how great you are?"

"It's just not the way I was raised," Michael replied. "I feel uncomfortable saying I'm great."

"I'm not suggesting that you run around telling everyone how great you are. I'm just doing my best to get you to say it to yourself. The best know they're great. They carry themselves in a way that everyone knows when they look at them that they're great. Do you know who Derek Jeter the baseball player is or the golfer Rory McIlroy?

"Sure."

"They're excellent examples of what I'm talking about. They know they're great. They tell no one about it, and they are always humble in public, but they know they're great. And that knowing has them showing up in a way that has everyone else knowing they're great."

"But how do I act like I'm great?"

"I'm not talking about acting great. Acting occurs in the behavior field. There are lots of people who act great, oftentimes to cover up the fact that they see themselves as far less than great. I'm talking about the self field. I'm talking about seeing yourself as great—knowing you're a great leader." Again, Michael sat in silence, listening closely.

"From my perspective, this is the last piece of work I need to help you accomplish," I went on. "You know who you are and for what you stand, but you just don't yet know how great you are, or you do and you just don't have the balls to say it. And the best way I know to help you recognize you're great is to get you to acknowledge it to yourself from time to time. Are you hearing what I'm trying to tell you?"

"That I'm great," Michael replied. "That I'll be a more effective leader if I know that and embrace it. And that doesn't mean I have to brag about it. It just means I see myself that way."

"Yes! Exactly! Keep saying that to yourself until you know it . . . until, when you look into the mirror, you see yourself as a great leader."

I leaned toward Michael, making sure to meet his eyes. "It's important that you finish this last piece of work. When you're standing in front of industry leaders down the road, enrolling them in your vision, you want to walk onto that stage and be like Jeter and McIlroy, with the presence of a great leader. And that comes from within you; it can't be an act."

Michael sat nodding in thought. I glanced at my watch and remembered he had to get to a meeting. After a short time, he stood and walked behind his desk to retrieve his tablet for his next appointment. Michael moved toward the door.

"Walk with me to the elevator," he said. I stood and joined as he stepped into the hallway and walked toward the elevator.

"So, we've circled back to the first leadership lesson you taught me—that the only person who needed to change was me. We're all the way back to Forrest Gump, aren't we?"

"In a way, yes. You need to know who you are, what you believe, and what you stand for."

"Just like Forrest," Michael declared. He pushed the up button, summoning the elevator.

"Exactly. You see, Michael," I said, almost whispering, "the big leadership lesson is this: we trump everything."

"We? You mean you and me?"

"You, me, and every other human being on this planet. We all possess the potential to turn around the performance of organizations, transform industries, give birth to nations, and even change the world. That's the big secret we all once knew but which most of us have allowed to be schooled out of us."

We stood waiting silently for the elevator as Michael considered the enormity of what I'd just said. Several times, he started to speak but stopped himself and returned to thought. I imagined him thinking back to our first meetings, connecting the pieces of the journey he'd taken—a path that wound back around to something he'd known when he was just a kid, knowledge he'd spent most of his life unlearning. On his face, I saw the gravity of our work coming together.

The ding of the elevator's bell interrupted his thoughts.

Michael turned to me, shook my hand, and proceeded to enter the elevator. When he turned back around, I noticed his eyes were gleaming.

"Thanks for helping me reeducate myself," Michael said.

"My pleasure, sir," I replied, as the elevator doors closed and we parted ways. I knew at that moment I was no longer Michael's guide and protector. Michael was in every sense of the word an All-In Leader, capable of leading his people from the future on his own.

Epilogue:
The Turnaround

"I changed."

> —Henry Turner, played by Harrison Ford in the movie
> *Regarding Henry*

Michael's business unit designed, planned, executed, and completed every well on its schedule on budget, on time, the first time, for the next calendar year—a first in the business unit's history. In fact, so many of the wells were delivered ahead of schedule that Michael's business unit created problems for those upstream and downstream in the corporation. "We're outperforming their ability to keep up with us, and that's a nice problem to have," Michael said.

These improvements were reflected in key measures for the organization. For example, productive time improved from less than 50 percent to nearly 80 percent—not bad for an organization that, when they started the journey, believed the 74 percent industry benchmark was "unachievable for an operation as complex as ours." This efficiency increase, combined with other improvements, drove a bottom-line annual impact of over $325 million in cost avoided, in addition to cash savings of $75 million. In short, before Michael's intervention, his business unit's performance was falling well short of his stakeholder's expectations. Eighteen months later, they had begun to clearly separate themselves from the best in their industry while saving their company $400 million.

Michael has deservingly been the recipient of frequent acknowledgments from his counterparts and superiors. He and his people have not yet achieved their ultimate goal of "perfect execution," but they are well on their way to that aspiration. Shifting his attention to transforming his industry is the next step in his leadership journey. However, as I have shared in previous chapters, shouldering the burden of leadership, especially in a high-stakes situation where hundreds, if not thousands, of people's futures are in your hands, can be exhausting.

During my last interaction with Michael, his unit was consumed by the challenge of weathering an unprecedented downturn in oil prices—from $110 to less than $40 a barrel—and his company was hit extremely hard. Transforming the industry would have to come later, if ever. This frustrated Michael, and I attempted to console him by asserting that "Many authors of great visions rarely live to see them fully realized. I have no doubt that the wakes you've created will hit the shore someday."

Near the end of our engagement, one of Michael's key stakeholders related to me a concern I also shared. She said, "I only hope our executives realize that Michael's growth as a leader is the reason for this turnaround. They seem to think the answer is always some new initiative or program. What I've learned from watching you coach Michael is the difference a change in one single leader can make." This person experienced firsthand what one All-In Leader can accomplish and the value of coaching.

Too often, I find that companies are oblivious to what real leaders are or how they can be identified, nurtured, and utilized to their full potential. They squander resources in trying to teach leadership to their managers, in the hope that somehow a few might grow from that effort. But that's not how leaders come into being.

Only events and circumstances can truly call forth a leader's full potential. The Civil War sculpted Lincoln; women's suffrage, Anthony; racial injustice, King; the death of their children, Mothers Against Drunk Driving; and Macondo, Michael.

That's where I come in. Through the experiences and mentors I've shared in this book, I have developed the unique capacity to recognize when the circumstances and individual are present for an All-In Leader to be born. And when I do and that emerging leader signs up with me, I mentor, challenge, and help that person develop into a leader who creates extraordinary performance while promoting humanity in the workplace.

In the weeks after returning home from my final visit with Michael, I couldn't help but begin to direct my gaze outwards, looking for that next emergent All-In Leader—a special individual who is stuck or stymied, facing a daunting challenge.

It is at this time, as a coach, I feel the greatest anticipation. What will she be like? What will he want me to help him take on? What will she and I accomplish together?

Maybe it's someone who can see a better way but is surrounded by peers ready to burn her at the stake. Or perhaps it's someone like Patel who's called to serve those less fortunate. Or possibly, it will be another Lamar who wants to leave a legacy while proving something to his bosses.

Or, just maybe, it will be someone ready to begin an entirely new enterprise or eager to pioneer a history-making movement. Regardless of who my next partner is, it is I, and not my partner, who will gain the most.

I take great pride and solace in having spent the majority of my life following through on my commitment to the men and women who design, build, operate, and maintain the world. I know I've contributed significantly to the well-being and happiness of the dozens of leaders I've coached and the thousands of men and women they served. And since I tend to coach primarily their leaders, I also know only a small fraction of the people I've affected will ever be aware of the role I've played.

But I'm alright with that, because I've benefited as much as they. For some reason, I am wired to get extraordinary satisfaction out of helping others succeed and thrive. Serving others, especially those who are servant leaders themselves and poised to take the hero journey, is my cocaine.

Someone made me this way. Maybe it was God, maybe it was Mother Nature, or maybe it was my mom and dad, family, preachers, teachers, and experiences that have created who I am. I have no idea how or why I'm this way, but I also can't imagine a more perfect path for someone like me than the one I've had the good fortune to live. I've been truly blessed to benefit from the mentors who have guided me and to coach the others who have invited me into their lives.

I can't wait to meet whoever is around the next corner—the next emerging leader poised for the big adventure, whom I will guide on his or her hero journey.